D1116580

Follies of Power

The election of Barack Obama notwithstanding, the political imagination of America's elites remains deeply attracted to a unipolar view of
world politics. In this way of looking at the world, peace and prosperity in the global system require a reigning superpower. Great Britain
is imagined to have played this role in the nineteenth century and the
United States to have inherited it in the twentieth. America's interest and
duty are thought to lie in fulfilling this fate that history has thrust upon
us. The vision persists but is more and more false. In reality, today's
disposition of international power and wealth is increasingly plural.
Our unipolar vision grows progressively dysfunctional as much of the
world fears and resists it. Chapter 1 spells out these themes. Chapters
2 and 3 look at the disastrous consequences of the unipolar vision at
work – in the Middle East and in Europe. Chapters 4, 5, and 6 assess
the nature and limits of American power – soft, military, economic, and
moral. Chapter 7 discusses the problems of order and coexistence in a
plural world. It speculates on the possible contributions of "Old America" and "New Europe" as models for organizing the future. America's
own constitutional equilibrium, David P. Calleo argues, increasingly
requires friendly balancing from Europe. To face their responsibilities
to the world and to each other, both sides of the West will need to
liberate their imaginations from thralldom to past triumphs.

David P. Calleo is University Professor at The Johns Hopkins University
and Dean Acheson Professor at its Nitze School of Advanced International Studies (SAIS). Before coming to SAIS, he first taught at Brown
University and then for several years at Yale University. He has also
been a visiting professor or research Fellow at several American and
European universities and institutes. He also once served as Consultant
to the U.S. Under Secretary of State for Political Affairs.

His previous books include *Rethinking Europe's Future* (2001), *The
Bankrupting of America: How the Federal Deficit Is Impoverishing
the Nation* (1992), *Beyond American Hegemony: The Future of the
Western Alliance* (1987), *The Imperious Economy* (1982), *The Ger-
man Problem Reconsidered* (1978), *America and the World Political
Economy* (with Benjamin M. Rowland, 1973), *The Atlantic Fantasy*
(1970), *Britain's Future* (1968), *The American Political System* (1968),
Coleridge and the Idea of the Modern Nation State (1966), and
Europe's Future (1965).

Follies of Power

America's Unipolar Fantasy

DAVID P. CALLEO

Nitze School of Advanced International Studies
The Johns Hopkins University

CAMBRIDGE UNIVERSITY PRESS

CAMBRIDGE UNIVERSITY PRESS
Cambridge, New York, Melbourne, Madrid, Cape Town, Singapore, São Paulo, Delhi

Cambridge University Press
32 Avenue of the Americas, New York, NY 10013-2473, USA

www.cambridge.org
Information on this title: www.cambridge.org/9780521767675

First published 2009

Printed in the United States of America

A catalog record for this publication is available from the British Library.

Library of Congress Cataloging in Publication data
Calleo, David P., 1934–
Follies of power : America's unipolar fantasy / David P. Calleo.
p.   cm.
Includes bibliographical references and index.
ISBN 978-0-521-76767-5 (hardback)
1. Hegemony – United States.   2. United States – Foreign relations.   I. Title.
JZ1312.C35   2009
327.73 – dc22   2008043036

ISBN 978-0-521-76767-5 hardback

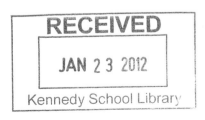

For my beloved Yale ghosts:

Lewis Perry Curtis

Joseph Toy Curtiss

Eugene V. Rostow

Frederick Watkins

Teaching that grows more vivid with the years.

Contents

Acknowledgments

Throughout nearly forty years of intensive teaching at SAIS, I have enjoyed remarkable support from teams of highly competent and often brilliant researchers drawn from SAIS's cosmopolitan mix of bright graduate students. Their help has not only made extensive writing possible for me, but also highly pleasurable. This book, which has evolved extensively over time and been through several versions, is certainly no exception. I should particularly like to thank the following: David Beffert, Timo Behr, Kai Behrens, Daniil Davydoff, Necmeddin Bilal Erdogan, Frederick Hood, Brian Hoyt, Mark Huberty, Kelly O'Malley, Jan Martin Witte, and Marco Zambotti. I hope they have enjoyed learning from me as much as I have enjoyed learning from them.

The book has also profited greatly from my disputatious family. My wife, Avis, has a long and rich experience with serving our government. That experience greatly adds to my own insight. My brother Patrick and sister-in-law Celestine Bohlen both have broad experience with the world beyond America and have been generous with their advice at critical moments along the way. So have a band of colleagues and friends – in particular Dana Allin, Christopher Chivvis, Erik Jones, Michael Steurmer, and Jenonne Walker. Lastly, I have had a fine editor – John Berger, an old student and friend from my early days at SAIS, with whom it is a great pleasure to be working once more.

Preparing this book has resulted in a number of journal articles and chapters in collective studies, and I have greatly profited from these collaborations. I should particularly like to note the following: "Do

Economic Trends Unite or Divide the Two Sides of the Atlantic?"
Geir Lundestad (ed.), *Just Another Major Crisis?: The United States
and Europe Since 2000* (Oxford, NY: Oxford University Press, 2008)
pp. 182–209; "Twenty-First Century Geopolitics and the Erosion of
the Dollar Order," Eric Helleiner and Jonathan Kirshner (eds.), *The
Future of the Dollar* (Ithaca, NY: Cornell University Press, 2009)
pp. 289–336; "How Europe Could Save the World," *World Policy
Journal*, Vol. 25 (3), Fall 2008, pp. 3–12; and "The Tyranny of False
Vision: America's Unipolar Fantasy," *Survival*, Vol. 50 (5), October–
November 2008, pp. 61–78.

Follies of Power

PART I

AMERICA'S GEOPOLITICAL ILLUSIONS AND THEIR CONSEQUENCES

I

The Unipolar Fantasy

America's Dysfunctional World View

This book appears just as the United States has installed a new president, Barack Obama. His victory has triggered a remarkable burst of enthusiasm and good will not only across a wide spectrum of the American public, but around the world. He takes office at a moment of severe crisis in America's policies. The economy is in a shambles that recalls the 1930s. Since World War II, our foreign policy has never been so bereft of foreign support. In effect, the United States, which professes to lead the world, has grown deeply out of tune with it.

It is tempting to see Obama's election as evidence, in itself, of a great turning point – the moment when the United States will begin to regain its geopolitical footing and economic success. But, as the new president has himself said so eloquently, meeting today's challenges calls for bold and doubtless painful rethinking of fashionable shibboleths. Undoubtedly, the new administration has assembled an impressive array of intellectual and administrative talent, but the new may not be as different from the old as we expect. Foreign policies are formulated and conducted by elites whose fundamental ideas often change very little from one administration to the next. What the present situation calls for is not merely a more expert and refined application of familiar ideas, but also accommodation to a different way of looking at the world.

For the past two decades, the American political imagination has been possessed by what has become a hazardous geopolitical vision. In it the United States is defined as the dominant power in a closely integrated and "unipolar" international system. Several decades of mostly successful history has done much to encourage Americans toward this view. World War II favored seeing the United States as the free world's natural leader. The cold war reinforced this identity and planted it deeply in Americans' view of themselves. With the collapse of the Soviet Union, the world seemed ready for a new and closely integrated world order. As the surviving superpower, the U.S. was the avatar for the new order. A "bipolar" world had grown "unipolar." To function properly, the new system required a hegemonic leader to take charge. Duty and interest alike seemed to compel the U.S. to play that role. Successive administrations have oriented American policy toward fulfilling it. By now a whole generation of Americans has scarcely known any other view of their country's place in the world.

Americans have had trouble realizing how revolutionary their unipolar vision can appear to others. A world system dominated by one superpower is a bold and radical program. If successful, it would mean for the first time in modern history a world without a general balance of power. Pursuing such a goal implies numerous confrontations with other nations. It antagonizes states that fear decline and states that anticipate improvement. Nevertheless, the American political imagination now finds it difficult to entertain any other view of the world. Americans have been slow to see, let alone accept, what to many others seems a more probable and desirable future – a plural world with several centers of power. Recent experience suggests that America's aggressive geopolitical stance is proving not merely unpopular but also dysfunctional. America's hegemonic pursuits have aroused a swarm of antagonists. Thus, we find ourselves not only at war in the Middle East but also alienating the Russians, the Chinese, and the Europeans. Surveys of public opinion throughout the globe show an alarming popular disaffection from America. Used to thinking of their nation as a friend and benefactor of all humankind, Americans have seen themselves resented and even hated in much of the world.[1]

It is tempting to believe that America's recent misadventures will discredit and suppress our hegemonic longings and that, following the presidential election of 2008, a new administration will abandon them. But so long as our identity as a nation is intimately bound up with seeing ourselves as the world's most powerful country, at the heart of a global system, hegemony is likely to remain the recurring obsession of our official imagination, the *idée fixe* of our foreign policy. America's hegemonic ambitions have, after all, suffered severe setbacks before. Less than half a century has passed since the "lesson of Vietnam." But that lesson faded without forcing us to abandon the old fantasies of omnipotence. The fantasies merely went into remission, until the fall of the Soviet Union provided an irresistible occasion for their return. Arguably, in its collapse, the Soviet Union proved to be a greater danger to America's own equilibrium than in its heyday.

Dysfunctional imaginations are scarcely a rarity – among individuals or among nations. "Reality" is never a clear picture that imposes itself from without. Imaginations need to collaborate. They synthesize old and new images, concepts, and ideas and fuse language with emotions – all according to the inner grammar of our minds. These synthetic constructions become our reality, our way of depicting the world in which we live. Inevitably, our imaginations present us with only a partial picture. As Walter Lippmann once put it, our imaginations create a "pseudo-environment between ourselves and the world."[2] Every individual, therefore, has his own particular vision of reality, and every nation tends to arrive at a favored collective view that differs from the favored view of other nations. When powerful and interdependent nations hold visions of the world severely at odds with one another, the world grows dangerous.

Periods of fundamental geopolitical change are particularly challenging – charged, as they usually are, with confusing, fanatical, and frightening possibilities. Comprehending and mastering big shifts in historical forces requires creative leaps of national imagination. Today, with the world rapidly growing more plural in its distribution of power and wealth, a lingering unipolar worldview isolates the United States from the reality to which it should be adapting. Accordingly, the United States becomes a danger to the world and to itself. When a nation as powerful as the United States defies – Canute-like – the onrushing historical tide, all the makings of a grand historical tragedy are at hand. Adding the United States to the world's list of failed hegemons would be a depressing outcome for America's long and rich experiment with federal constitutionalism. But avoiding such a fate requires a resolute reshaping of the country's geopolitical imagination. This is a work of genuine national patriotism, requiring a firm turning away from the bombastic chauvinism of recent years. It means a tranquil acceptance of other great nations, a sympathy for their accomplishments and sorrows, along with a lively sensitivity to the original sin that we all share. Like other great Western democracies, the United States has a healthy tradition of self-criticism that, with luck, rouses itself to spare the nation from egregious folly. This book aspires to provide a modest contribution to a resurgence of that indispensable tradition.

We should start our collective examination of conscience by reflecting on why we have come to commit ourselves so deeply to the unipolar worldview and why we have been so oblivious to its manifest inadequacy.

America's Unipolar Gene

Were the United States a traditional great power of the nineteenth century, its current preoccupation with hegemony, however injudicious, might not be so surprising.[3] But as a constitutional republic, blending democracy and federalism, the United States has traditionally supposed itself to be beyond such temptations. Historically, we have tended to view ourselves as aloof from power politics – with a strong predilection for isolationism. That view is, however, an incomplete reading of our nation's genetic code. Our past is not as innocent of global ambition as we are fond of believing.[4] At the very birth of the Republic, Alexander Hamilton, from today's perspective the most influential of the Founding Fathers, was already promoting the idea of America's global hegemony. At the time of the Civil War, faith in America's global destiny was a critical part of Abraham Lincoln's dedication to preserving the Union. At the start of the twentieth century, Hamilton's vision revived to stimulate the imperial tastes of Theodore Roosevelt and the coterie of geopolitical strategists around him. Woodrow Wilson gave the Hamiltonian vision a liberal gloss and used it to induce America to join World War I.[5] By World War II, Franklin Delano Roosevelt (FDR) had melded Wilsonianism and the geopolitical enthusiasms of his cousin, Theodore, into the vision of a global *Pax Americana*.[6] Roosevelt's early vision of today's unipolar vision had wide bipartisan appeal. Wendell Willkie, the Republican presidential candidate in 1940, possessed by an almost chiliastic sense of American omnipotence, conducted his electoral campaign around the theme of "One World" led by the United States.[7] Henry Luce, publisher of *Time, Life*, and *Fortune* magazines, and a major light in the Republican firmament, trumpeted the "American Century" throughout the wartime years.[8]

Not surprisingly, as FDR began to sketch his postwar vision, even America's closest allies grew uneasy. Charles De Gaulle was outraged by the small role left not only for France but also for Europe in general. Roosevelt, he thought, illustrated a familiar phenomenon in history – the "will to power cloaked in idealism."[9] Winston Churchill, compelled as he was to rely on the American alliance, was dismayed at the heavy financial price desperate Britain was being forced to pay. "Lend-Lease," the British soon realized, was a system patently ensuring that postwar Britain would not return to its prewar global preeminence. As soon as the war ended, moreover, Lend-Lease was brutally terminated, despite Britain's devastated finances. The United States, it was clear, had little interest either in preserving Britain's global empire or in assisting the socialist experiments of the new Labour government.[10] Nor was the United States much interested as continental European states tried to finance radically ambitious plans to invigorate their economies and transform their societies.[11]

By 1947, American policy had taken a more generous course. Europeans had mainly Joseph Stalin to thank. The iron-willed Soviet dictator made American expectations of a unipolar world premature. The Soviets rivaled the Americans not only in China, which Americans would soon "lose," but also in Europe itself – the great prize of the Cold War struggle. The Soviet threat gave West European states much more leverage against their anxious transatlantic protector. Given the strong leftist parties in the major continental countries, the United States felt it could ill afford to alienate European governments or publics. Roosevelt's triumphal vision of postwar American policy – unipolar, global, and aloof from Europe – gave way to Harry Truman's defensive vision, which included "containment" of the Soviets, above all, in Europe.[12]

The American political imagination soon transformed containment into a "bipolar" paradigm in which two superpowers contested the world between them. Mindful of European sensitivities, however, Americans emphasized the multilateral character of the West's Cold War alliances. The United States saw itself not as competing with the Soviets to dominate the world but as joining defensively with others to prevent their enslavement. Ultimately mindful of its own vulnerability to nuclear attack, the United States grew wary of radical ambitions that threatened the bipolar status quo. Thus, although there was recurring support for "rolling back" and defeating the Soviets, the predominant official view favored pursuing peaceful coexistence within a stable bipolar system. Nor was the United States much inclined to vaunt its own strength. In the 1970s and even in Ronald Reagan's jingoish 1980s, American analysts seemed more alive to the long-term weaknesses of the United States than to those of the Soviet Union. The United States was thought to be losing ground geopolitically, with Europeans increasingly inclined toward "Eurocommunism" and "Finlandization." Military strategists were greatly concerned about America's own "window of vulnerability" to Soviet nuclear attacks.[13] Foreign-policy intellectuals were embroiled in a debate over "declinism" – the view that superpower status, with its heavy military and financial burdens, was inexorably leading the American economy to "overstretch" and decay. America's disorderly finances in the Reagan years made the declinist syndrome seem uncomfortably relevant.[14]

In summary, even though we can now see more clearly the great weaknesses of the Soviet Union, the bipolar system was nevertheless balanced. Not only was Soviet power contained but American power toward Europe was contained as well. Part of this was undoubtedly owed to America's own self-restraint as a constitutional republic, as well as to generosity and respect for the cultural homelands of many Americans. But America's better instincts came to the fore in a geopolitical framework in which fear of Soviet power encouraged attentiveness to the European allies.

The Soviet Demise: Back to the Future

With the demise of the Soviet Union in 1991, the unipolar vision of 1945 returned with a vengeance. Public discourse was puffed once more with triumphal assessments of America's military and economic prowess. Within a few years, Americans had changed their self-image from the world's reluctant defender into its "indispensable nation."[15] For the third time in the twentieth century, a sort of Hegelian nationalism arose to convince Americans that all modern history had been incubating America's global leadership.[16] It helped that, just as the Soviet Union was abandoning its European empire, America's military power, recklessly enhanced by Reagan's outsized defense budgets, was being brilliantly displayed in the Gulf War of 1990–1991.[17]

In the succeeding Clinton years, however, the content of America's triumphal self-image was more economic than military. The Soviet economy's demise was read as a definitive validation of American capitalism, whose own traditional problems were temporarily forgotten. Europe's communitarian capitalism and social democracy were bundled with Soviet communism – all seen as tainted ideals in decline.[18] America's triumphalism waxed further with its economy's remarkable run of success. Whereas the later 1980s had been years of financial instability in the United States, followed by a recession in 1991, the mid-1990s saw a boom, built around the most modern technologies of the time and fueled by huge inflows of foreign investment. In short, the triumphal America of the 1990s seemed the very center of rampant globalization.[19]

Given such a run of political, military, and economic success, imaginations habituated to seeing the world as *bipolar* found it only natural to see the new world order as *unipolar*. Previously, two superpowers had divided the world between themselves. The collapse of one was seen as the triumph of the other. Now that only one superpower remained, the struggle for world predominance was over. The United States could take up its true historic role – to lead and integrate the world's nations into a liberal and peaceful world system.[20]

False Metaphors and Bad History

In retrospect, it is easy to see how the transposing of bipolar to unipolar metaphors involved a geopolitical sleight of hand that was treacherously misleading. Why should a unipolar world be expected to follow inevitably from the collapse of a bipolar world? Why not expect a multipolar or nonpolar world instead?[21] After all, the Cold War's bipolar imagery was itself a considerable distortion of reality. The two blocs were internally less unified than the imagery implied. The notion of a single integrated Soviet bloc had long been an egregious mischaracterization of the larger communist world, in which the Soviet Union had come close to an open war with China.[22] And certainly it was never accurate to describe the West merely as a bloc dominated by the Americans. True, the United States had assumed the role of hegemon within the Atlantic Alliance and sometimes attempted to act unilaterally, but Western Europeans had habitually preferred to see the relationship more as a concert of allies. Throughout the Cold War, Europeans were quite successful in holding their own. They quickly learned to be "free riders," not only on the American troops that contained the Soviets militarily but also on the Soviet troops that balanced the Americans politically. Moreover, Western Europe, organized into the European Economic Community, became an increasingly successful economic competitor. In some respects, therefore, it was more accurate to speak of the Cold War's transatlantic relationship as a "tripolar" rather than a bipolar balance.

Meanwhile, powerful signs indicated that the broader global system was growing more plural as the Cold War proceeded. Major states were rising beyond the Atlantic and Soviet blocs. By the 1970s, Japan, its security assured by the United States, had become a major economic power, with Americans growing increasingly fearful of its competition.[23] Asia's other potential superpowers, China and India, had carefully kept themselves detached from either superpower's bloc. By developing their own political and economic independence first, and thereafter only gradually incorporating themselves into the "world economy," they were ensuring their own enduring self-determination and signaling a plural global system in the future.[24]

Given such trends, the world of the late Cold War was already too pluralistic to make a unipolar outcome the inevitable result of the Soviet demise. The American geopolitical imagination was setting off on the wrong track. The collapse of one bipolar pole did not automatically mean a world dominated by the other. Leaping to such a conclusion suggested a national imagination hankering for hegemony. Different outcomes were clearly possible. One was a certain restructuring of the "West" itself. West Europeans, pursuing their own vision of a "European Europe," could be expected to try both tightening their own integration and extending it to Eastern Europe. An enlarging European Union would naturally cultivate its own ties with the new Russia and a rapidly evolving China. Such trends were all the more likely if the United States, imagining itself in a unipolar world, began to throw its weight around.

In short, the implosion of the Soviet Union should not have been expected to lead automatically to a docile world yearning for American direction. In place of the Cold War's bipolar system, with its carefully tended balances, an unstructured and volatile world, given to random outbursts of violence, was more likely to follow.[25] That is the world in which we now live and for which our unipolar imagination has left us dangerously unprepared.

Unipolar Strategy and 9/11

Between the Soviet collapse and the atrocities of 9/11, American pretensions to global hegemony emphasized economic predominance more than military prowess. Indeed, maintaining the former depended on limiting the latter. President Clinton's greatest economic accomplishment – the return to fiscal balance – depended at the outset on radical cuts in military spending. It was America's "peace dividend" that started the United States on the road to fiscal balance. Himself a refugee from the Vietnam War, Clinton was at first leery of military adventures that would threaten a return to the chaotic fiscal conditions of the past.

Logically, lower defense spending called for a correspondingly restrained foreign policy. Military interventions were to be limited by the "Powell Doctrine," designed to keep American forces from getting bogged down in other people's local wars.[26] Such a military posture implied cooperative rather than antagonistic relations with Russia and China, together with a serious effort to resolve the Palestinian conflict. It meant encouraging European powers to strengthen and pool their military forces to take primary responsibility for security in their own region. The Clinton administration pursued these aims with varying consistency and success, but, in due course, it found itself increasingly drawn into military commitments. Early in his presidency, Clinton became a fierce partisan of enlarging the North Atlantic Treaty Organization (NATO) to add former members of the Warsaw Pact, and even former parts of the Soviet Union, enthusiasms that predictably poisoned relations with the new Russia. Nevertheless, enlarging NATO, extending its reach, and maintaining America's leading role within it became major goals of the Clinton administration's foreign policy.[27]

The administration's military proclivities were further encouraged by the European Union's lamentable failure to stop the genocidal killing that accompanied the disintegration of Yugoslavia. The United States was pressured to take charge – first in Bosnia and then in Kosovo. America's success after Europe's failure led to a wave of military triumphalism in the United States. Weakened by scandal, the administration began adjusting its rhetoric to please neoconservative sensibilities. By the end, it had started bombing Iraq and was proposing significant increases in military spending.[28]

Ironically, George W. Bush, in his campaign, criticized the Clinton administration for supercilious meddling in other nations' affairs.[29] In practice, the Bush presidency that followed shared none of Clinton's initial diffidence toward the use of military power. The terrorist attacks of 9/11 permitted the growing fancy for exercising military power to be transformed into a compulsion. The pursuit of global hegemony was recast into a War on Terror, a decisive step toward militarizing American diplomacy. Bush's neoconservative prophets presented the nation's political imagination with a new bipolar system – with a terrorist "axis of evil" on one side and a coalition of the virtuous on the other.

Bush's new bipolar paradigm was, however, very different from that of the Cold War. Unlike in the Cold War, there was little real balance within the War on Terror. The Cold War was a heavily armed truce, in which neither the United States nor the Soviets ever directly fought the other. Despite all the recurring alarms of the period, containment and coexistence were the real strategies of each side. Consolidating this coexistence required accepting some effective and stable theory of mutual deterrence. "Mutually assured destruction" provided the necessary strategic doctrine. It made all sides shrink from confrontations that risked escalating into nuclear war. Even though American policymakers tended to interpret the two wars in which the United States was deeply involved – Korea and Vietnam – as bipolar confrontations, the Soviets were, in fact, careful not to be directly involved in either. The Cold War finally ended not because the Americans won but because the Soviets lost.[30] The Soviet system was felled not by an American assault but by its own inner weaknesses and dissatisfactions, exacerbated by the strains of the long but bloodless confrontation with the United States and Europe. Arguably, the Soviets were defeated more than anything else by pluralist national forces arising within their own empire.

Bush's War on Terror presented an entirely different paradigm. Whereas Cold War boundaries were closely drawn and the status quo was respected by both sides, the indeterminate character of "terrorism" precluded any stable doctrine of deterrence. With terror, the United States was presented with an amorphous enemy to be eradicated rather than a precisely located antagonist to be "contained." Without a theory of deterrence to compel mutual self-restraint, the War on Terror provided no internalized check on the assertion of American military power. Quite the contrary, it provided the rationale for a continued projection of American power into every nook and cranny of global space. It enabled rather than restricted the unipolar instinct. It was, in brief, the ideology for a particularly intrusive form of global hegemony. The United States thereby transformed itself from the world's favorite protector into its leading disturber of the peace. American policy, informed by such an unstructured vision, pointed toward a series of catastrophes. The rest of the world has sensed this and has feared the consequences.[31]

The next two chapters examine our dysfunctional unipolar vision in action. The past decade has provided a rich example of the damage that can follow from applying self-indulgent bad ideas and bad history. Americans, of course, expect to play a major role in shaping the new century. But it is ironic that for all the hyperbolic vaunting of American strength, this past decade has seen a precipitous decline in American power. Our military is bogged down; our economy is in a shambles; the legitimacy of our leadership could scarcely be lower. Worse yet, it is hard to escape the conclusion that America's loss of power is not as great a misfortune for humankind as most of us might have wished. We can hope, of course, that, as in all great countries, serious adversity can provoke a cleansing reaction. We have a new administration. We can hope for a new foreign policy. But we will not really get one, so long as our American political imagination remains enchanted by its unipolar fantasy.

Notes

1. Surveys of international opinion by the Pew Global Attitudes Project show a precipitous decline in favorable opinion of the United States during the early years of the George W. Bush presidency. Early 2008 saw some improvements in various countries, but of four West European countries surveyed (France, Germany, Spain, and the UK), only Britain had a majority (53%) with a favorable opinion of the United States. Favorable opinion remained very low in most Muslim countries and deteriorated sharply in Japan and Mexico but improved significantly in Poland (to 68%), Russia (to 46%), South Korea (to 70%), India (to 66%), and China (to 41%). Large majorities in Western Europe "among people who have been following the election" believed U.S. foreign policy would improve with a new president (France 68%, Spain 67%, and Germany 64%). Among those following the election, Obama ranked higher in every country surveyed

except Jordan and Pakistan, "where few people have confidence in either candidate" and in the United States itself.

The following tables are from a report by the Pew Global Attitudes Project in March 2007 titled, "America's Image in the World: Findings from the Pew Global Attitudes Project." All Pew Global Attitudes Project reports can be found online at www.pewglobal.org.

The report "Global Economic Gloom – China and India Notable Exceptions," a Pew Global Attitudes Project that was published in June 2008, offers more recent world opinions about the United States and its presidential candidates. The survey results are on p. 15.

Favorable Opinions of the U.S.

	1999/2000 %	2002 %	2003 %	2004 %	2005 %	2006 %
Great Britain	83	75	70	58	55	56
France	62	63	43	37	43	39
Germany	78	61	45	38	41	37
Spain	50	--	38	--	41	23
Russia	37	61	36	47	52	43
Indonesia	75	61	15	--	38	30
Egypt	--	--	--	--	--	30
Pakistan	23	10	13	21	23	27
Jordan	--	25	1	5	21	15
Turkey	52	30	15	30	23	12
Nigeria	46	--	61	--	--	62
Japan	77	72	--	--	--	63
India	--	54	--	--	71	56
China	--	--	--	--	42	47

1999/2000 survey trends provided by the Office of Research, U.S. Department of State

Dangers to World Peace

% saying 'great danger'	Iran %	US in Iraq %	North Korea %	Israeli-Palestinian conflict %
U.S.	46	31	34	43
Great Britain	34	41	19	45
France	31	36	16	35
Germany	51	40	23	51
Spain	38	56	21	52
Russia	20	45	10	41
Indonesia	7	31	4	33
Egypt	14	56	14	68
Jordan	19	58	18	67
Turkey	16	60	6	42
Pakistan	4	28	8	22
Nigeria	15	25	11	27
Japan	29	29	46	40
India	8	15	6	13
China	22	31	11	27

Favorable Opinion of Americans

% very/somewhat favorable	2002 %	2003 %	2004 %	2005 %	2006 %
Great Britain	83	80	73	70	69
France	71	58	53	64	65
Germany	70	67	68	65	66
Spain	--	47	--	55	37
Russia	67	65	64	61	57
Jordan	53	18	21	34	38
Indonesia	65	56	--	46	36
Egypt	--	--	--	--	36
Pakistan	17	38	25	22	27
Turkey	31	32	32	23	17
Nigeria	--	67	--	--	56
Japan	73	--	--	--	82
India	58	--	--	71	67
China	--	--	--	43	49

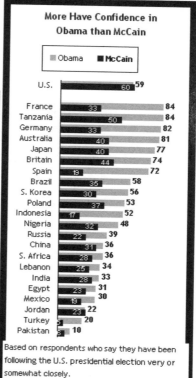

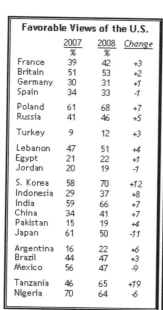

2. Walter Lippmann, *Public Opinion* (New York, NY: Macmillan, 1965), p. 10.

3. Great powers of the nineteenth century, however, were generally careful to limit their ambitions. See Henry Kissinger, *Diplomacy* (New York, NY: Simon & Schuster, 1994) or A. J. P Taylor, *The Struggle for Mastery in Europe, 1848–1914* (Oxford, UK: Clarendon Press, 1954).

4. For America's long-standing "liberal" aggressiveness, see Robert Kagan, "Cowboy Nation: Against the Myth of American Innocence," *The New Republic*, Vol. 235, 2006, pp. 20–23.

5. For the Hamiltonian school, see John Lamberton Harper, *American Machiavelli: Alexander Hamilton and the Origins of U.S. Foreign Policy* (Cambridge, UK: Cambridge University Press, 2004) and Walter Russell Mead, *Special Providence: American Foreign Policy and How It Changed the World* (New York, NY: Alfred A. Knopf, 2001), pp. 99–131. For a discussion of Theodore Roosevelt and his imperialist circle, see Warren Zimmerman, *First Great Triumph: How Five Americans Made Their*

Country a World Power (New York, Farrer, Straus and Giroux, 2002), and David P. Calleo and Benjamin M. Rowland, *America and the World Political Economy* (Bloomington, IN, and London, UK: Indiana University Press, 1973), Ch. 3. For Woodrow Wilson's liberal imperialism, see Arthur S. Link, *Wilson the Diplomatist* (New York, NY: New Viewpoints, 1974), Ch. 5.

6. For Franklin Delano Roosevelt's personal melding of the energetic foreign policy of his cousin Theodore and the liberal internationalism of Woodrow Wilson during the ideological battles of 1914–1919, with the consequences for World War II and beyond, see John Lamberton Harper, *American Visions of Europe: Franklin D. Roosevelt, George F. Kennan, and Dean G. Acheson* (Cambridge, UK: Cambridge University Press, 1994), Chs. 1–3.

7. Wendell L. Willkie, *One World* (New York, NY: Simon & Schuster, 1943).

8. Henry Luce founded *Time Magazine* in 1923. By 1940, one in five Americans, mostly from the East Coast middle class, was exposed to a Luce publication each week. "The American Century," appeared in *Time* on February 7, 1941. America, Luce urged, should "accept wholeheartedly our duty and our opportunity as the most powerful and vital nation in the world and in consequence to exert upon the world the full impact of our influence, for such purposes as we see fit and by such means as we see fit."

9. Charles de Gaulle, *The Complete War Memoirs of Charles de Gaulle: Salvation*, Jonathan Griffen and Richard Howard (trans.). (New York, NY: Carroll & Graf, Inc, 1998), Vol. II, pp. 573–574.

10. For early indications of Anglo-American disagreement, see Francis L. Loewenheim, Harold D. Langley, and Manfred Jonas, *Roosevelt and Churchill: Their Secret Wartime Correspondence* (New York, NY: The Saturday Review Press, 1975). For Britain's difficulties negotiating post-war economic aid from the United States and the role of Lend-Lease in weakening Britain's economy, see Robert J. A. Skidelsky, *John Maynard Keynes: Fighting for Britain, 1937–1946* (London, UK: Macmillan, 2000), Vol. 3, pp. 180–181 and Chs. 11–12. See also Richard N. Gardner, *Sterling-Dollar Diplomacy in Current Perspective: The Origins and the Prospects of our International Economic Order* (New York, NY: Columbia University Press, 1980). See also Randall Bennett Woods, *A Changing of the Guard: Anglo-Saxon Relations, 1941–1946* (Chapel Hill, NC: University of North Carolina Press, 1990). For a rancorous recollection of old Anglo-American conflicts in the light of the Iraq invasion of 2002, see Francis Beckett, "What Has America Ever Done for Us?" *New Statesman*, Vol. 132 (4627), 2003, p. 18.

11. For early U.S. reactions to postwar European plans, see Federico Romero, Alan Steele Milward, and George Brennan, *The European Rescue of the Nation-State* (London, UK: Routledge, 2000), and John Lamberton

Harper, *Postwar US Foreign Policy: Patterns and Prospects*, Johns Hopkins University, Bologna Center, Occasional Papers no. 40 (Bologna: The Johns Hopkins University Bologna Center, 1982).

For a general discussion, see Benjamin M. Rowland, ed, *Balance of Power or Hegemony* (New York, NY: NYU Press, 1976), in particular, Rowland's own Ch. 5, "Preparing the American Ascendancy: The Transfer of Economic Power from Britain to the United States, 1933–1944."

12. Disappointment of American unipolar expectations began in the waning days of Roosevelt's presidency, as he appears already to have decided that Stalin could not be counted on to fulfill the promises made at Yalta regarding the postwar treatment of Eastern Europe. Arthur Schlesinger, Jr. explains that although senior statesmen in the United States hoped to find a long-term *modus vivendi,* the USSR was, for historical and ideological reasons, resistant to such an idea. The conflict between American and Soviet expectations for the postwar order festered until the 1947 Soviet withdrawal from the Marshall Plan proceedings, and subsequent Communist advances in Eastern Europe led to a frozen confrontation. See Lloyd Gardner, Arthur Schlesigner, Jr., and Hans Morgenthau, *The Origins of the Cold War* (Lexington, KY, and Toronto: Xerox College Publishing, 1970), pp. 41–77.

13. For American fears of Eurocommunism and Finlandization, or Cold War debates over nuclear strategy and the evolution of nuclear warfighting, see Dana Allin, *Cold War Illusions: America, Europe and Soviet Power, 1969–1989* (New York, NY: St. Martin's Press, 1994), pp. 110–111. For the strategic debates, see also Fred M. Kaplan, *The Wizards of Armageddon* (Palo Alto, CA: Stanford University Press, 1991).

14. For declinism in general and Reagan's financial vulnerabilities in particular, see David P. Calleo, *Beyond American Hegemony* (New York, NY: Basic Books, 1987), Ch. 7, and *The Bankrupting of America: How the Federal Budget Is Impoverishing the Nation* (New York: William Morrow and Company, 1992), Chs. 6 and 8–10; and Paul Kennedy, *The Rise and Fall of the Great Powers* (New York, NY: Random House, 1987). For the idea of a "declinist" school, see Peter Schmeisser, "Taking Stock: Is America in Decline?" *The New York Times*, Section 6 April 17, 1988, p. 24, http://query.nytimes.com/gst/fullpage.html?res=940DE2DD143AF934A25757C0A96E948260&scp=10&sq=Beyond+American+hegemony&st=nyt.

15. President Clinton first used this phrase on the occasion of his second Inaugural Address. It was later picked up by Madeline Albright, who expanded it into a justification for the use of force in the Balkans and on February 19, 1998, said, "If we have to use force, it is because we are America. We are the indispensable nation. We stand tall. We see further into the future." For Clinton's address, see http://www.presidency.ucsb.edu/ws/index.php?pid=54183. For Albright's comments, see transcripts

from the February 19, 1998, broadcast of "The Today Show," from the National Broadcasting Company, New York, NY.

16. Francis Fukuyama, "The End of History?" *The National Interest*, Vol. 16, 1989, p. 3, and the expanded book version, *The End of History and the Last Man* (New York, NY: The Free Press, 1992), provided sophisticated encouragement for American triumphalism.

17. U.S. military expenditures were 4.7% of GDP in FY 1981 and at 5.9% in FY 1988, having peaked in FY 1986 at 6.3% of GDP. For the consequences of our internationally outsized military spending, see David P. Calleo, *The Bankrupting of America, op. cit.*, Ch. 4. See also data from *NATO Burdensharing After Enlargement* (Washington, DC: The Congressional Budget Office, 2001), p. 30.

TABLE A.1. *Defense Spending as a Percentage of Gross Domestic Product in Selected Years, 1990–2000*

	1980	1985	1990	1995	1996	1997	1998	1999	2000[a]
Belgium	3.3	3.0	2.4	1.6	1.6	1.5	1.5	1.4	1.4
Canada	1.9	2.2	2.0	1.5	1.4	1.2	1.3	1.3	1.2
Czech Republic[b]	n.a.	n.a.	n.a.	n.a.	n.a.	n.a.	n.a.	2.2	2.3
Denmark	2.4	2.2	2.0	1.7	1.7	1.7	1.6	1.6	1.5
France	4.0	4.1	3.6	3.1	3.0	2.9	2.8	2.7	2.7
Germany	3.3	3.2	2.8	1.7	1.6	1.6	1.5	1.5	1.5
Greece	5.7	7.1	5.8	4.4	4.5	4.6	4.8	4.8	4.9
Hungary[b]	n.a.	n.a.	n.a.	n.a.	n.a.	n.a.	n.a.	1.6	1.7
Italy	2.4	2.7	2.1	1.8	1.9	2.0	2.0	2.0	1.9
Luxembourg	1.0	1.1	1.1	0.8	0.8	0.8	0.8	0.8	0.7
Netherlands	3.1	3.1	2.7	2.0	1.9	1.8	1.7	1.8	1.6
Norway	2.9	3.3	3.2	2.4	2.2	2.1	2.3	2.2	1.9
Poland[b]	n.a.	n.a.	n.a.	n.a.	n.a.	n.a.	n.a.	2.0	2.0
Portugal	3.5	3.1	3.1	2.6	2.4	2.4	2.2	2.2	2.2
Spain[c]	n.a.	2.7	1.8	1.5	1.4	1.4	1.3	1.3	1.3
Turkey	4.7	4.5	4.9	3.9	4.1	4.1	4.4	5.4	6.0
United Kingdom	5.0	5.3	4.0	3.0	3.0	2.7	2.7	2.5	2.4
United States	5.1	6.7	5.7	3.8	3.5	3.3	3.1	3.0	3.0
NATO Average	3.5	3.6	3.1	2.4	2.3	2.3	2.3	2.2	2.2
NATO European Average[d]	3.4	3.5	3.0	2.3	2.3	2.3	2.3	2.3	2.3

Notes: n.a. = not applicable.

   Averages are weighted by GDP.

   Iceland is excluded because it has no armed forces.

[a] Estimated by NATO on the basis of available data.

[b] Poland, Hungary, and the Czech Republic did not join NATO until 1999.

[c] Spain did not join NATO until 1992.

[d] Excludes the United States and Canada.

Source: Congressional Budget Office based on data from the North Atlantic Treaty Organization (NATO).

18. Robert J. A. Skidelsky, *The Road from Serfdom: The Economic and Political Consequences of the End of Communism* (New York, NY: Viking Penguin, 1996).

19. Thomas Friedman, *The Lexus and the Olive Tree* (New York, NY: Farrar, Straus and Giroux, 1999); Zbigniew Brzezinski, *The Choice* (New York, NY: Basic Books, 2004); or my colleague Michael Mandelbaum, *The Case for Goliath: How America Acts as the World's Government in the Twenty-First Century* (New York, NY: Public Affairs, 2005).

20. The 1992 Defense Planning Guidance document projected indefinite U.S. military dominance. In controversial early drafts, later amended, it counseled the United States to prevent the rise of rivals. Patrick E. Tyler, "U.S. Strategy Plan Calls for Insuring No Rivals Develop," *The New York Times*, March 8, 1992: A1; Barton Gellman, "Keeping the U.S. First, Pentagon Would Preclude a Rival Superpower," *The Washington Post*, March 11, 1992: A1.

21. For a nonpolar future, see Richard Haas, "The Age of Nonpolarity," *Foreign Affairs*, Vol. 87(3), 2008, pp. 44–56.

22. For the strategic context of the near-war between China and Russia, and its aftermath, see Dittmer Lowell, *Sino-Soviet Normalization and Its International Implications, 1945–1990* (Seattle, WA: University of Washington Press, 1992), Chs. 11 and 12.

23. The Japanese economy grew at an annual rate of 9.1% between 1953 and 1960, whereas the U.S. growth rate was 3.2%. Japan's per capita GDP finally exceeded that of the United States in 1987, although subsequent economic stagnation reduced Japan to thirteenth in the world by 2003 (the United States was second). All along, however, Japan continued to run a large current-account surplus with the United States. For early postwar growth figures, see *Yearbook of National Accounts Statistics 1965* (New York, NY: UN Department of Economics and Social Affairs, 1966), p. 46; for 1980s data, see *National Accounts Statistics: Analysis of Main Aggregates 1988–9* (New York, NY: UN Department of Economic and Social Affairs, 1991) pp. 6–7. Per-capita GDP rankings are taken from *CIA World Factbook 2004* (Washington, DC: Central Intelligence Agency, 2004). For early postwar Japanese growth and its broader implications, see Herman Kahn, *The Emerging Japanese Superstate* (Englewood Cliffs, NJ: Prentice Hall, 1970) and David P. Calleo and Benjamin M. Rowland, *America and the World Political Economy* (Bloomington, IN: Indiana University Press, 1973), Ch. 8. For American reactions (that now seem paranoid), see Leon Hollerman, ed; *Japan and the United States: Economic and Political Adversaries* (Boulder, CO: Westview Press, 1980), and Pat Choate, *Agents of Influence: How Japan's Lobbyists Manipulate America's Political and Economic System* (New York, NY: Knopf Books, 1990).

24. For a review of the conditions underpinning the rise of the Asian economies, and their current state, see Indermit Singh Gill, Yukon Huang, and Homi J. Kharal, editors, *East Asian Visions: Perspectives on Economic Development* (Washington DC: The International Bank for Reconstruction and Development, The World Bank and The Institute of Policy Studies, 2007). See also Chapter 7, footnote 23.

25. See John J. Mearsheimer, "Back to the Future: Instability in Europe after the Cold War," *International Security*, Vol. 15(4), 1990; John Lewis Gaddis, *The United States and the End of the Cold War: Reconsiderations, Implications, Provocations* (Oxford, UK: Oxford University Press, 1992). For my own analyses, see *Rethinking Europe's Future*, *op. cit.*, Chs. 10–12 and 16 and "Afterword." For earlier versions, see "Restarting the Marxist Clock? The Economic Fragility of the West," *World Policy Journal*, Vol. 13(2), 1996, pp. 57–46.

26. Powell's doctrine, first proclaimed during the Persian Gulf War of 1990–1991, argued that American forces should not be sent into combat without a precise and limited objective tied to clear American national security objectives with comprehensive support at home and abroad and the ability to deploy overwhelming force to assure an American victory. The doctrine was designed explicitly to avoid repeating the sort of engagements the United States had made in Vietnam in the 1960s or Lebanon in the early 1980s. See Colin L. Powell, "U.S. Forces: Challenges Ahead," *Foreign Affairs*, Winter Vol. 71, 1992/93, pp. 32–45.

27. See my *Rethinking Europe's Future. op. cit.*, pp. 309–314, notes 26–35.

28. For more information on "Operation Desert Fox" see Romesh Ratnesar et al., "What Good Did It Do?" *Time*, Vol. 152(6), 1998/1999, p. 68, http://search.ebscohost.com/login.aspx?direct=true&db=aph&AN=1378913&site=ehost-li. For information about President Clinton's 1999 proposal to increase defense spending see "Clinton to Seek $100 Billion, 6-Year Defense Spending Boost," *The Washington Post*, January 3, 1999: A12.

29. "Presidential Debate," *Online NewsHour*, October 12, 2000, November 9, 2008 <http://www.pbs.org/newshour/bb/politics/july-decoo/forpolicy_10-12.html.>

30. For my own selective survey of the vast literature on the Soviet collapse, see *Rethinking Europe's Future, op. cit.* pp. 131–134. Important recent studies include Anders Aslund, *Building Capitalism: The Transformation of the Former Soviet Bloc* (Cambridge, UK: Cambridge University Press, 2002).

31. Much of the world prefers the terminology "fight against terror" to the Bush administration's War on Terror. The former suggests a complex,

many-sided struggle requiring many levels of professional expertise but within a more or less normal, peacetime society. The latter implies the total mobilization of a nation at war and can easily be counterproductive for the detection and prosecution of terrorism at home and to civil liberties more generally. See, for example, the concerns by the former British Director of Public Prosecutions, Sir Ken MacDonald, in Clare Dyer, "There Is No War on Terror," *The Guardian*, January 24, 2007. For U.S. debate on the prediliction to "make war" on a host of evils, including poverty, cancer, drugs, and illiteracy, see Guy Raz, "Defining the War on Terror," *All Things Considered*, November 1, 2006 (Washington, DC: National Public Radio, 2006). For a more general discussion of why the "war" analogy does not fit the security problems posed by terrorism and how its use may damage U.S. public diplomacy, see Max Rodenbeck, "How Terrible Is It?," *The New York Review of Books*, Vol. 52(19), 2006.

Hubris in the Middle East

America's Liabilities

America's War on Terror, together with its unipolar assumptions, are all intimately linked to the Middle East. The region, with its variety of politically divided and undeveloped states, richly endowed with oil resources needed by the rest of the world, is an inviting venue for relieving hegemonic compulsions. It is not surprising that the most significant of America's recent wars have taken place there – two with Iraq and one with Afghanistan. Ironically, before going to war the United States gave important support to each, although in markedly different ways. Starting in the late 1970s, the U.S. upheld the Afghan resistance to a Soviet-backed government. Throughout most of the 1980s, the U.S. was a principal backer of Saddam Hussein's regime in its war with Iran. The collaboration was rudely broken in 1990, when Saddam, finally at peace with Iran, seized the neighboring oil state of Kuwait. Whatever the merits of the historic case for attaching Kuwait to Iraq, the invasion was a direct challenge to the widely supported principle that borders should not be changed by force, as well as to long-standing Anglo-American oil interests. The administration of the elder George Bush intervened massively but only after carefully garnering the support of the European allies and most of Iraq's regional neighbors while eliciting the forbearance of the Soviet Union.

Arguably, the intervention in Iraq might not have occurred had the Cold War not been ending. In any event, something of the Cold War's habits of self-restraint persisted. Iraqi forces were ejected from Kuwait, but Iraq itself was not deeply invaded nor was Saddam's regime toppled. A decade later, within a year after 9/11, U.S. forces invaded Afghanistan directly and a new war against Iraq followed the year after. The second Bush administration presented both of its invasions as campaigns in the War on Terror. Both demonstrated how much traditional Cold War restraints had been discarded. In each case, the U.S. destroyed the sitting regime and began redesigning the invaded nation's politics, economics, and culture. As these policies unfolded, the rest of the world grew doubtful. At the start, attacking the Afghan regime was easy to present as an appropriate response to 9/11. The Taliban regime was, after all, al Qaeda's host. By normal international law, the U.S. had the right to topple it to preempt further attacks. The second invasion of Iraq, however, elicited a quite different reaction. Much of the world could see no immediate threat to the United States. Although the attack on Saddam's regime was presented as "preemptive" – blocking an imminent threat of attack on the U.S. or Israel. To many others it seemed "preventive," specifically, to remove a potential military threat or remove an obstacle to America's regional dominance.[1] As such it appeared not only a clear violation of international law but also, more disturbingly, a flat declaration of America's unipolar hegemony over the Middle East. Many observers saw it as the first step in a revolutionary American grand design to transform the entire region. With the exception of the British and Japanese, most of the world's other major powers – not only China and Russia but even old allies like France and Germany – were greatly alarmed. In effect, the U.S. was proclaiming a global hegemony that could threaten anyone. Public opinion around much of the world turned deeply hostile.[2]

The most obvious explanation for America's extraordinary new assertiveness was the impact of 9/11 on our elite and public. Compared to many European countries and Japan, U.S. home territory had been relatively untouched by international terrorism before September 2001. Prescient analysts did warn earlier that the U.S. was highly vulnerable to terrorist attacks made easy by modern technology.[3] In its final years, the Clinton administration itself was growing seriously alarmed. But although many defense intellectuals and bureaucrats saw counterterrorism as a promising growth industry, neither the Clinton nor the early Bush administrations publicized it as an urgent priority.[4]

When the attacks did materialize, they came as a great shock to the public. Americans were brutally confronted by fanatical, murderous, and self-righteous foreign enemies. What could explain such venomous hatred?

Part of the answer could doubtless be found in the particular culture and pathology of Osama bin Laden and his followers.[5] Al Qaeda, however, is not merely a random band of fanatics but a global network of dedicated and disciplined zealots, backed by considerable public sympathy throughout the Muslim world. Why is there such sympathy? One obvious cause is America's historic role as Israel's devoted and all-powerful protector. While sustaining Israel for nearly half a century, the U.S. has never succeeded in brokering a compensatory settlement for the displaced Palestinians.[6] Among Arabs, and throughout the broader Islamic universe, the never-ending conflict with Israel has fed a widespread and deep-seated hostility to the United States. That hostility fuels global anti-Americanism and constitutes a major American geopolitical liability.

Anti-Americanism throughout the Middle East has, however, broader causes than Israel. Islam, not unlike Christianity, has had great trouble coming to terms with the modern world. But the Arab world, unlike the Christian one, has been far less able to use nation-states as frameworks and instruments for social, cultural, and economic advancement and reconciliation. This is not least because the existing Arab states lack the legitimacy of Western nation states. For this fatal deficiency, many Arabs find it both plausible and convenient to blame the West. Most Middle Eastern states, unlike European states, are not the natural outgrowth of several centuries of indigenous conflict and reconciliation. Rather, they are artificial structures imposed on the Arab world, principally by Britain and France after the breakup of the Ottoman Empire in World War I.[7] Such imposed states, lacking a natural consensus and legitimacy, are necessarily fragile and tyrannical. Typically, they are controlled by minorities ruling more by coercion and inertia than by active consent. Many Arab reformers detest their own governments and regional state systems and hold the West responsible for installing and sustaining them.

By now, "West" has come to mean, above all, the United States. After supporting Israel's implantation, the U.S. replaced Britain and France as the principal sustainer of the region's imposed state system. Accordingly, the U.S. is widely resented. Ironically, America's own clients are sometimes themselves major contributors to anti-American feeling. Unpopular traditionalist regimes curry popular favor by supporting fundamentalist Muslim foundations, often disseminators of rancorous anti-American propaganda. Al Qaeda itself springs and derives much of its nourishment from unofficial Saudi Arabian sources.[8] Modernist tyrannies, like Syria, use similar populist tactics at America's expense. Anti-Americanism helps them to gain the popular support they otherwise lack.

Successive administrations have searched for some new formula to stem the growing anti-Americanism in the Islamic world. An obvious course would be to achieve a settlement between Israel and the Palestinians. One administration after another has tried and failed.[9] Terrorist organizations, feeding on popular hatred for Israel and the U.S., are the principal beneficiaries. They grow increasingly difficult for the Arab states themselves to manage. In short, the U.S., ostensibly the dominant force in the region, has been trapped in an inexorably declining position. It has been tied both to an Israel that so far cannot reconcile itself with its neighbors and to authoritarian Arab allies, driven to seek popular legitimacy through covert accommodations with terrorists and anti-American forces generally.

Bush's Attempt to Escape

Not surprisingly, the Bush administration began searching for a radical policy to escape. By the summer of 2003, it was moving in two directions. On the one hand, it proclaimed its "road map" – a renewed effort to push Israel and the Palestinians into a stable settlement.[10] On the other hand, it had invaded Iraq, with a new policy of "regime change" aiming to achieve "democratization."[11] Although prompting an Israeli–Palestinian accord was a familiar "realist" goal, albeit never fulfilled, bringing democratic regime change to Iraq was a more recent enthusiasm, "neoconservative" rather than realist. Neoconservative partisans, and occasionally even the president himself, made clear their inclination to favor regime change elsewhere – soon perhaps in Lebanon, Syria, and Iran and later perhaps in Saudi Arabia and Egypt.[12] In effect, democratization was a policy to outflank the anti-American revolutionaries like al Qaeda. It offered the Arab world a competing ideal – unapologetically "modern" and Western – and put the military and economic power of the United States actively behind it. In extreme cases, like Iraq or Afghanistan, direct military power seemed ready to smash an old regime to create a new one.

The boldness of such a grand strategy is difficult to exaggerate. America's military predominance is the policy's vital precondition, but its success ultimately depends on the Middle East's receptivity to the modernist Western models introduced by American arms. Such a gamble suggests an old-fashioned liberal, neo-Wilsonian view of politics: Liberal capitalism, democracy, and Western-style human rights are seen as universal values, waiting to be released everywhere.[13] Destroying old tyranny automatically opens the way to asserting these values. American power imposes an enlightened liberal dictatorship until counterrevolutionary forces are purged or exhausted.

Among Americans, there was never any shortage of expert critics of this policy.[14] Many intellectuals and scholars familiar with Arab and Muslim cultures denied the universality of liberal Western values or at least rejected trying to implant them by military force. For many, the Bush policies were merely the latest clumsy and brutal Western intrusion, an imposition of alien Western ideals on a resistant culture. Ironically, Iraq was among the most "modernized" and secular societies in the region and therefore among the least susceptible to the wiles of Islamic terrorism. Saddam's regime was a brutal tyranny but had little use for Islamic-based political parties, let alone for terrorists like Osama bin Laden. Saddam's Iraq was also the region's most powerful and dedicated enemy of Islamic Iran – potentially the region's dominant power and also the most hostile to the United States. In short, from a realist perspective the Bush administration's strategic rationale for invading Iraq was deeply puzzling. This helps to explain the vehement criticism of most professionals who entered into the public debate.

Critics within the military saw the administration's policy as a reckless use of assets with little prospect of long-term success. Critics among professional diplomats saw it as a hubristic rush to national disaster, guaranteed to alienate old allies and rapidly undermine America's global influence. Such criticisms, however, took hold only slowly with the American public at large and even more slowly among America's political classes. For several years, the Bush administration continued to enjoy massive public support. Even in late 2004, when the problems of the American position should have been clear, Bush easily won a second term as president while the Republicans kept control over both houses of Congress.[15]

Whatever the Bush administration's practical failings, its neoconservative apologists were able to put together a vision of America's role in the world that resonated strongly among the nation's public. The war on terrorism provided the American political imagination with a new Manichean enemy. For much of the public, this updating of the familiar bipolar vision greatly simplified an otherwise complex and confusing world scene. Bush's new version of bipolarity, however, no longer reflected a conservative policy of containment.[16] Instead it envisaged a revolutionary policy of regime change, fusing neo-Wilsonian idealism and unipolar triumphalism. It had numerous critics but was difficult for traditional Democratic politicians to attack, perhaps because its liberal Wilsonian provenance was more a Democratic than a Republican heritage.[17] In any event, the administration was highly effective at intimidating its critics. In the heated atmosphere following 9/11, liberals criticizing the Bush policies were made to seem apologetic about defending America's national interest. Traditional conservatives – followers of Eisenhower rather than Reagan – seemed better suited and more disposed to criticize the Bush policies. Some conservative notables did speak out forcefully against launching the war in Iraq but made little headway.[18] The general public, like the administration, felt enabled by widespread feelings of unipolar omnipotence and threw diplomatic caution to the winds.

Bush's Reckoning

Early results seemed to justify the gamble; America's military victory in Iraq was swift and brilliant, as it had been over the Taliban in Afghanistan. But the triumph in Iraq soon dissolved into an increasingly bloody insurrection. Thereafter, events began to bear out the worst predictions of the war's critics. By 2004, the position of the invaders was growing increasingly uncomfortable. Not only was their legitimacy widely questioned but their grip on the country was alarmingly tenuous. The Bush administration pressed impatiently to "democratize" Iraq, so that U.S. forces might withdraw but leave behind a stable and friendly regime. A provisional government was named in June 2004 and elections for a constitutional assembly were held in January 2005.[19] A constitution was agreed on and ratified by the public in 2006. Shiite and Kurdish groups decided to participate in the new regime and, in the end, even some Sunni groups joined. All this seemed a considerable triumph for American policy. Nevertheless, finding and implementing a constitutional structure acceptable to all the warring elements has remained an elusive goal.[20]

Meanwhile, prospects for a Palestinian settlement have plunged still further. Palestinian elections in January 2006 resulted in an overwhelming victory for Hamas – a group still formally dedicated to eradicating the Jewish state. Israel responded by invading Lebanon to attack the Hezbollah guerrillas based there.[21] The military gains were minimal. Heavy casualties among Lebanese civilians fueled general outrage throughout the world. Meanwhile prospects for an early American withdrawal from Iraq grew more and more unpromising. By the end of 2006, talk of America's military "defeat" was widespread in Washington itself. Finally, after three years of surprisingly uncritical support, mass opinion in America began to turn abruptly. Polls showed only 22% of the American public approved of President Bush's conduct of the war. Slightly more than half believed the U.S. was losing; only 34% believed the United States was winning.[22] The Democrats gained a narrow victory in the Congressional elections of November 2006. Their own divisions, however, were soon patent. They were unanimous in condemning the administration's conduct of the war and the mendacious way in which the invasion had been justified. They were eager to investigate the financial and judicial abuses that the war had entailed. Many also favored withdrawing American forces, although with a wide variety of timetables. At the same time, however, many Democrats in Congress had voted for the war initially and found it unacceptable that the U.S. should acknowledge defeat.

Immediately following the Congressional elections of 2006 came the long-awaited *Iraq Study Group Report*, the product of a distinguished group of traditional and experienced moderates and conservatives from both parties. It was time, the *Report* argued, to shift responsibility for national reconciliation, security, and economic progress to the Iraqi government itself.[23] American forces should aim to be mostly gone by early 2008. A diplomatic offensive should engage Iraq's key neighbors, including Iran and Syria, as well as the major European states, in a consensus to avoid a general regional breakdown. The consensus would have to encompass a resolution of the Palestine question.[24]

Although all these ideas were common among the old establishment, they had little appeal for President Bush. Although he had fired Defense Secretary Rumsfeld, the principal architect of the administration's Iraq policy, the President remained reluctant to abandon the war. No doubt he was encouraged in this course by the reactions of the Democratic leaders in Congress – whose own support for *The Iraq Study Group Report* was, in many cases, as lukewarm as his own. The Democratic reaction was surprising, as polling data revealed broad public support for the *Report's* principal proposals. Analysts spoke of a notable dichotomy between public support for the plan and the ambivalent or hostile reception from the political classes in Washington. The *Report*, it seemed, was a "political orphan in Washington with little backing from either party."[25]

Bush Regains the Initiative

By early 2007, the president had regained the initiative by dispatching a "surge" of 21,500 additional troops.[26] This reflected a basic change in the Pentagon's approach to the war – a shift to counterinsurgency tactics discussed presently in Chapter 4. The shift implied a heavier commitment of troops trained to be an army of long-term occupation.[27] The American public, however, showed little enthusiasm for greater and longer engagement. Democrats in Congress were mostly opposed but unable to bind the administration. Fortunately for America's own domestic tranquility, Bush's surge proved a sufficient military success, at least in the short run, to avoid an immediate constitutional crisis.[28] Instead, the confrontation over Iraq policy was pushed into the presidential election of 2008.

At the outset of the campaign, the Republican candidate, John McCain, not only supported the war firmly but also adopted a rationale with considerable public appeal and great potential for sowing dissension among the Democrats. According to McCain, Bush's surge had reversed the precipitous decline of the military situation. A low-grade insurrection might persist but its cost was bearable and certainly

preferable to an ignominious withdrawal. With more patience, history
would vindicate Bush's war after all. Iraq could be transformed at a
bearable cost. This view also began to find support abroad, notably
in Israel, where respected analysts were claiming that Bush's invasion had brought about a fundamental and favorable shift in the
geostrategic balance in the Middle East – "a tectonic movement."
Iraq was a humanitarian and political disaster internally, to be sure,
but regionally, with Saddam out of the way, strategic threats were
much less than before. Chances were greatly improved for deals among
neighbors that would lower risk all around. Iran would be more
inclined to abandon its nuclear pursuits; Sunni and Shia would be
more likely to find a *modus vivendi*. Admittedly, prospects for an
Israeli settlement with the divided Palestinians were slight. Indeed,
no sooner was Obama elected than the Israelis bombarded and then
invaded Gaza. But the new American administration was counseled
to live with an imperfect Middle East, be content with conflict management rather than conflict resolution, and exploit the favorable new
geostrategic balance Bush had left behind.[29]

Many among *realist* foreign-policy elites may be inclined toward
these minimalist but nevertheless highly optimistic views. For others,
of course, such an outcome will seem an outrageously costly "victory,"
given the hundreds of thousands of dead Iraqis, the terrible degradation
of life for the remaining population, the suffering among our own
forces, and the trillions of dollars misspent. Above all, the implicit
presumption of a long-term occupation is likely to prove difficult for
much of the public to accept with complacency. As Barack Obama was
fond of saying while a candidate, the Iraq invasion was "the greatest
strategic blunder in the recent history of American foreign policy."
Much of the American public agreed and was eager to put the whole
experience behind it.

By the summer of 2008, Obama was preoccupied with trying to craft
a position that responded to the popular eagerness for withdrawal but
avoided advocating an American "defeat," as the McCain Republicans were ready to claim. The U.S. "would be as careful getting out of
Iraq as we were careless in getting in," Obama promised. An Obama
administration would renounce any "misguided" plan to establish
permanent bases in Iraq. It would initiate a phased withdrawal, spread
out over 16 months. Beginning to withdraw, Obama argued, would,

in itself, press the fledgling Iraqi regime to reach the domestic political accommodations needed to bring stability and security. Failure to pursue a stable and predictable withdrawal was what was blocking progress. In other words, starting withdrawal would create the conditions that would make withdrawal a success. With Iraq settled, Obama was careful to add, the U.S. would then be able to concentrate on the real war against terror – in Afghanistan. What if withdrawal failed to produce the effects Obama predicted? Obama's timetable would be subject to "technical adjustments." Residual forces would perform "limited missions," including "going after any remnants of Al-Qaeda in Mesopotamia."[30]

Obama's caution was doubtless sensible but it also revealed the weakness of his position. Like many other Democratic politicians, he found it easier to blame the "incompetence" of the Bush administration in pursuing its goals than to repudiate the goals themselves.[31] As a result, the election campaign may well prove to be less about America's place in the world than about who will manage that place better. This, of course, is not a trivial issue. But the real differences between Republicans and Democrats are likely to be less than expected. Neither is willing to risk Iraq's retrogressing into a hostile or failed state. Neither is pressing to reduce America's heavy involvement in the Middle East. Indeed, Obama is pressing for a major new effort in Afghanistan, not necessarily a promising project. In effect, both parties are caught in the unipolar mindset, where setbacks are the result of tactical mismanagement rather than strategic overstretch. So long as this unipolar mindset predominates in the nation's political imagination, Americans are unlikely to turn back their own geopolitical clock. The U.S. will remain an imperial power firmly engaged in the Middle East. Bush will be the election's real victor. What Bush has done probably cannot or, in any event, will not be undone. All this will leave many Americans feeling frustrated and betrayed, even if they do not exactly know why. And, of course, it will have major effects on America's relations with the rest of the world, above all perhaps in Europe.[32]

Notes

1. The distinction between preemptive and preventive war is critical to explaining the lack of foreign support for America's second invasion of

Iraq. To define a war as preemptive requires an imminent and certain threat to the invader's security. Such a war is a defensive action not banned under international law or the laws of war. Preventive war, by contrast, is military action to impede the rise of some potential threat in the future. Whether mere possession of "weapons of mass destruction" – a category that somewhat disingenuously includes chemical and biological weapons as well as nuclear arms – justifies a preemptive war is a matter of hot dispute. In any event, because no weapons of mass destruction were found in Iraq, the administration's effort to invoke preemption was ultimately not convincing – still less as the ongoing inspections of the International Atomic Energy Agency appeared to have been efficacious in frustrating Iraq's nuclear ambitions. Nor was serious evidence found for other so-called weapons of mass destruction, chemical or biological. For an account and analysis by the UN's chief weapons inspector, see Hans Blix, *Disarming Iraq* (London, UK: Bloomsbury Publishing PLC, 2005). For more information regarding preemptive and preventive war see Richard Betts, *Surprise Attack: Lessons for Defense Planning* (Washington, DC: Brookings, 1982), pp. 145–147.

2. See Chapter 1, footnote 1. The U.S. not only implied a new doctrine but also stated it clearly in the 2002 *National Security Strategy of the United States*. For example, President Bush declared, "the United States will use this moment of opportunity to extend the benefits of freedom across the globe.... The United States possesses unprecedented – and unequaled – strength and influence in the world. Sustained by faith in the principles of liberty, and the value of a free society, this position comes with unparalleled responsibilities, obligations, and opportunity. The great strength of this nation must be used to promote a balance of power that favors freedom.... While the United States will constantly strive to enlist the support of the international community, we will not hesitate to act alone, if necessary, to exercise our right of self defense by acting preemptively against such terrorists, to prevent them from doing harm against our people and our country." The White House, September 17, 2002, http://www.whitehouse.gov/nsc/nssall.html. An updated version of the National Security Strategy appeared in March 2006, at http://www.whitehouse.gov/nsc/nss/2006/.

3. For earlier expert warnings, see Ian O. Lesser et al., *Countering the New Terrorism* (Santa Monica, CA: The RAND Corporation, 1998), Daniel Benjamin and Steven Simon, "America and the New Terrorism," *Survival*, Vol. 42(1), 2000, pp. 59–75. See also Daniel Benjamin and Steven Simon, *The Age of Sacred Terror: Radical Islam's War against America* (New York, NY: Random House, 2003).

4. *The 9/11 Commission Report: Final Report of the National Commission on Terrorist Attacks upon the United States* (New York, NY: W. W.

Norton & Company, 2004), criticized the first Bush and Clinton admin-
istrations for not paying enough attention to the terrorist threat. The
Clinton administration did step up efforts. *The Presidential Decision
Directive 39*, U.S. Policy on Counterterrorism (http://www.fas.org/irp/
offdocs/pdd39.htm), June 21, 1995, tried to formulate a more coherent
approach to "reduce vulnerabilities at home and abroad." See Richard
Clarke, *Against All Enemies: Inside America's War on Terror* (New York,
NY: Free Press, 2004), pp. 90–92.

5. Osama bin Laden founded al Qaeda soon after the end of the Afghan
   struggle against the Soviets. He had joined the Afghan resistance in 1979
   and soon become a commander. After the Soviet collapse he shifted his
   focus to opposing the Western world in general and the U.S. in particular.
   Al Qaeda today is a loose and decentralized organization of militant small
   terrorist groups, inspired by figures like Osama bin Laden and Ayman
   el-Zawahiri and spread around the world. In 2000, al Qaeda was behind
   the attacks on the U.S. embassy in Nairobi and against the U.S. warship
   USS *Cole*. It then organized the September 11, 2001 attacks on the World
   Trade Center and the Pentagon. Bin Laden's primary aim in the early 1990s
   was securing the withdrawal of U.S. and other foreign troops from Saudi
   Arabia, from which he was himself expelled. He declared a holy war on
   the United States, using religious language invoking Islamic resistance to
   the medieval European crusades, to fuse and mobilize the Muslim world
   against today's "neocrusaders," seen as an alliance of Zionist Jews and
   Christians.

   For more information on al Qaeda and its leader, see Lawrence Wright,
   The Looming Tower: Al Qaeda and the Road to 9/11 (New York, NY:
   Knopf, 2006), and Peter L. Bergen, *The Osama bin Laden I Know: An
   Oral History of Al-Qaeda's Leader* (New York, NY: Free Press, 2006).
   Michael Scheuer, *Through Our Enemies' Eyes: Osama bin Laden, Radical Islam, and the Future of America* (Washington, DC: Potomac Books,
   2006) compares al Qaeda's vision to that of the eighteenth-century American colonists fighting the British. For information on more recent developments, see "Curbing al-Qaeda: the group may be weaker but jihadism still
   spreads," *Financial Times*, July 6, 2007, p. 14 and "Winning or Losing:
   A Special Report on al-Qaeda," *The Economist*, July 19, 2008, after
   p. 50ff.

6. For a history of the U.S.–Israeli relationship, see David Schoenbaum, *The
   United States and the State of Israel* (Oxford, UK: Oxford University
   Press, 1993). For recent critical analyses of the relationship and what
   sustains it, see Anatol Lieven, *America Right or Wrong: An Anatomy
   of American Nationalism* (Oxford, UK: Oxford University Press, 2004),
   Ch. 6. See also John J. Mearsheimer and Steven Walt, *The Israel Lobby and
   U.S. Foreign Policy* (New York, NY: Farrar, Straus, and Giroux, 2007).

For additional information see letters "The Israel Lobby" by Alan Dershowitz and the comments from Robert Pfaltzgraf in the *London Review of Books*, Vol. 28(8) April 20, 2006, pp. 4–5). See also Eliot A. Cohen, "Yes, It's Anti-Semitic," *The Washington Post*, April 5, 2006, A23; Glenn Frankel, "A Beautiful Friendship: In Search of the Truth about the Israel Lobby's Influence on Washington," *The Washington Post*, July 16, 2006: W13; and Tony Judt, "A Lobby, Not a Conspiracy," *The New York Times*, April 19, 2006: A21.

7. At the treaties of Sèvres with the Ottoman Empire (1920) and Lausanne with the Turkish Republic (1923), Britain and France carved up the Ottoman Empire's Arab territories much as they had divided up Africa following the Berlin Conference of 1885. Winston Churchill, advised by the exotic academic adventurer T. E. Lawrence, was the driving force behind the final settlement. The former Empire's Arab possessions were transformed into the Kingdoms of Iraq, Transjordan and Saudi Arabia, the Republic of Lebanon, and the British Mandate of Palestine. Iraq and Palestine (the latter included the Transjordan) were made British mandates. Syria and Lebanon were French mandates. All gained independence in the 1940s but remained artificial creations superimposed on peoples of disparate language, religions, and sects. For T. E. Lawrence's own account, see his *Seven Pillars of Wisdom: A Triumph,* (Garden City, NY: Doubleday, Doran & Company, 1935.) For the misperceptions that informed British and French territorial ambitions, see David Fromkin, *A Peace to End All Peace: The Fall of the Ottoman Empire and the Creation of the Modern Middle East* (New York, NY: Avon Books, 1990). For a broad historical survey of accumulating Muslim failure and dissatisfaction, see Bernard Lewis, *What Went Wrong: Western Impact and Middle Eastern Response* (Oxford, UK: Oxford University Press, 2002). My colleague, Fouad Ajami, in his *The Foreigner's Gift: The Americans, the Arabs, and the Iraqis in Iraq* (New York, NY: Free Press, 2006) argues that the U.S. intervention in Iraq was essentially a moral enterprise, one that history will portray either as a "noble success" or a "noble failure." For a contrasting view of the Middle East conflict, see Edward W. Said, *From Oslo to Iraq and the Road Map: Essays* (New York, NY: Vintage, 2005), and Said's foreword to the 25th anniversary edition of his *Orientalism* (New York, NY: Vintage, 2004).

8. See *The 9/11 Commission Report: Final Report of the National Commission on Terrorist Attacks upon the United States* (New York: W.W. Norton & Company, 2004); Council on Foreign Relations, *Terrorist Financing* (New York, NY: CFR Press, 2002); Christopher Blanchard and Alfred Prados, *Report for Congress: Saudi Arabia: Terrorist Financing Issues,* Congressional Research Service, December 2004; Barry Rubin, "The Truth

about US Middle East Policy," *The Middle East Review of International Affairs*, Vol. 5(4), 2001, pp. 1–25.

9. For surveys of U.S. diplomacy toward Israel, see Dennis Ross, *The Missing Peace: The Inside Story of the Fight for Middle East Peace* (New York, NY: Farrar, Straus, & Giroux, 2005). Charles Enderlin and Susan Fairfield (trans.), *Shattered Dreams: The Failure of the Peace Process in the Middle East, 1995–2002* (New York, NY: Other Press, 2003), David Schoenbaum, *The United States and the State of Israel* (Oxford, UK: Oxford University Press, 1993).

10. Bush's road map was proposed in the summer of 2003, with support from the UN, the EU and Russia. It foresaw progression from a cease-fire to a provisional Palestinian state to final negotiations on permanent borders followed by recognition of the two states by the international community. Originally the process was to be completed by the end of 2005. Each side has accused the other of bad faith. See David Makovsky, "Gaza: Moving Forward by Pulling Back," *Foreign Affairs*, vol. 84 May/June 2005, pp. 52–62.

11. President George W. Bush, in 2003, before the National Endowment of Democracy: "Iraqi democracy will succeed – and that success will send forth the news, from Damascus to Teheran – that freedom can be the future of every nation. [...] Therefore, the United States has adopted a new policy, a forward strategy of freedom in the Middle East. This strategy requires the same persistence and energy and idealism we have shown before [...]. The advance of freedom is the calling of our time; it is the calling of our country" (http://www.whitehouse.gov/news/releases/2003/11/20031106–2.html).

12. For a general study of the neoconservative group around Bush, see my colleague James Mann's *Rise of the Vulcans: The History of Bush's War Cabinet* (New York, NY: Viking, 2004).

13. The younger Bush's triumphalism has many Wilsonian aspects, in particular the idea that the American political system is the world's best and can be exported elsewhere, by force if necessary. But Wilson put great faith in global public opinion, whereas recent American policymakers disregard it. Similarly, he had great hopes for a League of Nations, whereas the Bush administration has low expectations for the UN. And although Wilson counted the U.S. the world's leading power, he avoided unipolar imagery and preferred to present a plural global system of nation states coexisting harmoniously. He was less Hobbesian and more liberal than today's neoconservative Wilsonians and perhaps also more of a realist. Interestingly, the one insight neoconservatives borrow from contemporary realists is the idea that international institutions and international law are largely useless. Taking this into account, one could say that

neoconservatives represent the worst of both the Wilsonian and realist models.

14. Cultural, military, and diplomatic critics of the Bush administration's foreign policy are by now legion, even among neoconservatives themselves. See Gary Rosen (ed.), *The Right War? The Conservative Debate on Iraq* (Cambridge, UK: Cambridge University Press, 2005); or Francis Fukuyama, *America at the Crossroads: Democracy, Power, and the Neoconservative Legacy* (New Haven, CT: Yale University Press, 2006). See also General Tony Zinni and Tony Koltz, *The Battle for Peace: A Frontline Vision of America's Power and Purpose* (New York, NY: Palgrave Macmillan, 2006).

15. In the 2004 elections, George W. Bush won 50.7% of the popular vote and 286 electoral votes. John F. Kerry won 48.3% of the popular vote and 251 electoral votes. *USAToday*/Gallup Polls showed consistent majority support for the President until the middle of 2005, with significant wavering in 2004. By February 1, 2007, twice as many disapproved as approved "of the way George W. Bush is handling his job as president" (65% versus 32%). See Jeffrey M. Jones, "Bush Approval Dips to 32%," *The Gallup Poll*, February 6, 2007, http://www.galluppoll.com/content/?ci=26413. For the shift in public reaction to the war and the president's handling of it by the end of 2006, see footnotes 21 and 26.

16. See, for example, the letter from thirty professors of international relations urging the administration to contain Iraq but avoid an invasion. See the advertisement "War with Iraq Is Not in America's National Interest," *New York Times*, September 26, 2002, http://johnmearsheimer.uchicago.edu/pdfs/P0012.pdf.

17. For the difficulties of the Democrats, see David P. Calleo, "Dilemmas of Liberal Realism," *Survival*, Vol. 47(1), Spring 2005, pp. 167–171, a commentary on Zbigniew Brzezinski's *The Choice: Global Domination or Global Leadership* (New York, NY: Basic Books, 2004). For a rich historical study of the multiple roots of American nationalism and imperialism, including its appeal to Democrats, see Anatol Lieven, *America Right or Wrong: An Anatomy of American Nationalism* (Oxford, UK/New York, NY: Oxford University Press, 2004).

18. Notable for opposing the Iraq war was the older Bush's National Security Adviser, Brent Scowcroft, "Don't Attack Saddam," *Wall Street Journal*, August 15, 2002: p. A12. See also Brent Scowcroft with his Clinton counterpart, Samuel R. Berger, *In the Wake of War: Improving U.S. Post-Conflict Capabilities* (New York, NY: Council on Foreign Relations Press, 2005). Several other members of the first Bush administration, including the elder Bush himself, never seemed enthusiastic about the 2002 invasion of Iraq, at least not as it was actually conducted. The elder Bush's Secretary of State, James Baker, took his distance early on. See

James A. Baker III, "The Right Way to Change a Regime," *The New York Times*, August 25, 2002: D9. During 2006, Baker was co-chairman of the bipartisan and Congressionally mandated *Iraq Study Group Report* that urged American military disengagement from Iraq and a broad settlement of Middle Eastern issues in negotiation with all interested parties.

19. For the Iraqi elections of January 30, 2005, see BBC News, "Shia parties triumph in Iraq poll," February 14, 2005 (http://news.bbc.co.uk/2/hi/middle_east/4261035.stm). For expert analysis see "Iraq after the Elections," *The Brookings Institution*, February 10, 2005, http://www.brookings.edu/comm/events/20050210.pdf.

20. For information on Iraq's constitutional development during 2007, see Christina Parajon, "The Iraq Hydrocarbon Law: How and When?" U.S. Institute of Peace Briefing, June 2007. www.usip.org. See also Steven Lee Myers and Alissa J. Rubin, "U.S. Scales Back Political Goals for Iraqi Unity," *New York Times*, November 25, 2007, http://www.nytimes.com/2007/11/25/washington/25policy.html; Daniel Serwer and Sam Parker, "Iraq After the Surge: Options and Questions," U.S. Institute of Peace Briefing, April 6, 2008, http://www.usip.org/pubs/usipeace_briefings/2008/0406_iraq_surge.html#improved.

21. For an interesting article on the shared real interests between Israel's Olmert government and Hamas, see Robert Malley and Aaron David Miller, "For Israel and Hamas, a Case for Accommodation," *The Washington Post*, May 15, 2006: A17. Formerly, Malley was special assistant to President Clinton for Arab–Israeli affairs and Miller a State Department Middle East negotiator.

22. An article that summarizes poll results, in particular the *Washington Post-ABC News* survey released on December 12, 2006, put President Bush's general approval rating at 36% and his handling of Iraq at 28%. Overall 52% believed the U.S. to be losing the war. The article also discusses the public's skepticism toward the Democrats and complicated reaction to the Baker/Hamilton Iraq Study Group findings. Peter Baker and John Cohen, "Americans Say U.S. Is Losing War," *The Washington Post*, December 13, 2006: A1.

23. The Report appeared immediately following the Congressional elections of November 2006 and was meant to present a coherent and bipartisan way out of Iraq. It called for a radical acceleration of American withdrawal. The primary mission of U.S. forces should be "supporting the Iraqi army, which should take over primary responsibility for combat operations" (p. 70). American combat units should "be deployed only in units embedded with Iraqi forces" (p. 72). Further American support should depend on how resolutely and successfully the regime was restoring order and pursuing a policy of national reconciliation. In any event, American troops should be mostly gone by early 2008. James A. Baker III

and Lee H. Hamilton, *The Iraq Study Group Report* (New York, NY: Random House, 2006), p. 70.

24. *Ibid.*, p. 39.

25. Quoted in Peter Baker and Jon Cohen, "Americans Say U.S. Is Losing War," *The Washington Post*, December 13, 2006: A1.

26. For President Bush's announcement of the surge, see "President's Address to the Nation," *The White House*, January 2007, http://www.whitehouse.gov/news/releases/2007/01/20070110-7.html. For an optimistic view of the surge, see Pete Hegseth, "Give the Surge a Chance," *The Wall Street Journal*, July 9, 2007: A15; and Cesar G. Soriano, "Patraeus Says Security Crackdown Working," *USA Today*, June 13, 2007. For a critique of the surge, see Mike Bruton, "Troop Surge Comes with Criticism," *The Philadelphia Tribune*, January 21, 2007, Vol. 4, p. 3C.

27. For more information on broader changes in training and strategic goals from Iraq see Michael R. Gordon, "After Hard-Won Lessons, Army Doctrine Revised," *New York Times*, February 8, 2008, http://www.nytimes.com/2008/02/08/washington/08strategy. html. See also Jeffrey P. Bialos, *Ideas for America's Future: Core Elements of a New National Security Strategy* (Washington, DC: Center for Transatlantic Relations, 2008).

28. Although the "troop surge" did not quickly effect any considerable change in the American public's views about the wisdom of the Iraq War, during 2007 more and more people saw the current situation getting better as a result of the surge. By December 5, 2007, 40% of the population held this view. See Lydia Saad, "U.S. Troop Surge in Iraq Receives a Bit More Credit," *Gallup*, December 5, 2007, http://www.gallup.com/poll/103057/US-Troop-Surge-Iraq-Receives-Bit-More-Credit.aspx.

29. For a discussion with Ehud Yaari and Shlomo Avineri, see Jonathan Marcus, "Bush's Mid-East Legacy," *BBC News,* July, 15, 2008, http://news.bbc.co.uk/2/hi/middle_east/7507880.stm.

30. Barack Obama, "My Plan for Iraq: It's Time to Begin a Troop Pullout," *International Herald Tribune*, July 15, 2008: 8.

31. For the early positions of the three leading presidential candidates concerning Iraq see "The Candidates on Iraq," Council on Foreign Relations, May 30, 2008, http://www.cfr.org/publication/14761/candidates_on_iraq.html.

32. See Ch. 1, footnote 1.

3

The Broken West

Strategic Dissonance in the West

Over the past several years, West European public opinion, by very large majorities, has been more deeply critical of American policy than at any time since World War II.[1] The Democrats freely criticized the Bush administration's failure to cultivate the European allies, but it was not clear that they were themselves any more willing to defer to European views. At times, the two halves of the West have almost seemed programmed for mutual alienation. Arguably, this is the Iraq War's heaviest cost – for both Europe and for the United States. The Obama administration will hope to restore transatlantic comity. But it will soon confront fundamental geopolitical differences that will require more than a change in atmosphere to manage. These differences have been emerging over the past three administrations.

The European public was leery of the Bush administration from the start, but it was horrified at the terrorist atrocities of 9/11. There followed a spontaneous outpouring of sympathy and solidarity. European publics strongly supported America's retaliatory invasion of Afghanistan. European governments proposed making the invasion a NATO project in which they would participate. Ironically, the U.S. turned down the offer.[2] By contrast, the war in Iraq never was popular with European publics. The governments of France and Germany refused to support the invasion within the UN Security Council. As a result the invasion was initially illegal under international law.[3] So

39

dramatic a repudiation by two of our principal allies came as a great
political shock in the U.S. and caused a remarkably bitter reaction from
the American government.[4] It also quickly divided European governments from one another, although public opinion in most of Europe
remained deeply hostile to the Iraq war.[5]

The Security Council debates around the invasion revealed the depth
of the disagreements. The formal Anglo-American resolution to autho-
rize the invasion prudently avoided proposing regime change per se,
because it was a goal rejected out of hand by most Security Council
members. Instead, the U.S. and Britain emphasized the danger that Iraq
was about to acquire weapons of mass destruction and claimed their
own intelligence reports validated such fears.[6] UN inspectors in Iraq
found scant evidence to support the Anglo-American claims. Thus,
for many governments and world public opinion generally, the Anglo-
American position lacked credibility.[7] An invasion might eventually
be needed, the French agreed, but Iraq posed no immediate threat.
And if, as preliminary UN reports indicated, inspections continued to
frustrate Iraqi ambitions, a Western invasion could not be justified.
The risks were too high both for the region and for the West. France's
private advice to the U.S. was: Don't invade, but if you must, don't
ask for our formal support.[8]

Escalation

The French logic was powerful so long as Iraq's putative weapons
of mass destruction were the main concern. As the French rightly sus-
pected, however, the dominant American preoccupation was to change
the regime; the search for weapons was merely a pretext. The French
were diffident about condoning a use of American military power jus-
tifiable neither by the letter nor by the spirit of normal international
law. Above all, they feared the practical consequences of an invasion.
The French view was fervently shared in Germany, France's principal partner in building the European Union and formerly America's
closest continental ally.[9] Ultimately standing together with France and
Germany in the Security Council were the two principal Eurasian military powers – China and Russia. A nascent Great Eurasian coalition
suddenly emerged, Cheshire-cat–like, to oppose the unipolar ambitions
of the United States.[10]

The United States escalated the transatlantic conflict by launching a campaign to isolate France and Germany from the rest of Europe.[11] Despite the public hostility to the war across Europe, the official Anglo-American bandwagon soon loaded on the governments of Italy, Spain, Poland, and most of the smaller Eastern European members and candidate members of the EU.[12] An Anglo-American-led "New Europe" thus broke openly with the traditional French-and-German-led "Old Europe." The stakes suddenly were very high. American officials began talking about "punishing France" or breaking up the French–German alliance. There followed a very bad period for intra-European and transatlantic relations. Meanwhile, the American and British invasion of Iraq was duly launched, joined initially by token forces from Australia and Poland. By 2003, the administration claimed support from a coalition of 49 countries.[13]

Second Thoughts

By 2005, events in the Middle East were encouraging greater caution in Washington. The Iraqi insurrection was gaining strength and hopes for a quick coalition victory had vanished. The Bush administration launched its second term with a flurry of diplomacy to mend its European fences. Europeans were themselves eager to welcome the new American overtures. *Schadenfreude* over America's discomfiture was limited by growing concern over the consequences of an Iraq abandoned to ever greater chaos. Meanwhile, Europeans were struggling to repair their own fragmented Union. The EU's highly charged agenda included enlarging the membership, instituting a "constitutional treaty" that might permit coordinated diplomacy and defense – (along with more rapid and transparent decision-making in general), finding a common policy toward immigration, and installing policies to anticipate expected demographic changes as well as to augment competitiveness and employment generally. Collective European aspirations suffered a severe blow in May 2005, as the EU's proposed new constitutional treaty failed in French and Dutch referenda.[14] The result has been several years of constitutional drifting with a third failed referendum during June 2008. With Europe itself in such disarray, patching up transatlantic relations seemed all the more prudent. Confronting each other over Iraq had led Americans and Europeans to the edge of a geopolitical abyss. Neither side liked what it saw there and each began trying to appease the other. Although still refusing to contribute combat forces to Iraq, the French and Germans had taken up serious peacekeeping roles in the Balkans, Afghanistan, and Africa, thus relieving indirectly some of the strain on American forces.[15] Although most European states that had originally sent troops to Iraq soon withdrew them, Europeans did take a major role in training an Iraqi police force and formally cancelled significant portions of Iraq's large debts.[16]

Containing the United States

European diplomacy was much concerned with heading off American plans for military strikes against any more countries in the region, most particularly Iran, a popular target in neoconservative circles close to the Bush administration.[17] Prospects for a negotiated *modus vivendi* had grown dimmer as the Iranian election of June 2005 resulted in a populist and fundamentalist president, Mahmoud Ahmadinejad, whose inflammatory rhetoric greatly alarmed the Israelis.[18] Nevertheless, the French, German, and even British governments all made clear their strong opposition to an American or Israeli military intervention. At the same time they all firmly acknowledged the need to prevent Iran from acquiring nuclear weapons.[19] Iranians claimed to be pursuing nuclear enrichment technologies for civilian purposes. Although not illegal according to the Non-Proliferation Treaty, their secretive progress in these technologies did advance their capabilities for producing nuclear weapons.[20]

To remove the ostensible *casus belli*, Britain, France, and Germany, with wide support from the rest of the EU, negotiated jointly to dissuade the Iranians from pursuing the offending technologies. Russia and China joined in to press both Iran and the United States to negotiate directly. Insofar as Iran, surrounded by nuclear powers, feared for its own security, Europeans dangled the distant prospect of a multilateral security organization devised for the region. Iran also wished to join the World Trade Organization. Promoting its membership was part of the elaborate diplomatic game. Although diplomatic progress was limited, the direct military confrontation that Europeans feared was avoided.[21]

In summary, transatlantic relations did improve superficially in Bush's second term, but underlying serious differences continued.

Europeans and Americans were divided by conflicting approaches to the future that went beyond Iraq and the Middle East. France and Germany, deeply committed to the EU, were on one geopolitical wavelength; the U.S. and Britain, at least under Blair, were on another. As a result, France and Germany were taking their distance from American global positions, whereas the U.S. and Britain were more frankly unenthusiastic about having the EU emerge as a strong and independent world force.[22] Britain, in any event, saw its role as a balancer between the U.S. and the EU.

NATO, the EU, and Russia

The potential for conflict had been clear at the start of the 1990s, during the administration of the elder Bush.[23] America's ambitions for the post-Soviet world revealed themselves in the "Two Plus Four" negotiations, held in 1990 to settle Germany's future status.[24] With the Soviets retreating from the front line of their European empire, the administration was determined to keep NATO unchanged and a unified Germany firmly within it. Promises were apparently made to the Soviets not to extend NATO further, but the promises were quickly ignored in the Clinton administration, in which plans were soon germinating for expanding the Alliance. By 1992, newly elected President Clinton had himself publicly endorsed NATO's expansion. In due course, NATO's "Partnership for Peace," although engaging the Russian military in token cooperation, was busy installing America's military presence deep into what the Russians saw as their "near abroad."[25] NATO's formal enlargement to ex-Soviet states began in 1999. By 2006, the new members included the three Baltic states, Poland, the Czech Republic, Slovakia, Hungary, Romania, and Bulgaria. The U.S. was pushing to add Ukraine, Georgia, and various Central Asian states.[26]

Meanwhile, NATO's planners had been busy searching for a new "concept" to rationalize the Alliance after it had lost its enemy. Taking in new members was seen as a major way to stabilize the fledgling democracies of Eastern Europe.[27] It was assumed that NATO membership would guarantee peace among them. In this respect, NATO might be transformed from an anti-Russian alliance into a pan-European security system. Such a project, however, implied membership for the new Russia. The other former communist states were vehemently opposed, whereas the Russians themselves professed to be uninterested. They did, however, participate eagerly enough in the North Atlantic Cooperation Council but complained that it was devoid of any real substance. With Russia at arm's length, NATO's potential for becoming a pan-European security system was greatly curtailed.[28]

Another rationale for perpetuating the Alliance was encapsulated in the fashionable nostrum "out of area or out of business." NATO was promoted as a "toolbox" of European forces available for American-led expeditions around the world. NATO did play an important military role of this kind, as American forces came into the Balkans in the 1990s, later in Afghanistan and in the War on Terror generally. West European allies, however, grew increasingly leery of remote NATO entanglements. NATO's support in Europe depended heavily on those former communist states who remained preoccupied with old and new fears of Russia. The military forces of these states were, however, relatively undeveloped and of limited use to the Americans.[29]

Maastricht Europe

Meanwhile, the more advanced European states were tending toward a quite different view of post-Soviet security arrangements. The Maastricht Treaty of 1991 spelled out a deeper and more complete European Union. Alongside the familiar economic projects – a single market, a European Monetary Union, and the euro – there was to be common foreign and security policy and common defense, tied together with a general constitutional overhaul. By early 1993, the EU's Copenhagen Agreement also called for gradually extending membership to most of what had been Soviet Europe.[30]

Although frequently depicted as complementary, American and European strategies pointed toward quite different geopolitical results. The Franco-German–led Maastricht strategy implied a more autonomous EU, a development that in itself implied a plural rather than unipolar world. American leaders were conscious of what was at stake. By early 1991, the U.S. was openly seeking to limit EU plans for an independent military force. In December 1992, the first President Bush himself angrily denounced the European schemes.[31] And from the start, the rival visions were implicitly competing for the loyalties of the newly liberated East Europeans.

Clinton's European Détente

The advent of the Clinton administration in 1993 encouraged a temporary transatlantic détente. Clinton himself shared little of the elder Bush's enthusiasm for military power and traditional geopolitics. Instead, he was preoccupied with the global economy and with restoring America's competitiveness and fiscal stability. Restoring fiscal balance, Clinton's greatest achievement, depended in the first instance on deep cuts in defense spending. Logically, these ruled out an aggressive foreign policy involving major military interventions. In principle, a stronger, more autonomous European defense suited Clinton's own strategy.

Following Maastricht and Copenhagen, the European Union was, like America, preoccupied with its own internal and regional economic projects – in particular monetary union and enlarging its membership. Neither side was vigorously pressing military issues and neither was eager for confrontations over fundamental strategic questions. Possibly neither side was fully conscious of the longer term geopolitical implications of the different plans for European security arrangements. Probably Clinton's Americans did not see themselves using NATO to cement an imperial hegemony over Europe. And although most European governments welcomed the prospect of more European self-sufficiency, they were loath to part with an American military protection that had served them well in the Cold War, cost them very little, and given them some voice in American policy. Nevertheless, as the elder Bush had grasped early on, building the new EU of Maastricht was not a project easily compatible with preserving and extending NATO as a hegemonic alliance.

Events soon overtook both sides. The Soviet collapse had spawned a whole variety of new military threats. Even as Maastricht was being negotiated at the end of 1991, an appalling ethnic conflict was exploding in Yugoslavia. By August 1992, Europeans had decided to intervene under a UN mandate. But left to themselves, the Europeans soon revealed a lamentable lack of collective will to sustain an effective military intervention. The French refused to act forcefully without a major ally. Because the Germans remained unwilling and perhaps unable to assume a serious military role in the Balkans, this left the French partnered with John Major's Britain, which was unenthusiastic about acting outside of NATO and forever limiting and qualifying its terms of engagement.[32] Under these circumstances, American leadership did prove indispensable. An American-led military intervention was successful in stopping the fighting and culminated in the Dayton Agreements in December 1995.[33]

The Persistence of Europe

Blessed with a fresh military and diplomatic triumph, the Clinton administration began to look more like its predecessor.[34] Americans grew more assertive and less attentive to European views or interests. As noted earlier, NATO was admitting its first group of new members in 1998 with several more scheduled in the new decade.[35] The year 1999 also saw America's second major Yugoslav intervention – in Kosovo, traditionally a Serbian province but with an Albanian Muslim majority. The Serbian police were waging war on their own Muslim citizens. If the earlier genocidal horrors were not to be repeated, intervention was clearly required. The Americans commanded the operation – using air power exclusively – mostly their own. Unlike the earlier Balkan interventions, the Kosovo intervention was organized and legitimated by NATO rather than the UN. Both Americans and Europeans were ultimately dissatisfied with the arrangements. The American military resented having to share with Europeans control over targeting the aerial missions.[36] Europeans found the air campaign needlessly destructive and ill suited for protecting the populations at risk.

More fundamentally, Europeans, particularly after the EU's spectacular success in launching its common currency, began to find an American-led alliance an unreliable, inappropriate, and indeed unworthy arrangement for dealing with security problems in Europe's own region. European projects for a more autonomous defense continued, however, to be regularly frustrated by disagreements among Europe's national governments. Europe's aspirations for collective defense have, nevertheless, refused to go away. Anglo-French military conversations and projects have continued, with the Germans increasingly involved. Even the bitter falling out among the three over Iraq will perhaps prove only a temporary setback. By 2005, a European Security and Defense Initiative (ESDI) called for a European rapid reaction force of 60,000 troops. By 2008, the forces appeared to be taking form.[37]

In summary, as Europe's integration accelerated after the Soviet demise, tensions mounted between Europe's aspirations for regional autonomy and America's unwillingness to give up its Cold War position. Political, economic, and military ambitions on both sides of the Atlantic grew increasingly divergent. At the root of the differences were radically different visions of the world's future geopolitical order. Throughout the 1990s the issues separating the visions could never be resolved decisively because neither side was really strong enough to prevail. An enlarged Europe was itself too diverse to sustain its pretensions to a common foreign and defense policy. Each of Europe's major military powers had its own hesitations. The British, even if progressively unhappy with American policy, were themselves only slowly being drawn into a full European role. The Germans were too pacifist to allow the Franco-German axis to become the foundation for Europe's military dimension. France, for centuries a leading global power in rivalry with Britain, was drawn to global military roles but, with Germany holding back, was wary of depending on the British (or the Americans). Short of some severe crisis, it will, at best, take considerable time for the EU's military partners to grow sufficiently cohesive in their strategies and practices to endow the European Union with an effective military dimension.

The former communist states may, with time, also come to see the advantages of a more European defense. So far, their experiences with NATO have not been particularly encouraging. They are likely to see their own national success bound up more and more with the success of Europe as a whole. As their national identities grow more "European," they may come to see the advantages of cordial relations with Russia, as well as the dangers of being too closely identified with American global policies.

Europe, Its Neighbors, and the United States

It is interesting to speculate on whether the Iraq war will eventually speed European military integration. Among the major inducements for Europe to have an effective military force of its own is the need for secure relations with surrounding regions. These include Russia, the Muslim Middle East, and Africa. Europe has a vital strategic interest in preserving friendly relations with all these neighbors. All seem essential to a secure and prosperous Europe – as suppliers of energy and raw materials, as markets for European trade, or, in the case of Russia and the Middle East, as suppliers of capital for Europe's financial industry. Accordingly, a return to the old Cold War hostility with Russia is certainly not in Europe's interest. And a "war of civilizations" with the Muslim world would have catastrophic consequences, not only for Europe's trade and investment but for its own domestic stability. Insofar as a close alliance with the United States makes these catastrophes more probable, Europeans will be inclined to keep their distance.

Europeans, of course, are well aware of the advantages to them of an American military presence. An effective military balance is generally a necessary foundation for good relations and for this reason many Europeans are not eager to see NATO disappear. Europeans, however, tend to define military balance as mutual containment rather than as the clear superiority of one side over the other. And Europeans tend to see military balance as only the precondition for a successful foreign policy, not as the foreign policy itself. For Europe, foreign policy generally involves mutual appeasement, where both sides join to cultivate the possibilities for collective gain. Hard bargaining is to be expected, but neither side should grow fixated on issues that provoke mutual irritation or fear.

The United States has long played a useful role in this sort of European strategy. Throughout the Cold War, America's military presence not only contained Soviet Russia but also permitted Europe's postwar states the confidence to integrate as intimately as they have. American security, of course, comes with risks: Sometimes a would-be hegemonic protector develops a vested interest in regional bad relations. Too aggressive protecting against neighbors may block possibilities for good relations with them.

New Geostrategic Calculations: Europe and America Forever?

In the heyday of the Soviet Union the American alliance was clearly a good bargain for Europe. Today, with a different Russia and an emerging Islamic world – not to mention rising Asian superpowers and a deeply troubled Africa, the calculation for Europe is more complex. The war in Iraq emphasizes the risks of Europe's American connection. With no Soviet Union, Europe has lost its transatlantic leverage. Europe's natural recourse is to build up its own capabilities to help to restore the transatlantic equilibrium that has been disturbed by the Soviet collapse. A stronger and more autonomous defense will also help to give Europe more leeway for appeasing diplomacy with its neighbors. Better relations with neighbors will lessen dependency on the United States.

Would a more autonomous European Union point to the end of the Atlantic Alliance? This does not need to happen. It could mean a healthy rebalancing that would strengthen the West and help make both the U.S. and the EU better adapted for life in an increasingly plural world system. Undoubtedly, however, Europe's unhappiness with the Alliance since the Cold War should be taken as a friendly warning. The leading states of the EU, and much of the European public, are not enthusiastic about the vision of a global *Pax Americana* that successive U.S. governments have been nurturing; neither, for that matter, are the Russians, Chinese, and Arabs. All have dreams of their own for the new century. America's aspirations have seemed inhospitable to them all. It is not, therefore, surprising that the United States has grown progressively isolated and embattled.

The U.S. likes to think of itself as the passive victim of the malevolence of others. Although there is no gainsaying the malevolence of those who carried out the attacks of 9/11, the widespread opposition to the U.S. in the world represents something much broader than a coalition of the envious or the unenlightened. In recent years, the U.S. has launched a variety of bold and ambitious policies that conflict frontally with the interests and aspirations of many other powers. In the Middle East, the U.S. has embarked on a radical policy of destroying regimes it does not like and has been trying to replace them with a new political, social, and economic model of American provenance. In Europe, the U.S. has been fearful of the EU and increasingly put itself in conflict with the two principal European continental powers – France and Germany.

Americans, of course, are not the only people who harbor outsized ambitions. The postwar Franco-German vision of a strong and self-sufficient European Union is itself radical and ambitious. But although ambitious, it is not unreasonable: Europe's states are seeking to organize themselves and project peace and prosperity to their own neighborhood. They are trying to conciliate the world, not to dominate it. Europeans may, in the end, lack the political will to succeed, particularly if they are opposed by the United States. But what they are attempting is probably in everyone's best interest. If they fail, it will most likely be bad for them, bad for the world, and bad for the United States. A uniting Europe has become a great pole of stability and prosperity for the world. A quarrelling Europe would be a menace to itself and to everyone else.

By comparison with Europe's project, the *Pax Americana,* conceived of as global hegemony, with the right, indeed the obligation, to intervene anywhere, is a program that seems a good deal less attractive or attainable. The costs are bound to be high. Installing and maintaining global hegemony will almost certainly require a more authoritarian government than Americans are used to. It seems unlikely to bring out those traits that embody the best of American civilization. It seems an improbable way to enrich our national life. It points toward a disappointing outcome for two centuries of American democracy. For the U.S. to pursue unipolar power also means accepting the duty to preserve it and to thwart any regional power or grouping that might threaten America's predominance. This is a task that automatically makes the U.S. hostile toward rising new powers, including a rising European Union. In a world increasingly diverse and dynamic, this seems an unpromising course.

Historians will wonder how the U.S., led by the second President Bush, acquired the moral and intellectual confidence for so aggressive a global agenda. The answer is circular: America inclines toward the unipolar agenda when it believes it has unipolar power. As America emerged from World War II much stronger than Europe, FDR projected a unipolar future. Stalin's aggressive opposition forced Roosevelt's successors to retreat into "containment." Once the Soviet Union was dead, unipolar visions revived among American elites like an epidemic fever. At the heart of the present U.S. affinity for unipolar policy is, once again, proud faith in our own strength. That faith derives from four broad assumptions:

• America's "soft power" is irresistible.
• America's "hard power" is incomparably superior.

- America's economic power is invulnerable to the "overstretch" that has regularly defeated the hegemonic ambitions of others.
- America's power is intrinsically legitimate.

Before betting our future, we should perhaps examine these assumptions more carefully.

Notes

1. Only eleven days after the "troop surge" was announced, a global poll showed even further drops in world opinion favoring U.S. influence abroad. Only 29% of those polled across eighteen countries thought the United States had a generally positive influence on world affairs. The year before (2006), the favorable percentage was 36%. "World View of U.S. Role Goes from Bad to Worse," World Public Opinion.org, January 22, 2007, http://www.worldpublicopinion.org/pipa/articles/international_security_bt/306.php?lb=btvoc&pnt=306&nid=&id=. Recent polls show a slight improvement with the favorable percentage increased to 32%. "Global Views of USA Improve," World Public Opinion.org, April 1, 2008, http://www.worldpublicopinion.org/pipa/articles/views_on_countriesregions_bt/463.php?lb=btvoc&pnt=463&nid=&id.

   A Pew Research poll published June 16, 2008, shows solid majorities in France, Germany, and Spain that profess an unfavorable view of the United States. Only in Great Britain (the fourth West European country surveyed) was a majority (53%) favorable. Among the East European countries only Poland was surveyed and showed a solid majority (68%) favoring the United States. In all four West European countries, among those following the presidential campaign, solid majorities believed U.S. foreign policy would change for the better with a new president. This optimistic view was not shared in Jordan, Egypt, Turkey, Russia, or Japan. The West Europeans very strongly preferred Obama (Britain, 74%; France, 84%; Germany, 82%; and Spain, 72%). Fifty-three percent of Poles also favored the Democratic candidate. For a more detailed breakdown, see Ch. 1, footnote 1.

2. See Christina Torsein and Ian Davis, "The 'Old Cold War Dog' and the War against Terrorism: Continuing NATO's Shift Toward Collective Security?" BASIC Notes, November 19, 2001, http://www.basicint.org/pubs/Notes/2001wardog.htm.

3. The prevailing view on the legality of the Iraq war was given in 2004 by Kofi Annan, then Secretary-General of the UN, who said that the war did not conform to the UN charter. "Iraq War Illegal, Says Annan," *BBC News*, September 16, 2004, http://news.bbc.co.uk/2/hi/middle_east/

3661134.stm. Much has also been made of Richard Perle's admission that the war was illegal by standards of international law. See Oliver Burkeman and Julian Borger, "War Critics Astonished as U.S. Hawk Admits Invasion was Illegal," *The Guardian*, November 20, 2003, http://www. guardian.co.uk/uk/2003/nov/20/usa.iraq1.

4. See, for example, Secretary of State Colin Powell's statement, reported in Brian Knowlton, "Assertion That U.S. Will Punish France over Its Iraq Stance Strains Ties Again: Defiant, Paris Rejects Warning by Powell," *International Herald Tribune*, April 24, 2003, http://www.iht.com/ articles/2003/04/24/powell_ed3__o.php. Likewise, in 2003 the quotation "punish France, ignore Germany, forgive Russia" was attributed to Condoleezza Rice. See Philip H. Gordon, "'Punish France, Ignore Germany, Forgive Russia' No Longer Fits," *Brookings*, June 24, 2008, http://www .brookings.edu/opinions/2007/09europe_gordon.aspx. For more information, see Philip H. Gordon and Jeremy Shapiro, *Allies at War: America, Europe and the Crisis over Iraq* (New York, NY: McGraw-Hill, 2004), Ch. 5.

5. European public opinion polls in January 2003 indicated that Europe's public was more opposed to an invasion of Iraq than its leaders. Strong majorities in every EU country were against a unilateral U.S. intervention. A majority of those polled in Finland, Austria, Sweden, Greece, and Germany did not support U.S. intervention even with UN support. Support for war against Iraq, even in "New Europe," was low: only 38% of respondents in Romania, 28% in Bulgaria, and 20% in Estonia would support a war in Iraq if sanctioned by the UN. The figure for Russia was 23%. See William Horsley, "Polls Find Europeans Oppose Iraq War," *BBC*, February 11, 2003, http://news.bbc.co.uk/2/hi/europe/2747175.stm. See also footnotes 6 and 11.

6. In the late 1990s, both U.S. and UK intelligence communities began claiming that Saddam Hussein was trying to manufacture weapons of mass destruction (WMD). WMD, however, is a somewhat protean category, including chemical and biological weapons, as well as nuclear. Iraq did, of course, have chemical weapons supplied by the U.S. and others used in the war against Iran. Iraq also was discovered to have biological weapons in 1995 and some of the stocks were still unaccounted for. The critical question, however, was whether Iraq had restarted its nuclear weapons program of the 1980s. American and British intelligence reports claimed that it had. See the Key Judgments from the National Intelligence Estimate of October 2002, as well as the State Department's INR dissent at http://www.fas.org/irp/cia/product/iraq-wmd.html. A declassified version of the full NIE is found at http://www.fas.org/irp/cia/product/iraq-wmd-nie.pdf.

Prime Minister Tony Blair received much criticism for the February 2003 "dodgy dossier" that quoted unattributed material from a twelve-year-old scholarly article. See, for example, Charles Kennedy, "Blair Must Give Evidence or Lose Our Trust," *Financial Times*, July 8, 2003: 19.

In his 2003 State of the Union Address, President Bush featured documents claiming that Iraq was buying tons of uranium oxide from Niger. In its March 7, 2003, testimony to the Security Council, the UN's IAEA declared the documents forgeries.

On February 5, 2003, U.S. Secretary of State Colin Powell presented the Security Council with evidence derived from satellite images and alleged intercepted military communications. These included computer-generated images depicting mobile biological weapon production systems. Powell also sought to link Iraqi officials and the Al-Qaeda terrorist network and suggested that Iraq was planning to give the terrorist organization WMDs.

In 2004 the U.S. Senate Intelligence Committee's Report on prewar intelligence assessments on Iraq concluded that the "key judgments in the Intelligence Community's October 2002 National Intelligence Estimate (NIE)" were "either overstated, or were not supported by, the underlying intelligence reporting." Moreover, the report states, "much of the information provided or cleared by the Central Intelligence Agency (CIA) for inclusion in Secretary Powell's speech was overstated, misleading, or incorrect." See "Conclusions of Senate's Iraq Report: Report on the Prewar Intelligence Assessments," July 9, 2004, available at http://www. msnbc.msn.com/id/5403731/.

On February 14, 2003, UN Chief Inspector Hans Blix, in his report to the UN Security Council, questioned Powell's interpretation of the satellite images and reported that Iraqi officials were cooperating smoothly with the inspectors. In his final report to the UN Security Council on March 8, 2003, Blix refuted many of the claims made by the United States and the UK, although he remained skeptical that Iraq had destroyed its stockpiles of anthrax and VX nerve agent.

For a detailed account of the UN inspections and the evidence on WMD, see Hans Blix, *Disarming Iraq* (New York, NY: Pantheon Books, 2004). For an account less unfavorable to Anglo-American claims, see Kenneth Pollack, "Spies, Lies, and Weapons: What Went Wrong," *The Atlantic*, Jan/Feb 2004, Vol. 293(1), pp. 78–92. For Britain's Hutton Inquiry, which largely exonerated the British government of wrongdoing regarding the "September Dossier" and instead found fault with the BBC, see http:// www.the-hutton-inquiry.org.uk/.

7. The Pew Research Center concluded: "A year after the war in Iraq, discontent with America and its policies has intensified rather than diminished.

Opinion of the United States in France and Germany is at least as negative now as at the war's conclusion, and British views are decidedly
more critical. Perceptions of American unilateralism remain widespread
in European and Muslim nations, and the war in Iraq has undermined
America's credibility abroad. Doubts about the motives behind the U.S.-
led war on terrorism abound, and a growing percentage of Europeans
want foreign policy and security arrangements independent from the
United States. Across Europe, there is considerable support for the European Union to become as powerful as the United States.... The United
Nations itself engenders varied reactions around the world. Just 55% of
Americans have a favorable opinion of the world body. This is the lowest
rating the U.N. has achieved in 14 years of Pew Research Center surveys.
People in Russia and the Western European countries have a consider-
ably more favorable view of the U.N. But large majorities in Jordan and
Morocco hold negative views of both the U.N. and the man who leads it."
"A Year after Iraq War: Mistrust of America in Europe ever Higher,
Muslim Anger Persists," Pew Research Center, March 16, 2004 available
at http://people-press.org/reports/display.php3?ReportID=206.

8. See Philip H. Gordon and Jeremy Shapiro, *Allies at War: America, Europe
and the Crisis over Iraq* (New York, NY: McGraw-Hill, 2004), especially
Ch. 5.

9. For the German-American split, see Stephen F. Szabo, *Parting Ways:
The Crisis in German-American Relations* (Washington, DC: The Brook-
ings Institution Press, 2004), and Philip H. Gordon and Jeremy Shapiro,
Allies at War: America, Europe and the Crisis over Iraq (New York, NY:
McGraw-Hill, 2004).

10. Arguably, the war in Iraq eased China's integration into the global main-
stream as an antiwar *entente active* joined France, Germany, Russia,
and China. For the moment, all opposed the U.S. invasion of Iraq and no
major geopolitical conflict appeared to divide them across Eurasia.
Three putative strategic links were formed: the Sino-Russian strategic
partnership, the EU's "Common Strategy towards Russia," and "strategic
cooperation" between the EU and China. All were built with no declared
common enemy. See Lanxin Xiang, "China's Eurasian Experiment,"
Survival, Vol. 46(2). For earlier EU-Chinese-Russian links, see European
Union, "Common Strategy of the European Union on Russia," July 4,
1999, http://europa.eu.int/comm/external_relations/ceeca/com_strat/;
and Lowell Dittmer, "The Sino-Russian Strategic Partnership," *Journal
of Contemporary China*, Vol. 10(28), 2001, pp. 399–413(15).

11. Secretary of Defense Donald Rumsfeld: "Germany has been a problem
and France has been a problem. But you look at vast numbers of other
countries in Europe, they're not with France and Germany...they're

with the U.S. You're thinking of Europe as Germany and France. I don't. I think that's old Europe." "Secretary Rumsfeld Briefs at the Foreign Press Center," January 22, 2003, http://www.defenselink.mil/transcripts/2003/t01232003_t0122sdfpc.html.

On January 29, 2003, the governments of Denmark, Italy, Britain, Poland, Portugal, Spain, Hungary, and the Czech Republic published a joint letter supporting U.S. policies in Iraq. A second letter followed on February 5, 2003, from ten Central and Eastern European countries (Albania, Bulgaria, Croatia, Estonia, Latvia, Lithuania, Macedonia, Romania, Slovakia, and Slovenia), signed by their foreign ministers and said to be promoted by Bruce Jackson, an American arms lobbyist prominent in the campaign for NATO enlargement.

Germany, France, Belgium, and Luxembourg were not consulted beforehand and reacted angrily. President Chirac on February 18, 2003, observed that the Eastern European signers had missed a great opportunity to "remain silent" ("*se taire*"). The four held a summit meeting on April 29, 2003, and also called for greater defense integration among themselves, an independent European military headquarters, and greater European unity of action. On Chirac's comments see Laurent Zecchini, "M. Chirac fustige les pays candidats «pas très bien élevés» trop prompts à soutenir Washington," *Le Monde*, February 19, 2003; On the nuances of translating "*se taire*" see Eleanor and Michel Levieux, "No, Chirac Didn't Say 'Shut Up,'" *The New York Times*, February 23, 2003: D12.

Prospects for a common European position on Iraq, however, were unpromising from the start. Early on, the UK had decided unilaterally to give unrestricted support to the U.S. position, whereas the German Chancellor, Gerhard Schröder, publicly rejected absolutely any use of military force. Thus transatlantic differences over Iraq automatically translated into intra-European disputes.

For an overview of the Russian view, see Galia Golan, "Russia and the Iraq War: Was Putin's Policy a Failure?" *Communist and Post-Communist Studies*, Vol. 37, 2004, pp. 429–459. Nikolai Zlobini, "Iraq in the Context of Post-Soviet Foreign Policy," *Mediterranean Quarterly*, Vol. 15(2), 2004, pp. 83–102.

China's statements on the Iraq War were less unequivocal. However, China supported continued weapons inspections and coordinated its position with that of France, Russia, and Germany. China seemed to feel that if the U.S. were bogged down in the Middle East, it could not devote as much energy to its anti-Chinese containment policy. See Willy Lam, "China's Reaction to America's Iraq Imbroglio," *China Brief*, Vol. 4(8), 2004.

12. In March 2003, a Pew Foundation Poll reported that the populations of America's closest allies did not support the war. Even in Britain, initially 51% opposed, whereas only 39% supported. With the onset of hostilities, however, public opinion for a time swung behind the government. Opposition was higher in three other countries where governments strongly supported the war: Poland (73%), Italy (81%), and Spain (81%). In the U.S., by comparison, 59% supported the war, whereas 30% opposed it. In Europe, opposition to the war went hand in hand with a notable alienation from U.S. leadership in general. "America's Image Further Erodes, Europeans Want Weaker Ties. But Post War Iraq Will Be Better Off Most Say," Pew Global Attitudes Project, March 18, 2003, http://pewglobal.org/reports/display.php?ReportID=175.

13. See White House Press Release, "Operation Iraqi Freedom – Coalition Members," March 27, 2003, http://www.whitehouse.gov/news/releases/2003/03/20030327-10.html. At the outset, the United States, the UK, Australia, and Poland were directly involved in military operations, "Military Operations – Iraq," December 2007, http://www.european-defence.co.uk/iraq.html.

    On December 2003, coalition troop commitments reached 24,000. By May 9, 2007, a Government Accountability Office report stated that 12,600 coalition troops remained. Participating countries were Albania, Armenia, Australia, Azerbaijan, Bosnia and Herzegovina, Bulgaria, Czech Republic, Denmark, El Salvador, Estonia, Georgia, Japan, Kazakhstan, Latvia, Lithuania, Macedonia, Moldova, Mongolia, Poland, Republic of Korea, Romania, Singapore, Slovakia, Ukraine, and the United Kingdom. See, "Stabilizing and Rebuilding Iraq – Coalition Support and International Donor Commitments," *Government Accounting Office*, May 9, 2007, p. 9, http://www.gao.gov/new.items/d07827t.pdf. Separately, a May 31, 2007, version of the Multi-National Force – Iraq Web site listed twenty-one member-countries (excluding the U.S.). The MNF-Iraq list excluded Latvia, Moldova, Singapore, and Slovakia, MNF-Iraq, July 14, 2008, http://www.mnf-iraq.com/index.php?option=com_content&task=blogcategory&id=49&Itemid=129.

    As of June 2008, the two largest contingents of troops in Iraq were those of the U.S. and the UK, with 146,000 and 4,000, respectively. See Lolita C. Baldor, "As U.S. Military Buildup in Iraq Ends, What Next?" *The Associated Press*, June 23, 2008. However, there were rumors of British withdrawal by the end of 2008. See "Iraq Troops decision 'this year,'" *BBC News*, June 9, 2008, http://news.bbc.co.uk/2/hi/uk_news/politics/7444238.stm.

14. Andrew Moravcsik, "A Too Perfect Union? Why Europe Said 'No.'" *Current History*, November 2005. Moravcsik saw the vote as a protest – reflecting dissatisfaction with unpopular governments, economic and

cultural insecurity among poorer Europeans, and ideological extremism among those who actually voted. See also Eurobarometer, "The European Constitution: Post-referendum survey in France," Vol. 104(685), 2005, pp. 355–59, http://ec.europa.eu/public_opinion/flash/fl171_en.pdf. See also my general discussion in Chapter 7.

15. As of June 10, 2008, approximately 52,700 troops were taking part in NATO's International Security and Assistance Force (ISAF) in Afghanistan, of which about 25,500 were from Europe. Britain contributed about 8,500 troops, Germany contributed about 3,400, and France contributed about 1,700. Of the approximately 25,000 U.S. troops reported by NATO in Afghanistan, according to an International Institute of Strategic Studies report about 10,000 were under US CENTCOM control rather than part of the ISAF force. See "ISAF Key Facts and Figures Placemat," *NATO- International Security Assistance Force*, June 10, 2008, http://www.nato.int/ISAF/docu/epub/pdf/isaf_placemat.pdf and p. 38, International Institute for Strategic Studies, "North America," *The Military Balance*, Vol. 108(1), 2008, http://www.informaworld.com/10.1080/04597220801912762.

16. At the end of 2004, Iraq's overall public debt was estimated to be $120.2 billion in nominal value. The total debt owed to Paris Club creditors was estimated to be $38.9 billion, of which Russia held $8.5 billion, Japan $7.75 billion, France $5.5 billion, Germany $4.4 billion, and the U.S. $4 billion. On November 21, 2004, Paris Club members agreed on debt relief of 80% in three phases, reducing the Paris debt stock to $7.8 billion. Non-Paris Club countries, mostly Gulf countries, were owed $60–65 billion. See Martin A. Weiss, "Iraq: Paris Club Debt Relief," *Congressional Research Service Report*, January 19, 2005. As of December 2006, the Paris Club Debt Relief framework still held, while negotiations with non-Paris Club creditors were ongoing, and resolution of the commercial debt was largely complete. Martin A. Weiss, "Iraq's Debt Relief: Procedure and Potential Implications for International Debt Relief," *CRS Report*, December 6, 2006. Available at http://fpc.state.gov/documents/organization/79311.pdf. In 2008 the biggest hurdle to overcome was the reluctance of the Gulf States to forgive Iraq's debt at a UN conference in Sweden. See "Arab Nations Fail to Forgive Iraq's Debts," *The New York Times*, May 30, 2008, http://www.nytimes.com/2008/05/30/world/middleeast/30donors.html?ref=world. However, on July 6, 2008 the United Arab Emirates cancelled all debt owed to it by Iraq, some $6 billion, setting a precedent for the other Gulf States. See "UAE Waives Billions of Iraqi Debt," *BBC*, 6 July 2008, http://news.bbc.co.uk/2/hi/middle_east/7492115.stm. For police training, see Jeremy Shapiro and Christopher Blanchard, "Post-War Iraq: Foreign Contributions to Training, Peacekeeping, and Reconstruction," *CRS Report*, June 6, 2005.

After the installation of the new Iraqi government in May 2006, the European Union promised it €200 million. This was on top of €518 million already allocated by the Commission between 2003 and 2005. See Fidelius Schmid, "Baghdad set to get aid package from Brussels," *Financial Times*, 23 May 2006: 7.

In February 2007, the EU promised another €10.2 million in humanitarian aid to Iraq. See "EU Plans New Aid Package for Iraq," *Deutsche Presse Agentur*, February 15, 2007. Throughout 2007, the European Commission spent an additional €14 million on the Integrated Rule of Law Mission and €20 million to support the electoral process. See "External Cooperation Programmes–Iraq," European Commission, June 3, 2008, http://ec.europa.eu/europeaid/where/middle-east/country-cooperation/iraq/iraq_en.htm.

17. See Reuel Marc Gerecht, "Regime Change in Iran?," *The Weekly Standard*, Vol. 7(45), 2002, pp. 30–33; Frank J. Gaffney, Jr., "Worldwide Value," *National Review*, November 5, 2004, www.nationalreview.com/gaffney/gaffney200411051020.asp; William Kristol, "And Now Iran; We Can't Rule out the Use of Military Force," *The Weekly Standard*, Vol. 11(18), 2006; Richard Perle, "Why Did Bush Blink on Iran? (Ask Condi)," *The Washington Post*, June 25, 2006: B01; Charles Krauthammer, "The Tehran Calculus," *The Washington Post*, September 15, 2006: A19; Andrew C. McCarthy, "Negotiate with Iran?" *National Review Online*, December 8, 2006, http://article.nationalreview.com/?q=N2ViMTQ1NTllMjAxZDVmNjg3ZjIyMWRlMWU5OWE3N2M= See also the Iran Freedom and Support Act introduced in the Senate in 2004 at http://thomas.loc.gov/cgi-bin/cpquery/R?cp109:FLD010:@1(hr417).

18. Ahmadinejad's winning the presidency in 2005 disappointed neoconservative expectations that Iranians were yearning for liberation. Iran has long been playing a complex game. All in all, Iran seems to be the major beneficiary of the fall of Saddam Hussein. Closely linked to Shia elements in Iraq, it has so far seemed to play a circumspect role there, but is widely thought to supply Hezbollah forces in Lebanon, which were surprisingly effective against Israeli forces in the summer of 2006. On Ahmadinejad, see Ray Takeyh, "A Profile in Defiance: Being Mahmoud Ahmadinejad," *The National Interest*, 83, 2006: 13–15. On Iran's "emerging empowerment" as a result of the Iraq war, see Ray Takeyh, "The Rising Might of the Middle East Super Power," *Financial Times*, September 11, 2006, Asia edition: 11; and Christopher de Bellaigue, "Defiant Iran," *The New York Review of Books*, Vol. 53(17), November 2, 2006.

19. On European opposition to military action in Iran see Seymour M. Hersh, "The Iran Plans: Would President Bush Go to War to Stop Tehran from Getting the Bomb?" *The New Yorker*, Vol. 82(9), 2006, p. 30.

20. A November 2007 National Intelligence Estimate judged, with high confidence, that Iran halted its nuclear weapon program in 2003. However, the same report concluded, with moderate confidence, that through
peaceful nuclear development Iran would be able to produce enough
highly enriched uranium to build a weapon sometime between 2010
and 2015. "Iran: Nuclear Intentions and Capabilities," National Intelligence Estimate, November 2007, http://www.dni.gov/press_releases/
20071203_release.pdf.

21. Iran has insisted on developing its own nuclear fuel cycle capability, something not forbidden by the Non-Proliferation Treaty but a major step
toward being able to make nuclear weapons, a step vehemently opposed
by the U.S. and logically a rationale for preventive war.

    The EU-3 (Britain, France, and Germany) entered into tortuous
negotiations with Iran in October 2003. See Aldo Zammit Borda,
"The Iranian Nuclear Issue and E.U.-3 Negotiations," *Fornet Working
Paper*, No. 8, May 2005. For the E.U.-3 Nuclear Proposal to Iran, see
www.payvand.com/news/05/aug/1074.html.

    The Bush Administration announced on March 11, 2005, that it would
drop its previous opposition to Iran's applying for WTO membership. At
a WTO meeting in May 2005, no state opposed Iran's application, which
opened the way for accession talks. Kenneth Katzman, "Iran: U.S. Concerns and Policy Responses," CRS Report for Congress, updated September 29, 2008, www.fas.org/ssp/crs/mideastRL32048.pdf. For persisting
interest in a military intervention within the Bush administration, see
Seymour M. Hersh, "Preparing the Battlefield: The Bush Administration
Steps up Its Secret Moves against Iran," *The New Yorker*, July 7, 2008,
www.newyorker.com/reporting/2008/07/07/080707fa_fact_hersh.

22. For my own earlier analysis of this process, see David P. Calleo, "The
Broken West," *Survival*, 46(3), 2004, pp. 29–38.

23. See NATO, "Declaration on Peace and Cooperation," Rome, November
8, 1991, at http://www.nato.int/docu/comm/49–95/c911108a.htm; James
A. Baker III, "A New Europe, a New Atlanticism: Architecture for a
New Era," address to the Berlin Press Club, December 12, 1989; also
"Declaration on a Transformed North Atlantic Alliance," NATO, July 6,
1990, at http://www.nato.int/docu/basictxt/b900706a.htm.

24. See Stephen F. Szabo, *The Diplomacy of German Unification* (New
York, NY: St. Martin's Press, 1992); Philip Zelikow and Condoleezza
Rice, *Germany Unified and Europe Transformed: A Study in Statecraft*
(Cambridge, MA: Harvard University Press, 1995).

25. For a thorough account and spirited advocacy of NATO's extension,
see Ronald Asmus, *Opening NATO's Door* (New York, NY: Columbia
University Press, 2002). For the observations of a veteran French diplo-
mat, see Jacques Andréani, "Le devenir des institutions européenes et les

relations transatlantiques," Intervention au colloque de la Fondation Robert Schuman, organisé par Paris-1 et SAIS, January 17, 2003.

26. The NATO summit in Bucharest in April 2008 invited Croatia and Albania to join but not Macedonia, Ukraine, and Georgia. Macedonia was not admitted thanks to a naming dispute with Greece. The latter two were not upgraded from "intensified dialogue" to a "membership action plan" thanks to opposition by German chancellor Angela Merkel, who saw no need to provoke Russia. See "With Allies Like These," *The Economist*, Vol. 387(8574), April 3, 2008, http://www.economist.com/world/international/displaystory.cfm?story_id=10981434.

27. For NATO's preconditions, see: "Enlargement: What Does This Mean in Practice?" *NATO Topics*, February 12, 2008, http://www.nato.int/issues/enlargement/practice.html. For NATO expansion and East European military reform, see F. Stephen Larrabee, *Nato's Eastern Agenda in a New Strategic Era* (Santa Monica, CA: The RAND Corporation, 2003), Summary, http://www.rand.org/pubs/monograph_reports/2005/MR1744.sum.pdf.

28. See David P. Calleo, *Rethinking Europe's Future* (Princeton, NJ: Princeton University Press, 2001), pp. 309–314; Vladimir Baranovsky, "NATO Enlargement: Russia's Attitudes," IISS/CEPS European Security Forum, July 9, 2001, http://www.eusec.org/baranovsky.htm. For longstanding Russian proposals to join NATO or to create an alternative pan-European security organization, see: Amelia Gentleman, "Replace NATO by Pan-European Pact, Putin Says," The Guardian, July 19, 2001, http://www.guardian.co.uk/world/2001/jul/19/eu.russia; Vladimir Socor, "Medvedev Proposes All-European Security Pact during Berlin Visit," *Eurasian Daily Monitor*, June 9, 2008, http://www.jamestown.org/edm/article.php?article_id=2373127.

29. See Chris Donnelly, "Military Matters, Reform Realities," *NATO Review*, Vol. 49(3), 2001, pp. 13–15, available at http://www.nato.int/docu/review/2001/0103-11.htm.

30. From March 1998 to 2007, the EU added twelve new members: the Czech Republic, Estonia, Hungary, Poland, Slovenia, Cyprus, Bulgaria, Latvia, Lithuania, Malta, Romania, and the Slovak Republic. European Commission, "Enlargement of the European Union. An historic opportunity," European Commission, Brussels, 2003, http://europa.eu.int/comm/enlargement/docs/pdf/historic_opportunity_2003_en.pdf.

31. Rhetorical support for a stronger West European role within the Atlantic Alliance was regularly matched by warnings from prominent U.S. officials about the adverse impact of a European caucus on America's European commitment. During February 1991, the "Bartholomew Telegram," communicated directly to a West European Union ministerial meeting, set

forth U.S. preconditions for a European Defense Identity. Specifically, it warned against the creation of a European caucus within NATO, against discriminating against NATO members who were not in the European Community, and against any attempt to formulate an independent defense identity.

At the NATO summit in Rome on November 7–8, 1991, President Bush was reported to have said: "if your ultimate goal is to provide independently for your own defense, the time to tell us is today." Some U.S. officials were enraged by France's apparent encouragement for alternative structures to NATO, taken as a sign that Paris hoped and expected the U.S. would soon leave Europe.

See Simon Duke, *The Elusive Quest for European Security: From EDC to CFSP* (New York, NY: St. Martin's Press, 2000); Martin Walker, "The European Union and the European Security and Defense Initiative," *NATO & Europe in the 21st Century*, Woodrow Wilson International Center for Scholars, 2000; Jacques Andréani, "Le devenir des institutions européennes et les relations transatlantiques," *op. cit.*

32. See Craig R. Whitney, "Balkan Scenes Stir Europe, But Action Remains Elusive," *The New York Times*, August 8, 1992, http://query.nytimes.com/gst/fullpage.html?res=9 E0CE7DA123DF93BA3575BC0A964958260 &sec=&spon=&pagewanted=1. See also footnote 33.

33. Clinton's initial commitment of substantial American forces to Yugoslavia came as a pledge that American troops would help extricate the lightly armed UN peacekeepers if necessary. After UN forces were actually held as hostages at the end of May 1995, the newly elected French president, Jacques Chirac, publicly indicated that French troops would not remain in Bosnia for another winter without a more positive mandate. With breakdown of UNPROFOR (UN Protection Force) imminent the United States finally sent ground forces, mobilized NATO, and took charge to provide an impressive display of force. At the same time, Croat and Bosnian forces reoccupied large swathes of Bosnia. The Croatian offensive, paired with NATO bombardments and artillery support, finally brought the fighting to a halt. The Dayton Agreement of November 21, 1995 imposed a de facto partition, dressed up as a Bosnian federation. The Dayton Agreement provided an international peace implementation force (IFOR), 60,000 strong and NATO led. In contrast to the rules of engagement constricting the UN's peacekeeping operation in Bosnia during the war, IFOR could use decisive force against anyone violating the cease-fire agreement. See Dana Allin, "NATO's Balkan Interventions," *Adelphi Papers* (London, UK: International Institute for Strategic Studies, 2002); Richard Holbrooke, *To End a War* (New York, NY: Random House, 1998); and David Owen, *Balkan Odyssey* (Orlando, FL: Harcourt Brace, 1995).

34. After Dayton, NATO failed to devolve more commands to Europeans; the French, who had earlier seemed ready to reenter NATO's military structures, decided to remain outside. Elizabeth Pond, *The Rebirth of Europe* (Washington, DC: Brookings Institution Press, 1999), p. 83; Jonathan Marcus, "Adjustment, Recrimination: Franco-U.S. Relations and the New World Disorder," *Washington Quarterly*, Vol. 21(2), 1998, pp. 17–32.

35. After admitting the Czech Republic, Hungary, and Poland in 1999, NATO added seven other former Warsaw Pact countries in 2004: Bulgaria, Estonia, Latvia, Lithuania, Romania, Slovakia, and Slovenia. "Enhancing Security and Extending Stability through NATO Enlargement," NATO, http://www.nato.int/docu/enlargement/enlargement_eng. pdf. For later developments, see also Chapter 3, footnote 26. For a discussion of President Clinton's view that NATO needed to expand in light of European failures in Yugoslavia in 1992 and 1993, see Ronald D. Asmus, *op. cit.*, especially "Book II: The Debate Begins."

36. See Wesley K. Clark, *Waging Modern War: Bosnia, Kosovo, and the Future of Combat* (New York, NY: Public Affairs, 2001); Anthony Cordesman, *The Lessons and Non-Lessons of the Air and Missile War in Kosovo* (Washington, DC: Center for Strategic and International Studies, 1999); Benjamin S. Lambeth, *NATO'S Air War For Kosovo: A Strategic and Operational Assessment* (Santa Monica, CA: The RAND Corporation, 2001); Ivo H. Daalder and Michael E. O'Hanlon, *Winning Ugly: NATO's War to Save Kosovo* (Washington, DC: Brookings Institution Press, 2001).

37. The Balkan experience, together with Tony Blair's desire to redefine Britain's role in Europe, led to the Informal European Council at Pörtschach, Austria, in October 1998, where Britain for the first time dropped its objections to discussing defense matters in the framework of the European Union. This cleared the way for a wider Anglo-French agreement at Saint-Malo, in December 1998.

In 1999, the Cologne and Helsinki European Council meetings laid the groundwork for the European Security and Defense Policy (ESDP) to be constructed around the Helsinki Headline Goals. European countries pledged to create a European Rapid Reaction Force (ERRF) of some 50,000–60,000 soldiers, deployable within 60 days and able to sustain itself for one year. European member states supposedly committed some 100,000 troops, 400 combat aircraft, and 100 naval vessels, delineated 38 capability shortfalls, and, in 2001, set up the European Capabilities Action Plan (ECAP) to correct them. In due course, a series of new initiatives surfaced to increase European cooperation. In 2003, the ERRF reached its goal of 60,000 troops and became operational. Member states for the first time agreed to a European Security Strategy. An agreement among France, Germany, and Great Britain permitted an independent European Headquarters, and European member states agreed to set up so-called battle groups and a European Defense Agency. Later goals have stressed qualitative improvements and civilian capabilities.

For an overview of ESDP, see Nicole Gnesotto (ed.), *EU Security and Defence Policy: The First Five Years* (Paris: Institute for Security Studies, 2004); Simon Duke, *The Elusive Quest for European Security: From EDC to CFSP, op. cit.*; on the Saint-Malo process, See Jolyon Howorth, "Britain, France and the European Defence Initiative," *Survival*, Vol. 42(2), 2000, pp. 35–50.

On the Saint-Malo Process, ESDP, and Europe's armaments industry, see Burkard Schmitt, "European Armaments Cooperation – Core Documents," *Chaillot Paper*, 59, 2003; Burkard Schmitt, "The European Union and Armaments: Getting a Bigger Bang for the Euro," *Chaillot Paper*, 63, 2003; Francois Heisbourg, "From European Defense Industrial Restructuring to Transatlantic Deal?" *Stimson Center Working Paper*, 4, 2001, available at http://www.stimson.org/exportcontrol/pdf/paper4.pdf. See also David P. Calleo, *Rethinking Europe's Future, op. cit.*, ch. 14.; Antonio Missiroli (ed.), "From Copenhagen to Brussels. European Defence: Core Documents," *Chaillot Paper*, 67, 2003; Charles Grant, "Resolving the Rows over ESDP," *CER Opinion*, October 2003; Felix Neugart, "The EU and the Challenge of Iraq," presented at the workshop "The Role of the European Union in the Gulf Region" at the Gulf Research Center, Dubai, January 7–8, 2004. For more recent developments, see "ESDP and the EU's Emerging Role in Global Security," *Foreign Policy*, Jan./Feb. 2006; and C. Chivvis, "Birthing Athena: The Uncertain Future of European Security and Defense Policy," Security Studies Center, March 2008, http://www.ifri.org/files/Securite_defense/Focus_strategique_5_Chivvis_PESD.pdf. For a general study, see Emil J. Kirchner, "The Challenge of European Union Security Governance," *Journal of Common Market Studies*, Vol. 44(5), 2006. For a recent statement of French defense doctrine, see *Défense et Securité Nationale, Le Livre Blanc* (Paris: Odile Jacob, La Documentation Francaise, 2006).

PART II

THE NATURE AND LIMITS OF AMERICAN POWER

4

Assessing America's Soft and Hard Power

Soft Power – Exporting the American Way

A would-be hegemon should be well endowed with both hard and soft power; having one without the other can easily be self-defeating. Ambitious soft power, without hard power to guarantee respect, can make a nation seem pretentious and impotent. Hard power, without soft power to render it legitimate and welcome, is costly to sustain. How does this calculus apply to the United States?[1]

The U.S. certainly has abundant soft power. Its high culture can scarcely be considered inferior to anyone else's – in the arts and sciences or in higher education and research – not least because the polyglot U.S. has historically been a refuge for persecuted talent from around the world. But America's accomplishments in high culture are rivaled by others and scarcely justify America's claims to a unipolar status. American popular culture, however, is so widely diffused that it can claim a unique global stature. Does its attractiveness to the world's masses translate into usable soft power? Arguably, foreigners often find most appealing those aspects of American popular culture most vociferously in opposition to America's own political, social, and military establishments. In any event, admiration for American popular culture does little to obstruct populist anti-Americanism. Terrorists eat at McDonald's, wear blue jeans, and download popular music.

What of America as a model for the world's political, social, and economic development? During various stages of the Cold War, as

declinism regularly came in and out of fashion, many analysts feared
the U.S. was somehow losing the battle of ideals to Marxism – Soviet,
European, or Asian.[2] Naturally, the collapse of the USSR radically
devalued the appeal of Soviet Marxist models and indeed diminished
the appeal of socialist and communitarian models generally. As Marxism failed, capitalism was widely seen the winner by default. Its victory
seemed a special triumph for the United States, all the more because
America's leaders had grown fond of presenting their country as the
standard-bearer of global capitalism. Such a role, of course, has proved
a mixed blessing for America's soft power. Because global integration is widely believed to result in a growing inequality of incomes
within nations, opposition to it has been rising apace. And whereas
continental European-style capitalism is apologetic about the growing economic inequality, and emphasizes its continuing devotion to
those Christian, communitarian, and socialist ideals that are part of
its heritage, American capitalism ignores its own communitarian heritage and instead is more inclined to celebrate its social Darwinian
roots.

Long before the U.S. became the model for "globalization," however, it was capitalism's "land of opportunity" – the Old World's safety
valve – a country where enterprising immigrants, fleeing their own
class-bound societies, made new and sometimes richly successful lives
for themselves. Recent decades have seen that image of America spread
to Latin America and Asia.[3] Ironically, as the image has grown more
universally diffused abroad, it has grown less true at home. Recent
studies are inclined to show America's class and income structures
more unequal and rigid than those of Europe.[4] Greater inequality and
less social mobility seem the pattern of globalization generally. Britain
and America exhibit that pattern most vividly.

Nevertheless, the image of America as the land of opportunity
remains strong and, for millions of immigrants, is still very real. As
Chapter 2 observes, neoconservatives of the Bush administration have
tried to parlay this American image into a vigorous form of soft power,
exported as a revolutionary ideology to undermine economically illib-
eral and politically repressive regimes, particularly in the Middle East.[5]
The ideological appeal of American globalism, democracy, and upward
mobility, on occasion accompanied by hard military power, is supposed to pave the way for "democratization." Afghanistan and Iraq

are admittedly rather special tests for this American soft power. So far they are not very successful. To be sure, the time frame is still short. But what has happened so far belies hopes for quick success. In general, the American national model, with its enabling liberal culture, moral habits, entrepreneurial energy, and physical abundance, is not easy to transfer elsewhere. In effect, the Bush administration's promoters of these ideas are, at best, conservatives à la carte. Suspicious of social engineering at home, abroad they reason like old-fashioned liberal revolutionaries, determined to believe that economic and political free markets will work their magic once the evil obstructions of dictatorship and monopoly have been removed.

To reassure themselves, these "neoconservative" liberals point to the democratic transformations of postwar Germany, Italy, and Japan.[6] With enough will and time, they argue, the early postwar success achieved in those countries can be replicated in today's Middle East. The differences, however, are notable. Germany, Italy, and Japan were highly "modernized" cultures, societies, and economies. Before falling into totalitarian dictatorships, all three had enjoyed several decades of constitutional government and active parliaments. Arguably, their postwar incarnation was less Americanization than a return to their own frustrated constitutionalism. But certainly the return was strongly assisted by American power. It came after the total defeat of their dictatorial regimes and terrible devastation of their home territories. American occupation followed, together with an enormous and prolonged American effort to assist reconstruction, something hard to imagine without the threat of the Cold War to keep the U.S. engaged and its transforming allies faithful.[7] And although the American role in remaking postwar Germany and Italy was critical, the European Union, built around a special relationship between Germany and France, was certainly no less significant. In short, these postwar success stories involved far more promising countries and were helped in innumerable ways by the Cold War and by the enlightened regional initiatives of democratic neighbors.

Just to list these conditions makes obvious how greatly different were the prospects for democratization in postwar Western Europe from conditions in much of the "developing" world today. Iraq, for example, although rich in resources, is a country with very limited parliamentary experience. As a nation, it is, at best, a highly artificial construction, with deep ethnic, religious, and tribal divisions, often augmented by meddling neighbors. Its civil society lacks independent institutions used to operating within a framework of laws. Its dependency on the oil industry has reinforced an already powerful tradition of state tyranny, while denying many of the usual economic, social, and political benefits of more rounded economic development. Under the circumstances, it is not surprising that Iraq's military defeat and occupation have not been followed by a rapid transformation to political democracy and market freedom. Even without the prolonged and bitter military resistance to the occupation itself, ruling so divided, conflicted, and politically undeveloped a country inevitably requires a high degree of coercion.[8]

No one has a right to be surprised. Modern conservatism, after all, has its roots in those writers who reacted with profound skepticism to the ahistorical expectations of the French Revolution and Napoleon.[9] After two centuries of further experience, the conservative lessons should be clear: Modernizing societies abruptly is a painful, cruel, and generally dangerous process, all the more so when it is a conquering alien culture imposing the changes. The retrograde, obscurantist, populist forces of traditional societies are aroused and strengthened. The elites on whom modernization depends, caught up in the fury of a reactionary backlash, turn to dictatorship or save themselves by fleeing or otherwise abandoning their modernizing vocation.

The implications for America's adventure in Iraq are obvious: Imposing a liberal democracy will, at best, take a long time and great patience. It means maintaining a significant army of occupation, skilled in policing, as well as a substantial investment in creating the political, cultural, and linguistic expertise needed to govern so large and diverse a population. The odds for success are not impressive. Today's Western democracies are not notable for their ability to conduct steady long-term policies of this sort. Nor are they likely to tolerate for long the rough police practices needed to rule a country with a widespread and steadfast resistance. Even if sufficient order can be imposed long enough for democratic institutions to sprout, military force will have to remain on hand to protect the new regime and prevent its abrupt eradication. In other words, in Iraq and the Middle East generally, America's revolutionary unipolar agenda will depend heavily on the effectiveness and durability of America's own hard power – military and economic. Continuing to exercise raw hard power on a resisting population does not fit with those modern ideas of legitimacy common in the West. We can expect diffidence to persist and opposition to grow at home and among our allies. Nor are we in an era when non-Western societies are passive receptacles for Western tutelage. Is America's power adequate for such a test? Can the U.S. be shielded from the disdain its policies will arouse in the rest of the world? What will be left of America's soft power?

Hard Power: More Means Less

It is now common to say that never in modern history has one nation been so militarily predominant as the U.S. is today.[10] The First Gulf War gave a foretaste of America's burgeoning military superiority, thanks to advanced weaponry and communications. Impressive American military performances followed in Bosnia and Kosovo. The exceptions – Somalia and Haiti – could be blamed on an irresolute government rather than a weak military. America's successes continued through several years of sharply declining defense expenditures, with big cuts in forces and readiness training. Despite these reductions, the Clinton administration, preoccupied with technology in general, continued much of the Reagan era's research and development spending.[11] By the end of Clinton's second term, moreover, general defense spending had begun to rise.[12] The younger Bush sharply augmented the military budget after 9/11. A huge disparity grew rapidly between American and European defense spending, a gap that has made U.S. conventional military power seem unchallengeable and has strongly confirmed the unipolar vision.[13]

On closer examination, however, America's military predominance seems less secure than simple budgetary comparisons might suggest. To start with the high end of the military spectrum – the realm of nuclear weapons: The U.S. may well be more at risk from nuclear weapons than during the Cold War. True, the U.S. no longer has a nuclear superpower as its dedicated enemy. But the "bipolar" strategic system, with its elaborate network of inspected agreements and "hotlines," seems, in retrospect, more stable and less threatening than the supposedly unipolar world unfolding before us – a world of proliferating nuclear weapons and failed states.[14] Of course, the strategic dispensation of the Cold War was itself truly bipolar for only a short time. By the 1960s, Britain, France, China, and perhaps Israel had nuclear weapons, usually rationalized with strategies of "asymmetrical deterrence." According to these strategies, any country with a credible "second strike" should be able to deter a superpower. This meant being able to absorb a first strike and still have sufficient forces to retaliate. According to British and French theorists, being able to loose a dozen surviving nuclear warheads onto the cities of the Soviet Union (or the U.S.) was (and presumably remains) an adequate deterrent.[15] Even during the paranoid conditions of the Cold War, with huge conventional forces confronting each other in the middle of Europe, the strategic nuclear scenarios were sufficiently convincing and horrific to make improbable any major war that threatened the vital national interests of the nuclear powers.

For obvious reasons, neither superpower favored the spread of nuclear weapons, even to its closest allies.[16] American diplomacy, cooperating with the Soviets and using the rubric of the UN's Non-Proliferation Treaty of 1968, succeeded in severely limiting the further spread of nuclear arms. By the start of the twenty-first century, the U.S. and Russia still each retained a huge missile force. The only other countries that could be said to have a reliable second-strike strategic capability were Britain, France, and, marginally, China.[17] Several other countries, had or now have small-scale deterrents: Israel, and, more recently, India, Pakistan, and North Korea.[18] The Bush administration feared Iran is well on its way. Several major industrial countries (Germany, Japan, Italy, Canada, Australia, South Korea, Sweden, South Africa, Switzerland, and perhaps Brazil, Argentina, or Taiwan) could probably produce a significant nuclear deterrent if their national interest seemed to require it. But most of these countries have had these capabilities for several decades and have never chosen to exercise them. Most have not felt sufficiently threatened to face the domestic reaction, pay the financial costs, or risk the hostile diplomatic or military reactions of other powers. In short, while today's dispensation of nuclear strategic weapons has been multipolar for decades and could, hypothetically, be much more so, postwar conditions have not favored such widespread proliferation. Nevertheless, America's strategic position, in theory, has deteriorated greatly since the immediate postwar years, when it held an effective monopoly of nuclear weapons.

Thereafter, the global dispensation of nuclear weapons has served to check rather than enhance America's unipolar pretensions.

In principle, the Reagan administration's "Strategic Defence Initiative" of the 1980s – a vast project, in its most ambitious form aiming to produce an unbreachable missile defense covering the whole United States – could have radically changed America's strategic situation.[19] But after more than twenty years of trying, few experts believe so secure a system is possible. Most believe it will remain much easier to overwhelm a missile defense than to build one.[20] Nor does it seem likely that missile defense could deprive any of the five major nuclear powers of its second-strike capability. At best, missile defense might ultimately protect against a handful of missiles launched by a minor nuclear power.[21]

Not surprisingly, U.S. administrations have, in recent years, grown increasingly concerned about the proliferation of weapons of mass destruction, nuclear weapons in particular, to unstable states or terrorist groups. Here a perverse military logic works against the United States. The more America's overweening military power threatens smaller countries with forcible regime change, the more they will seek asymmetric solutions. Their options are terrorism, on the one hand, and rogue strategic weapons, on the other. Combining the two into terrorism using nuclear, biological, or chemical weapons offers still more striking prospects. These prospects, intrinsic to the post-Soviet strategic dispensation, bode ill for a unipolar America pressing regime change around the world. More interventions give incentive to more proliferation.

Strategic planners have long been conscious of America's particular vulnerability to enemies with nuclear weapons. Since the 1960s, the U.S. has tried to lessen its dependence on nuclear deterrence by maintaining a superior position in conventional forces. The Soviet Union's own massive armies made America's conventional superiority seem doubtful throughout the Cold War. This uncertainty inspired major American military buildups, notably during the Truman, Kennedy, and Reagan administrations. Throughout the entire postwar era, moreover, there has been a persistent opinion among experts – foreign and domestic – that the American military's organization and weaponry urgently need reform.[22] America's military failure in Vietnam gave new substance to the cry for a fundamental overhaul. Even earlier, military planners had grown dissatisfied with the huge deployments of heavily armored forces tied down in Europe.[23] Switching to a professional army in 1973 was a major step toward a new military configuration. By the 1990s, with the Soviet threat vanishing, American planners, liberated from their European commitments, felt free to start pursuing radical changes in force structure and weaponry. Without an immediate real enemy, planners had free rein imagining new threats.

As defense experts saw the new geopolitical climate of the 1990s, the U.S. no longer faced a single major opponent but rather a wide variety of turbulent conditions. Mastering them would call for rapid interventions around the world. These would require fewer, lighter, and more mobile forces. Technological developments were highly favorable. Satellites that gave remarkably detailed views of the battlefield provided "total battlefield awareness" – making possible vastly improved communications, command and control capabilities, as well as precisely guided projectiles. These improvements made possible a new kind of "network-centric" warfare. Intervention forces, protected by superior information systems allowing them to see and kill an enemy from afar, no longer needed heavy armor and could therefore be deployed rapidly to any part of the globe. The new technologies gave American conventional forces something analogous to the "shock and awe" achieved by the German *Blitzkrieg* in the early days of World War II. "Transforming" the American military into such a force has had great aesthetic and intellectual appeal.[24]

Trying to carry out such a transformation, however, assaulted a huge network of professional and economic interests oriented around the status quo. After an abortive early attempt to launch reform, the Clinton administration backed off, content to enjoy the beneficial fiscal effects of big cuts in military spending.[25] Before 9/11, the Bush administration's redoubtable Defense Secretary, Donald Rumsfeld, tried to resume major military reforms. Like the Clinton administration, the new Bush administration mostly failed.[26]

After 9/11, with America's military embroiled in Afghanistan and Iraq, overall spending was greatly augmented. Huge resources also began to be drawn off into a diffuse "war on terror." At the same time, Rumsfeld's Pentagon, by pursuing the vision of "jointless or seamless transformation" of air, naval, and ground forces, continued to fund a wide variety of advanced weapons systems.[27] America's security spending rapidly returned to Cold War levels and beyond.[28] Nevertheless, Rumsfeld firmly resisted calls from the military for more ground troops. His critics continued to claim that American forces were too few to control Iraq and not adequately equipped for the relatively low-tech tasks at hand.[29] Firing Rumsfeld after the Democratic victory in the Congressional elections of 2006 opened the door to change. By January 2007, with President Bush's enthusiastic support, a fresh "surge" of 21,500 ground troops was on the way to Iraq. It seemed clear, however, that the military was already greatly overstretched.[30] Serious increases in overall effective manpower seemed necessary – for ground forces particularly. But with budgetary outlays already beyond Cold War levels, it was not clear how significant increases could be financed.[31] The acute financial crisis raging in 2008 made major new military spending still more unlikely.

The Pentagon's dilemma was hardly new. Without a realistic and clear set of priorities, mammoth budgetary outlays for defense can easily become a source of national weakness rather than strength.[32] The bigger the military budget in relation to the economy and the nation's civilian priorities, the more questions arise over whether such a budget is economically and politically sustainable. To be sustainable, military spending has to be assessed and disciplined within some larger economic and geopolitical context. A nation's military resources have to be measured against its military commitments and more general geopolitical pretensions. Paradoxically, the loss of the Soviet enemy legitimized a vastly increased range of American commitments. Unipolar America implies a ubiquitous presence around the globe.[33] Global management calls for the political, economic, and cultural tools for "counterinsurgency operations" within resistant countries. Pretensions along such lines lead to more and greater long-term commitments. Conflicts grow more likely and the contingencies to be planned for grow more diverse.

Military prowess also has to be measured against the capabilities of likely opponents. Since World War II, the American military has not actually fought an adversary with a major modern army. Eventually, more serious opponents may emerge. Military high technology is not an American monopoly. The British and the French have been transforming their armed forces since the 1990s; the Germans have started recently.[34] Europeans expect major advances in airlift and satellite intelligence within the coming decade. Although Europeans and Americans are presumably not in an arms race, what Europeans can achieve relatively cheaply in a few years, others can be expected to acquire in due course. The Chinese and Japanese, for example, are rapidly upgrading their own forces and equipment.[35]

Very probably, however, the wars the U.S. actually fights in the next few decades will remain asymmetrical in most respects. In other words, the U.S. will not find cooperative enemies willing to engage America's modernized forces head on with weapons and tactics that will play to America's own strengths. Meanwhile, the U.S., despite its Rabelaisian military spending, lacks the means actually needed for real global management. By now, the Bush administration's experience in Afghanistan and Iraq has raised a profoundly disquieting strategic issue: The military transformation that Rumsfeld's Pentagon was pursuing may not be compatible with the unipolar global role to which the Bush administration aspired.[36]

Military posture and strategy during the Clinton years was geopolitically more coherent. Clinton's military outlook was strongly influenced by the "Powell Doctrine," according to which American forces were not supposed to be deployed anywhere without a clearly defined mission together with a clear exit strategy.[37] Powell's constraints were easily compatible with the forces, tactics, and weapons needed for "shock and awe" but not with a strategy aimed at "nation building" requiring long periods of occupation. Under Clinton, the danger of strategic misfit was already visible in Bosnia and Kosovo, where the absence of ground forces limited the overall effectiveness of American interventions.[38] Thereafter, the engagements in Afghanistan and especially Iraq pitilessly exposed this inner weakness of America's conventional military power. These wars have proved very different from those planned by General Powell.

To be sure, both wars went well at the start. Shock and awe did quickly defeat the Taliban in Afghanistan in the winter of 2001–2002, and routed the Iraqi army in 2003. That defeated Iraqi army was, of course, a mere shadow of what it had been in 1991, when it was also quickly defeated but by a much larger American force.[39] But in Iraq's second war with the Americans, the remnants of Saddam's old army quickly melted into the population and turned to irregular warfare and terrorism. Numerous sectarian militias and terrorist gangs soon joined the fray – fighting the coalition forces and each other. If there has been a coherent Iraqi resistance strategy it has been to create conditions so chaotic that a new pro-American regime could not be established and so costly that the Americans would finally withdraw. If that was Saddam's strategy, it had considerable success, diplomatically as well as militarily.[40] Whereas the First Gulf War saw Iraq isolated, the campaign of covert resistance attracted financial support and volunteers throughout the Arab world. The continuing disorder greatly inhibited the successful regime change that has presumably been America's geopolitical goal.

In effect, America's policy in Iraq replaced a rogue state that was being successfully contained with a failed state that threatened to require indefinite occupation. One can only imagine the desperate military consequences of extending the same policy to Iran, Syria, Saudi Arabia, or Pakistan. The effects would be unlikely to remain limited to the region itself. Widespread chaos in the Middle East could not help but seriously affect America's own domestic security. Replacing rogue states with failed states is a poor exchange for the United States. Failed states, societies in chaos obsessed with their grievances, are natural breeding grounds for global terrorism. Inevitably, ruined societies see themselves as victims and almost certainly they would see the United States as their principal enemy. Terrorism would be their strategy and, if at all possible, the U.S. would be their target. As 9/11 made clear, military power does not make America invulnerable to large-scale terrorism.

But terrorism, we Americans argue, is an illegitimate form of military power.[41] We should not be surprised if the argument carries little weight with the terrorists themselves. Terrorism is the ultimate populist weapon, the natural recourse of the weak and dispossessed of this world. It is entirely understandable why comfortable and powerful states find terrorism reprehensible. Undoubtedly, it is cruel and extremely inconvenient, which is what makes it effective. Although deliberately targeting civilians is a long step into barbarism, it is not so clear why bombs delivered by planes and rockets are less objectionable morally, at least to the victims of the "collateral damage," than bombs strapped onto the bodies of suicidal terrorists.[42] Surely the aggrieved weak are unlikely to renounce terrorism because they take seriously our self-serving moral distinctions between the intimate warfare of terrorist killers and the anonymous warfare of bombers and rockets. Terrorism is the world's great military equalizer, the ultimate asymmetrical defense for the weak against the strong.

As we wage our "war on terror" we discover that countering terrorism is a complex task. Success usually requires a combination of painstaking police work together with progress in alleviating the grievances that motivate the terrorists and give them wider support. Neither requirement falls easily within the ambit of conventional military tasks. Because terrorists are often linked internationally, enlisting the cooperation of other countries is critically important. Presumably all rich and established states share a common interest in discouraging the poor and dispossessed, as well as the vicious and crazy, from turning to this populist form of military power. But, in itself, antiterrorism is not necessarily an enduring foundation for efficacious alliances.[43] Uniting the rich and satisfied requires a deeper consensus than a shared distaste for terrorism. The allies should not have major differences among themselves. Moreover, there should be some credible policy to address the resentments that nourish support for the terrorists, otherwise the allies will tend to split. Those not directly involved will be reluctant to draw down on themselves the wrath of the terrorists, particularly to defend policies of which they themselves may not approve. In short, the U.S. will have to work hard to sustain effective international cooperation against terrorism. Meanwhile, despite America's vast conventional military power, or perhaps because of it, the United States will remain vulnerable to terrorism, both at home and abroad. Our large and spectacularly expensive military establishment is trained and equipped for attacking other military establishments that cooperate by meeting us head-on. It is of limited use against the enemies we actually have, as opposed to those we prefer to imagine.

By now, of course, the poor fit between America's current military configuration and its unipolar foreign policy has become a common observation. Pentagon planners cannot be said to have reacted with alacrity. Given intellectual commitments to network-centric warfare and the colossal economic interests involved, rapid adaptation is probably unlikely. Nevertheless, the American military have been in Afghanistan and Iraq for several years. Scholarly strategists, at least, have begun speculating on a new kind of army, suited for interventions in various forms of failed states. As is probably only to be expected, these new writings often use the language of yesterday's military reform – emphasizing flexibility, maneuverability, and rapid deployment. It is said that military planners have developed a fresh interest in the counterinsurgency doctrines of the 1960s – a not altogether reassuring development. Probably the most common lesson from the Iraqi experience is the need for more troops. It is worth remembering, of course, that the U.S. had more than a half million troops in Vietnam and still failed to win that war. Returning to the Vietnam model presumably also means a heavy investment in linguistic and cultural training, as well as psychological warfare, skills needed to control and win over a hostile population. The Pentagon is, for example, said to be considering a new force of 20,000 combat advisers to instruct our "soldier-diplomats" of the future – army officers trained to arbitrate, intimidate, and soothe.[44] As the Abu Ghraib scandals indicate, not to mention the notorious installations at Guantánamo, our military is already drawn to less benign forms of occupation. Having our military preoccupied with controlling civilian populations raises an awkward issue for a constitutional democracy such as ours, where "Homeland Security" increasingly presses against traditional rights of citizens.[45] How long can we expect our domestic political system to remain unaffected by our character abroad?

Not the least of our problems is that our military needs are outrunning our capacity to finance them. Quite apart from the self-defeating geopolitical results of our excessive and misshapen military power, there are the economic consequences. Cuts in military spending allowed the Clinton administration to escape the enormous fiscal deficits of the 1980s. But even in the Clinton era, the U.S. continued to run a very big external deficit with the rest of the world economy. In this new century, the external deficits have continued to grow, while the fiscal deficits have returned and seem fated to grow larger than ever. What are the consequences for the economy? This question confronts another fundament of the unipolar vision: America's supposedly boundless capacity to finance its world role.

Notes

1. For prominent assessments of American power, see Joseph Nye, *Bound to Lead: The Changing Nature of American Power* (New York, NY: Basic Books, 1990); Zbigniew Brzezinski, *The Grand Chessboard: American*

Primacy and Its Geostrategic Imperatives (New York, NY: Basic Books, 1997). For more on the concept of soft power, see Robert O. Keohane and Joseph S. Nye, *Power and Interdependence – World Politics in Transition* (Boston, MA: Little, Brown, 1977); Joseph S. Nye, *The Paradox of American Power, Why the World's Only Superpower Can't Go It Alone* (New York, NY: Oxford University Press, 2002); Joseph S. Nye, *Soft Power: The Means to Success in World Politics* (New York, NY: Public Affairs Press, 2004); Kurt Campbell and Michael O'Hanlon, *Hard Power: The New Politics of National Security* (New York, NY: Basic Books, 2006).

2. See Dana H. Allin, *Cold War Illusions: America, Europe and Soviet Power, 1969–1989* (New York, NY: St. Martin's Press, 1995); John Lewis Gaddis, *Strategies of Containment: A Critical Appraisal of Postwar American Security Policy* (New York, NY: Oxford University Press, 1982); Seyom Brown, *The Crises of Power: An Interpretation of United States Foreign Policy during the Kissinger Years* (New York, NY: Columbia University Press, 1979); James Burnham, *Suicide of the West: An Essay on the Meaning and Destiny of Liberalism* (New York, NY: The John Day Company, 1964); Robert Strausz-Hupé et al., *A Forward Strategy for America* (New York, NY: Harper, 1961); Jean François Revel, *How Democracies Perish* (London, UK: Weidenfeld & Nicolson, 1985).

3. In 2003 over half of the U.S. foreign-born population originated from Latin America (53.3%), 25% were born in Asia, 13.7% in Europe, and the remaining 8 percent in other regions of the world (Africa, Oceania, North America). See Luke J. Larsen, *The Foreign-Born Population in the United States: 2003. Current Population Reports* (Washington, DC: U.S. Census Bureau, 2004), pp. 20–551. The number of Latinos in the United States more than doubled between 1980 and 2000, accounting for 40% of the growth in the country's population during that period. Overall, the foreign-born comprise 11.9% of the U.S. population. See "Ranking Tables 2003: Percent of Population That is Foreign-Born," U.S. Census Bureau – American Community Survey, August 27, 2003, http://www.census.gov/acs/www/Products/Ranking/2003/R15T040.htm.

4. See "Meritocracy in America: Ever Higher Society, Ever Harder to Ascend," *The Economist*, December 29, 2004, pp. 22–24; and Aaron Bernstein, "Waking up from the American Dream," *Business Week*, 3860, pp. 54–58; also Anthony DePalma et al., *Class Matters* (New York, NY: Times Books/Henry Holt and Company, 2005); Jo Blanden, Paul Gregg, and Stephen Machin, "Intergenerational Mobility in Europe and North America," Centre for Economic Performance, April 2005, http://cep.lse.ac.uk/about/news/IntergenerationalMobility.pdf; Markus Jäntti, Knut Røed, Robin Naylor et al., "American Exceptionalism in a New Light: A Comparison of Intergenerational Earnings Mobility in the

Nordic Countries, the United Kingdom and the United States," Discussion Paper No. 1938, The Institute for the Study of Labor, January 2006, http://ftp.iza.org/dp1938.pdf.

5. On neoconservative thought and influence, see Max Boot, "The Case for American Empire," *The Weekly Standard*, Vol. 7(5), 2001, pp. 27–30; Robert Kagan, "The Benevolent Empire," *Foreign Policy*, No. 111, 1998, pp. 24–35; Sebastian Mallaby, "The Reluctant Imperialist: Terrorism, Failed States, and the Case for American Empire," *Foreign Affairs*, Vol. 81(2), 2002, pp. 2–7. On neoconservative influence in U.S. foreign policy, see also The Project for a New American Century, "Statement of Principles," June 3, 1997, http://www.newamericancentury.org/statementofprinciples.htm [accessed 11.09.2008]; William Kristol and Robert Kagan, "Toward a Neo-Reaganite Foreign Policy," *Foreign Affairs*, Vol. 75(4), 1996, pp. 18–32; Elizabeth Drew, "The Neocons in Power," *New York Review of Books*, Vol. 50(10), 2003, http://www.nybooks.com/articles/16378 [accessed 11.09.2008]; John Ehrman, *The Rise of Neoconservatism: Intellectuals and Foreign Affairs 1945–1994* (New Haven, CT: Yale University Press, 1996). Shadia B. Drury, *Leo Strauss and the American Right* (London, UK: Palgrave, 1997). Robert Devigne, *Recasting Conservatism: Oakeshott, Strauss, and the Response to Postmodernism* (New Haven, CT: Yale University Press, 1994); Clyde Prestowitz, *Rogue Nation: American Unilateralism and the Failure of Good Intentions* (New York, NY: Basic Books, 2003); James Mann, *Rise of the Vulcans: The History of Bush's War Cabinet* (New York, NY: Viking Penguin, 2004).

6. To quote President Bush himself: "America has done this kind of work before. Following World War II, we lifted up the defeated nations of Japan and Germany, and stood with them as they built representative governments. We committed years and resources to this cause. And that effort has been repaid many times over in three generations of friendship and peace. America today accepts the challenge of helping Iraq in the same spirit – for their sake, and our own." George W. Bush, *Address of the President to the Nation* (Washington, DC: September 7, 2003), http://www.whitehouse.gov/news/releases/2003/09/20030907-1.html [accessed 11.09.2008].

7. The Marshall Plan cost the United States $13.3 billion over a four-year period, about 4.5% of the GDP of that period or about $450 billion at today's GDP. William D. Nordhaus, "*The Economic Consequences of a War with Iraq*," NBER Working Paper No. W9361, National Bureau of Economic Research: Cambridge MA, December 2002, Yale University, 29 October, 2002.

8. Gen. (ret.) William E. Odom wrote in *What's Wrong with Cutting and Running?*, "Postwar Germany and Japan are not models for Iraq. Each

had mature (at least a full generation old) constitutional orders by the end of the 19th century. They both endured as constitutional orders until the 1930s. Thus, General Clay and General MacArthur were merely reversing a decade and a half of totalitarianism – returning to nearly a century of liberal political change in Japan and a much longer period in Germany. Imposing a liberal constitutional order in Iraq would be to accomplish something that has never been done before. Of all the world's political cultures, an Arab-Muslim one may be the most resistant to such a change of any in the world. Even the Muslim society in Turkey (an anti-Arab society) stands out for being the only example of a constitutional order in an Islamic society, and even it backslides occasionally." William I. Odom, "What's Wrong with Cutting and Running?," Nieman Foundation for Journalism, August 3, 2005, http://www.niemanwatchdog.org/index. cfm?fuseaction=ask_this.view&askthisid=129. General Odom died recently, depriving the country of one of its most insightful and courageous analysts.

9. See, for example, Charles Maurice de Talleyrand, *Memoirs of the Prince de Talleyrand* (1891); Edmund Burke, *Reflections on the Revolution in France* (1790); and Samuel Taylor Coleridge, *The Friend* (1809–1810), *Lay Sermons* (1816–1817), *On the Constitution of Church and State According to the Ideas of Each* (1830), and *The Collected Works of Samuel Taylor Coleridge* (23 volumes) (Princeton, NJ: Princeton University Press, 1991–2001).

10. For illustration and discussion of U.S. military primacy, see Stephen G. Brooks and William C. Wohlforth, "American Primacy in Perspective," *Foreign Affairs*, Vol. 4, 2002, pp. 20–33. See also William C. Wohlforth, "The Stability of a Unipolar World," *International Security*, Vol. 1, 1999, pp. 5–41; Michael Cox, "American Power before and after September 11: Dizzy with Success?" *International Affairs*, Vol. 2, 2002, p. 269; Henry Kissinger, *Does America Need a Foreign Policy?: Toward a Diplomacy for the 21st Century* (New York, NY: Simon & Schuster, 2001); Joseph S. Nye, *The Paradox of American Power* (New York, NY: Simon & Schuster, 2002); Dinesh D'Souza, "In Praise of American Empire," *The Christian Science Monitor*, April 26, 2002, p. 11; Jonathan Freedland, "Rome, AD...Rome, DC?," *The Guardian*, September 18, 2002, p. 2; Robert Kaplan, *Warrior Politics: Why Leadership Demands a Pagan Ethos* (New York, NY: Random House, 2001); Andrew J. Bacevich, *American Empire* (Cambridge, MA: Harvard University Press, 2002); Max Boot, "The Case for American Empire," *Weekly Standard*, October 15, 2001.

11. The Clinton administration reduced American military forces from 2.2 million to 1.45 million active soldiers between 1993 and 2002.

Aggregate U.S. outlays for military procurement during the 1990s were 76% of the total for the 1980s. As a proportion of GDP, defense expenditures amounted to an average of 3.5% of GDP between 1993 and 2002, a great deal less than the average of 5.8% of GDP during the 1980s (SIPRI Military Expenditure Database, October 2005). However, funding for advanced military technology like the Joint Direct Attack Ammunition (JDAM) program, the GPS-guided Tomahawk cruise missile, or unmanned aerial vehicles like the Predator and Global Hawk originated in the Clinton years.

12. In his State of the Union address of January 1999, President Clinton declared, "It is time to reverse the decline in defense spending that began in 1985." "Prepared Text of Clinton's State of the Union Speech," The Associated Press, January 19, 1999, available at http://www.cnn.com/ALLPOLITICS/stories/1999/01/19/prepared.text. Then, in a radio broadcast on January 2, 1999, President Clinton proclaimed the "start of a six-year effort that will represent the first long-term sustained increase in defense spending in a decade." President William Clinton, National radio address, January 2, 1999.

13. After the September 11, 2001, attacks, the Bush administration increased the defense budget substantially each fiscal year. By 2005, the combined defense budget of all 24 members of the European Defense Agency was approximately $193 billion dollars, less than half the $406 billion spent by the United States. The EU defense budget represented 1.81% of GDP compared to 4.06% in the United States (European Defense Agency, Defense Facts, European-U.S. Defense Expenditure in 2005, December 19, 2006). Ratios for the following countries were as follows: Britain (2.3%), China (1.9–2.4%) (RAND estimate), France (2.4%), Germany (1.3%), India (2.4%) (Defense Industry Daily), Russia (2.8%) (2004) (source for Britain, France, Germany, Russia: NATO-Russia Compendium of Financial and Economic Data Relating to Defense, Data Analysis Section, Force Planning Directorate, Defense Policy and Planning Division, Information for the Press, December 18, 2006, http://www.nato.int/docu/pr/2006/p06-159.pdf [accessed 11.09.2008]). For a view highly critical of the Europeans, see Robert Kagan, *Of Paradise and Power: America and Europe in the New World Order* (New York, NY: Knopf, 2003). See also footnote 20 below. According to the Stockholm International Peace Research Institute, in 2003 the United States spent approximately 47% of the world's total military spending of $956 billion. Even these figures may significantly understate U.S. relative spending. For a sharp critique of defense spending undisciplined by strategic priorities, see Gordon Adams, "Greater discipline required on defense spending," *Financial Times*, March 19, 2008. See also footnote 28.

14. Zbigniew Brzezinski has noted, however, that today's terrorist threats are far less apocalyptic than the hair-trigger nuclear threat of the Cold War, where the already programmed exchanges of the superpowers would predictably have killed approximately 160 million people. Zbigniew Brzezinski, The Annual Christopher J. Makins Lecture Series, Atlantic Council, Washington DC, May 31, 2006. Today the destructive threat is much smaller but arguably more probable, http://www.acus.org/files/060531-CJM-Lecture-Brzeziuski.pdf [accessed 11.10. 2008].

15. For a good survey of Anglo-French proliferation arguments, see Lawrence Freedman, *The Evolution of Nuclear Strategy* (London, UK: Macmillan/IISS, 1989). For a sophisticated defense of limited proliferation, see André Beaufre, *Deterrence and Strategy* (London, UK: Faber, 1965).

16. Britain tested its first bomb in 1952, France in 1960, China in 1964, India in 1974 and 1998, Pakistan in 1998, North Korea in 2006. The Soviets gave little help to the Chinese and, for a time, the U.S. tried to discourage the nuclear ambitions of the British and French – on the grounds that a proliferation of nuclear weapons increased the dangers of an "accidental" war. In due course, however, the U.S. came around to the view, at least officially, that the British and French nuclear forces did help to stabilize bipolar deterrence. Ultimately, the U.S. gave technical assistance to the French as well as to the British. Richard Ullman, "The Covert French Connection," *Foreign Policy*, No. 75, 1989, pp. 3–33; Lawrence Freedman, *Britain and Nuclear Weapons* (London, UK: Royal Institute of International Affairs, 1980); Edward A. Kolodziej, *French International Policy under De Gaulle and Pompidou: The Politics of Grandeur* (Ithaca, NY: Cornell University Press, 1974).

17. So far the Chinese have not upgraded their deterrent to a second-strike capability that would seem unchallengeable. In other words, if the U.S. attacked them first, they might not be able to retaliate against the U.S. directly. Chinese plans to field new submarines, however, appear to show that they are actively pursuing such capabilities. See William Choong, "China, India Lead the Pack in Buying More Sophisticated Submarine Models," *The Straits Times*, April 9, 2007; Toshi Yoshihara and James Holmes, "China's New Undersea Nuclear Deterrent: Strategy, Doctrine, and Capabilities," paper presented at annual meeting of the ISA's 49th Annual Convention, March 26, 2008, available at http://www.allacademic.com/meta/p254572_index.html. In January 2007, the Chinese also caused considerable consternation among strategic experts by demonstrating a capacity to shoot down orbital satellites. "China's Anti-Satellite Test: A New Arms Race in Space?" *The Economist*, January 25, 2007, available at http://www.economist.com/world/asia/displaystory.cfm?story_id=8596871 [accessed 11.11.2008].

18. Calculating the significance of the different nuclear arsenals is complicated by the widespread deployment of tactical (nonstrategic) nuclear weapons (TNWs). "TNWs constitute a large percentage of the arsenals of the nuclear weapon states: 30–40% of the American and Russian arsenals, nearly 100% of the Chinese and French arsenals, and all of the Israeli, Indian, and Pakistani arsenals; Great Britain, however, no longer has short-range nuclear weapons. TNWs are the category of weapons about which the least is known." Nikolai Sokov, *Issue Brief: Tactical Nuclear Weapons (TNW)*. Center for Nonproliferation Studies, May 2002, http://www.nti.org/e_research/e3_10a.html [accessed 11.10. 2008]. For a general survey of America's vulnerability to the very technology it so ardently pursues, see Max Boot, *War Made New: Technology, Warfare and the Course of History: 1500 to Today* (New York, NY: Gotham Books, 2006).

19. Reagan's Secretary of Defense, Caspar Weinberger, saw SDI as an alternative to the mutual assured destruction (MAD) doctrine that both the United States and the Soviet Union had accepted since the 1960s. A Strategic Defense Initiative Organization (SDIO) was established in the Pentagon to develop and manage the system but immediately faced budgetary and other problems. SDI was closely embroiled in the various arms control debates of the 1980s. For a contemporaneous analysis, see George Liska, Robert E. Osgood, David P. Calleo, and Robert W. Tucker, *SDI and U. S. Foreign Policy* (Boulder, CO: Westview Press, 1987).

20. See John E. Pike, "National Missile Defense: Rushing to Failure," *Public Interest Report* Vol. 52(6), 1999, http://www.fas.org/faspir/v52m6a. htm.; "Countermeasures: A Technical Evaluation of the Operational Effectiveness of the Planned U.S. National Missile Defense System," Union of Concerned Scientists, MIT Security Studies Program, April 2000, http://www.ucsusa.org/assets/documents/global_security/CM_all.pdf.; "Missile Defense: Actions Are Needed to Enhance Testing and Accountability," United States General Accounting Office, April 2004, http://www.gao.gov/new.items/d04409.pdf.; George N. Lewis and Theodore A. Postol, "The European Missile Defense Folly," *Bulletin of the Atomic Scientists*, Vol. 64(2), 2008, pp. 32–39, available at http://www.thebulletin.org/files/064002009.pdf. For an alternative view on missile defense, see James M. Lindsay and Michael E. O'Hanlon, *Defending America: The Case for Limited Missile Defense* (Washington, DC: Brookings Institution Press, 2001); Michael O'Hanlon, "Cruise Control: A Case for Missile Defense," *The National Interest*, No. 67, 2002, pp. 89–94.

21. Today's missile defense is different from Reagan's SDI. Experience now suggests that short-range systems occasionally work and long-range

systems seldom do; see "The Faith-Based Missile Shield," *The New York Times*, October 10, 2004, p. 10.

22. See Michael O'Hanlon, *Technological Change and the Future of Warfare* (Washington, DC: Brookings Institution Press, 2000). Nevertheless, the Pentagon has continued to invest heavily in Cold War military hardware such as the three major fighter programs [the F-35 Joint Strike Fighter (JSF), the F-22, and the F/A-18E/F], the Comanche helicopter, the DD(X) destroyers, and the CVNX aircraft carriers. Even the funding provided for Unmanned Aerial Vehicles (UAVs) is focused on the development of systems that are nonstealthy and, with the exception of Global Hawk, relatively short range; Steven M. Kosiak, *Analysis of the FY 2005 Defense Budget Request* (Washington, DC: Center for Strategic and Budgetary Assessment, 2004).

23. Phil Williams, *U.S. Troops in Europe* (London, UK: Routledge & Kegan Paul, 1984).

24. The concept of network-centric warfare (NCW) was presented in 1998 by U.S. Navy Vice Admiral Arthur K. Cebrowski and John J. Garstka, Assistant Director of the U.S. Office of Force Transformation, in their article "Network-Centric Warfare: Its Origins and Future," *U.S. Naval Institute Proceedings*, Vol. 124(1), 1998, pp. 28–35. Network-enabled capabilities (NEC) are "predominantly associated with operational and tactical levels of warfare, enabling various actors on the battlefield to interact with unprecedented effectiveness, agility and synchronisation. Advancements in cutting-edge, data-sharing technologies provide armed forces with exceptional situational awareness, increased operational tempo, accuracy, lethality and survivability. In network-centric combat operations, military units no longer need to maintain visual contact, a synchronised tactical offensive can be organised with small, dispersed battle groups, thus reducing the required number of soldiers and platforms, lowering the visibility, and raising survivability of troops. Countries possessing network-centric capabilities are thought to have a decisive war fighting advantage in the 21st century. A comprehensive and ambitious American NCW program for the period 2001–2016 was spelled out in the [Joint Chiefs of Staff's concept paper] 'Joint Vision 2020. America's Military: Preparing for Tomorrow,' June 2000. The United States is widely regarded as the undisputed global leader in developing the NEC. This, however, makes it difficult for US forces to operate jointly with most other NATO military forces." Pierre Claude Nolin, "Interoperability: The Need for Transatlantic Harmonisation," *NATO Parliamentary Assembly*, 177 STC 06 E, 2006, http://www.nato-pa.int/default.Asp?SHORTCUT-1004 [accessed 11/10/2008]. For a general survey of current issues, see John Gordon, "Transforming for What? Challenges Facing Western Militaries Today." *Focus stratégique*, no. 11, Paris, Ifni,

Novembre 2008. http://www.ifni.org/frontDispatcher/ifni/publications/
focusstrategique1192007544433.

25. The 1993 Bottom-Up Review (BUR), conducted by Clinton's first Secretary of Defense, Les Aspin, resulted in debates that produced the "Two Major Regional Contingency" (MRC) force-sizing model. The MRC aimed at adapting force sizing to a world where a global war against a single opponent seemed remote. However, the MRC strategy and its successor, the "Two Major Theater War" (MTW) strategy, required similar if smaller forces than the single global conventional war. Aspin was replaced in due course. For Clinton's declining defense expenditure, see footnote 11.

26. See Stan Crock, "Why the Hawks Are Carpet-Bombing Rumsfeld," *Business Week*, August 6, 2001, http://www.businessweek.com/magazine/content/01_32/c3744079.htm; Michael Duffy, "Rumsfeld: Older But Wiser?" CNN.com, August 20, 2001, http://edition.cnncom/ALLPOLITICS/time/2001/08/27/rumsfield.html.

27. "Seamless transformation" aims to integrate all military forces and commands into a comprehensive hierarchy of command structures and technologies, across all services and including civilian command authorities, as well as to integrate all force delivery systems on all platforms and among all military units. It exploits technology to achieve lean but centralized military forces. It bespeaks a worldview that is, I suppose, the polar opposite of constitutionalism.

28. The proposed budget for fiscal year 2007–2008 was about 12% higher than the average Cold War budget in real (inflation-adjusted) terms. The current United States military budget is larger than the military budgets of the next fourteen biggest spenders combined (see CIA World Fact Book 2007, http://www.odci.gov/cia/publications/factbook). The invasions of Iraq and Afghanistan were partly funded through supplementary spending bills and are therefore not necessarily counted in the conventional military budget. Original White House projections were $50 billion. By 2006, the Congressional Research Service (CRS) estimated the U.S. had appropriated well over $300 billion for the war in Iraq. See Amy Belasco, "The Cost of Iraq, Afghanistan, and Other Global War on Terror Operations since 9/11," *Congressional Research Service*, September 22, 2006, p. 9; see also Lionel Beehner, "The Cost of the Iraq War," *Council on Foreign Relations*, November 8, 2006, http://www.cfr.org/publication/11943 [accessed 11.11.2008]. Some economists have predicted that should U.S. forces remain in Iraq until after 2010 the entire war may cost over $1 trillion. Some find even this price tag inadequate because so much of the war appropriations have been off-budget supplemental requests, often with little time for congressional oversight or full disclosure of how the money is to be allocated. By early 2006, economists Linda Bilmes of

Harvard University and Joseph E. Stiglitz of Columbia University were estimating the final war cost could top $2 trillion, based on U.S. withdrawals from Iraq by 2010 to 2015 and accounting for the "value of statistical life" for troops killed. Joseph Stiglitz and Linda Bilmes, "The Economic Costs of the Iraq War: An Appraisal Three Years after the Beginning of the Conflict," *National Bureau of Economic Research Working Paper 12054*, February 2006, http://www.nber.org/papers/w12054 [accessed 11.11.2008]. By early 2008, they published *The Three Trillion Dollar War* (New York, NY: W. W. Norton & Company, 2008). See also footnote 13 and Ch. 5, footnote 35.

29. British General Rupert Smith argues that trying to fight an "industrial war" is a disastrous policy in an age where battles no longer take place against a people but instead seek to win them over. Today the best guides are anthropologists and the best forces are linguists and general police who can go among and understand the people. Therefore, the most appropriate military forces emphasize more infantry and intelligence personnel. General Rupert Smith, *The Utility of Force: The Art of War in the Modern World* (New York, NY: Knopf, 2005). See also, U.S. General Anthony Zinni and Tony Koltz, *The Battle for Peace: A Frontline Vision of America's Power and Purpose* (New York, NY: Palgrave Macmillan, 2006); Michael DeLong, Noah Lukeman, and Anthony Zinni, *A General Speaks Out: The Truth about the Wars in Afghanistan and Iraq* (St. Paul, MN: Zenith Press, 2007).

30. See, for instance, Colin Powell's bleak assessment of the effects on the military of the "surge" in U.S. forces in Iraq proposed by President Bush in late 2006: "...all of my contacts within the Army suggest that the Army has a serious problem in the active force, and it's a problem that will spread into the Guard and Reserves: backlog of equipment that is not being repaired, soldiers – especially officers and noncommissioned officers – going on repetitive tours. So if you surge now, you're going to keep troops who've already been kept there long even longer, and you're going to be bringing in troops from the United States who were going to be coming anyway but perhaps a little bit later. And so that's how you surge. And that surge cannot be sustained. The current active Army is not large enough, and the Marine Corps is not large enough, for the kinds of missions they're being asked to perform." Colin Powell on *Face the Nation* with Bob Schieffer, December 17, 2006, CBS Corporation, New York, NY.

For more on overstretch and dissent within the military see Peter Baker, "President Confronts Dissent on Troop Levels: Bush Indicates Military Won't Dictate Numbers, Top General to Retire," *The Washington Post*, December 21, 2006: A01.

National Defense (050) Budget Authority, FY
1979–FY 2011[a] (by fiscal year in billions of dollars)

Years	Current Dollars	FY 2007 Dollars	% Actual Change
1979	126.5	353.0	0.2
1980	143.9	358.7	1.6
1981	180.0	399.9	11.5
1982	216.5	442.2	10.6
1983	245.0	477.5	8.0
1984	265.2	498.7	4.4
1985	294.7	532.0	6.7
1986	289.2	511.4	(3.9)
1987	287.4	495.5	(3.1)
1988	292.0	486.0	(1.9)
1989	299.6	479.8	(1.3
1990	301.2	468.8	(2.3)
1991	296.2	443.8	(5.3)
1992	287.7	420.2	(5.3)
1993	281.1	402.9	(4.1)
1994	263.3	369.5	(8.3)
1995	266.4	366.1	(0.9)
1996	266.2	358.0	(2.2)
1997	270.4	355.6	(0.7)
1998	271.3	348.0	(2.1)
1999	292.3	365.7	5.1
2000	304.1	370.9	1.4
2001	334.9	396.8	7.0
2002	362.1	418.0	5.3
2003	456.2	511.6	22.4
2004	490.6	533.9	4.4
2005	505.8	533.1	(0.1)
2006[b]	561.8	575.4	7.9
2007[c]	513.0	513.0	(10.8)
2008	485.2	473.5	(7.7)
2009	505.3	481.4	1.7
2010	515.3	479.1	(0.5)
2011	526.1	477.2	(0.4)

[a] Excludes funding for the 1991 Gulf War and related allied cash contributions.

[b] Includes $70 billion supplemental appropriations request.

[c] Includes $50 billion administration expects to request as a downpayment on FY 2007 war costs.

Source: Center for Strategic and Budgetary Assessments, April 2006. Based on Office of Management and Budget, Congressional Budget Office, and Department of Defense data.

31. Figures starting with FY 2006 are presumably projections. Actual spending will probably be considerably higher because many Iraqi expenses are off-budget; Steven Kosiak, "Historical and Projected Funding for Defense: Presentation of the FY 2007 Request in Tables and Charts," Center for Strategic and Budgetary Assessments, April 7, 2006, http://www.

csbaonline.org/4Publications/PubLibrary/R.20060425.FY07Bud/R.
20060425.FY07Bud.pdf; see also Chapter 5, footnote 35.

32. For my own effort to analyze earlier defense spending, see David P. Calleo, *The Bankrupting of America* (New York, NY: Morrow, 1992), Chs. 3–5.

33. Chalmers Johnson examines the enormous world network of U.S. military bases and facilities, including naval bases, army garrisons, airfields, refueling stations, sites for prepositioned munitions and supplies, and various kinds of listening posts and other surveillance installations. The Department of Defense acknowledges such installations in thirty-eight countries, but Johnson claims that the actual number is considerably larger. This complex "has a definite – even defining – physical geography . . . creating not an empire of colonies but an empire of bases." In 2006, U.S. armed forces had five major regional commands around the globe: Northern Command (including mainland United States), Central Command (with nineteen countries in Southwest Asia, the Middle East, and East Africa), Oceania Command, Southern Command (with Central and South America), and European Command. An African Command was being planned. To advance the global war on terror, the U.S. army has hastened overseas deployment in recent years. It continues to reduce the number of troops stationed in Western Europe but is making urgent efforts to open new bases in Eastern Europe. Romania, Poland, Bulgaria, the Czech Republic and other states have agreed to the stationing of American servicepeople on their territories. In Central Asia, the United States has thirteen military bases in nine countries, including Afghanistan. In recent years, it has augmented its troops on Guam Island and increased the combat capabilities of its troops stationed in Japan and the Republic of Korea. Chalmers Johnson, *The Sorrows of Empire: Militarism, Secrecy, and the End of the Republic* (London, UK: Metropolitan Books, 2005), pp. 23, 31.

34. For a survey of European efforts, see Pierre Claude Nolin, "Interoperability: The Need for Transatlantic Harmonisation," *NATO Parliamentary Assembly*, 177 STC 06 E, 2006, http://www.nato-pa.int/default. Asp?SHORTCUT-1004 [accessed 11/10/2008].

35. For Chinese upgrading, see "Annual Report to Congress: The Military Power of the People's Republic of China," Council of Foreign Relations, July 2005, http://www.defenselink.mil/news/Jul2005/d20050719china. pdf. [accessed 11.11.2008]. For Japanese upgrading, see Stephanie Lieggi and Mark Wuebbels, "Will Emerging Challenges Change Japanese Security Policy?," Center for Nonproliferation Studies, December 2003, http://www.nti.org/e_research/e3_37a.html [accessed 11.11.2008].

36. See Lawrence Freedman, "The Transformation of Strategic Affairs" *Adelphi Papers* (London, UK: International Institute for Strategic Studies, 2006), Ch. 1; H. R. McMaster, "On War: Lessons to Be Learned,"

Survival, Vol. 50(1), 2008, 19–30.; Jeffrey P. Bialos, *Ideas for America's Future: Core Elements of a New National Security Strategy* (Washington, DC: Center for Transatlantic Relations, 2008).

37. See Colin L. Powell, "U.S. Forces: Challenges Ahead," *Foreign Affairs*, Vol. 72(5), 1992–1993, pp. 32–45. Ivo H. Daalder and Michael E. O'Hanlon, *Winning Ugly – NATO's War to Save Kosovo* (Washington, DC: Brookings Institution Press, 2000), pp. 212–213. Daalder and O'Hanlon summarize the Powell Doctrine as follows: "The United States should use military force only after exhausting all other alternatives and then only decisively, to achieve clearly defined political objectives." They insist that it differs from the "Weinberger Doctrine" that "force should only be used in defense of vital U.S. interests."

My colleague Michael Mandelbaum also posits a "Clinton Doctrine" of two parts: (1) the use of force on behalf of universal values instead of narrow national interests and (2) military intervention extending to the internal affairs of sovereign states rather than merely in response to cross-border aggression, as in the Gulf War of 1991. Michael Mandelbaum, "A Perfect Failure – NATO's War against Yugoslavia," *Foreign Affairs*, Vol. 78(5), p. 5.

38. Lawrence Freedman, "Why the West Failed," *Foreign Policy*, No. 97, 1994–1995, pp. 53–69; James Gow, *The Triumph of Lack of Will: International Diplomacy and the Yugoslav War* (London, UK: Hurst & Company, 1997), pp. 299–329; Susan Woodward, *The Balkan Tragedy: Chaos and Dissolution after the Cold War* (Washington DC: The Brookings Institution Press, 1995), pp. 317–332. See also Ch. 3, footnote 24. For a comprehensive and balanced study of the Bosnia and Kosovo interventions, see Dana Allin, *NATO's Balkan Interventions* (*Adelphi Papers*, Series No. 347, London, UK: Oxford University Press for The International Institute for Strategic Studies, 2002).

39. For accounts of Iraqi capabilities and performance, see Anthony H. Cordesman, *Iran and Iraq: The Threat from the Northern Gulf* (Boulder, CO: Westview Press, 1994); Anthony H. Cordesman, *Iraq's Military Capabilities in 2002: A Dynamic Net Assessment*, Washington, DC; *Center for Strategic and International Studies*, 2002; "Iraq: The Debate on Policy Options," Research Paper 02/53, House of Commons Library, September 20, 2002, pp. 33–34; *The Military Balance 2001–2002*, p. 134. (London: International Institute for Strategic Studies, 2002, available at http://www.parliament.uk/commons/lib/research/rp2002/rp02-053.pdf [accessed 11.11.2008].)

40. There seems no convincing evidence that Saddam planned the insurgency from the start, although circumstances, including American blunders (e.g., disbanding the Iraqi army and denying local elections), greatly facilitated

it; see Michael R. Gordon and Bernard E. Trainor, *Cobra II – The Inside Story of the Invasion and Occupation of Iraq* (New York, NY: Pantheon Books, 2006), pp. 504–506.

41. American doctrine proclaims all acts of terrorism illegitimate, "viewed in the same light as slavery, piracy, or genocide: behavior that no respectable government can condone or support and all must oppose." *The National Security Strategy of the United States of America*, The White House, September 2002, p. 6, available at http://whitehouse.gov/nsc.nss/pdf.

42. The numbers of casualties under the category of "collateral damage" are not trivial. According to a 2006 study by the Johns Hopkins Bloomberg School of Public Health there were 601,027 excess civilian deaths in Iraq due to the outbreak of the war. Of these, 13% were due to air strikes. See "The Human Cost of the War in Iraq: A Mortality Study, 2002–2006," Bloomberg School of Public Health and School of Medicine Al Mustansiriya University, October 11, 2006, http://web.mit.edu/CIS/pdf/Human_Cost_of_War.pdf. Another study concluded that over a million violent civilian deaths resulted from the conflict. See "More than 1,000,000 Iraqis Murdered," Opinion Research Business, September 2007, http://www.opinion.co.uk/Newsroom_details.aspx? NewsId=78. Drawing solely on official figures and records rather than on survey data, the "Iraq Body Count" project concluded that there have been 85,463–93,232 civilian deaths thus far; see "Iraq Body Count," July 5, 2008, http://www.iraqbodycount.org/. For an analysis of casualties resulting from Kosovo air strikes of 1999 see "Civilian Deaths in the NATO Air Campaign," *Human Rights Watch Report*, Vol. 12(1), February 2000, available at http://www.hrw.org/reports /2000/nato/.

43. For studies of international cooperation against terrorism, see Daniel S. Hamilton, "Tackling Terror: A Transatlantic Agenda," in: Daniel S. Hamilton (ed.), *Terrorism and International Relations* (Washington DC: Center for Transatlantic Relations, 2006), pp. 197–220; Daniel S. Hamilton et al. (eds.), *Protecting the Homeland: European Approaches to Societal Security-Implications for the United States* (Washington DC: Center for Transatlantic Relations, 2005); Daniel S. Hamilton and Anja Dalgaard-Nielsen, *Transatlantic Homeland Security* (London, UK: Routledge, 2006); Neyla Arnas et al., "Transatlantic Homeland Defense," Center for Technology and National Security Policy/National Defense University, May 2006, http://www.ndu.edu/CTNSP/pubs/324-005_PO6-20016.pdf [accessed 11.11.2008].

44. See Gordon Lubold, "U.S. Military Takes Lessons from Iraq 'Insurgent' War," *The Christian Science Monitor*, March 20, 2008, p. 23, available at http://www.csmonitor.com/2008/0320/p13s01-usmi.html.

45. For extensive coverage of civil liberties and human rights issues during the War on Terror, see "Safe *and* Free – Restore our Constitutional Rights," American Civil Liberties Union, http://www.aclu.org/safefree/index.html; "Amnesty International Report 2008 – USA," Amnesty International, 2008, http://thereport.amnesty.org/eng/regions/americas/usa. For the government position on these issues, see *National Strategy for Homeland Security*, The White House, October 2007, http://www.whitehouse.gov/infocus/homeland/nshs/2007/index.html.

5

Feeding American Power: The Economic Base

Decline?

Throughout the Cold War, America's giant economy greatly reinforced its global power. A decade after the Cold War, the economy seemed stronger than ever. With the turn of the century, however, things began to go badly. By 2007, the U.S. appeared to have led the world into an economic crisis perhaps as severe as the Great Depression of the 1930s. The country's economic strengths, however, remain obvious. Its GDP is by far the largest for any single nation-state and is roughly equivalent to the collective GDP of all the European Union countries together. The U.S. is also the world's largest single importer and vies with Germany to be the largest exporter.[1] America's foreign investments exceed anyone else's. The U.S. is also the largest single recipient of the rest of the world's foreign investment.[2] The majority of the world's major corporations are American.[3] The U.S. has unparalleled research facilities for developing and applying new technology. It also has an abundance of fine universities and attracts a large proportion of the world's best students and scholars.[4]

The U.S. also has a special role in the international institutions that oversee global finance. The U.S. has, for example, been the dominant country in the International Monetary Fund (IMF) and an American invariably has headed the World Bank (IBRD). Since before World War II, America's dollar has been the world's principal currency for international transactions and monetary reserves, as well as for pricing oil and most other raw materials. For decades, the dollar's international monetary role has kept it in high demand and thus given the U.S. great advantages in financing its debts at home and especially its deficits with the rest of the world. In effect, the U.S. has owned the printing press that produces the world's money. This capacity to generate practically unlimited credit for itself has been a critical assumption for the unipolar view of American power. Today's unfolding crisis raises the issue of whether, and for how long, the U.S. can continue to enjoy its customary access to unlimited credit. Without that access, America's power will be significantly curtailed.

Today's economic crisis and its geopolitical consequences have, in fact, long been anticipated. Despite plenteous advantages, the post-war American economy seldom fitted orthodox models of success. Throughout the Cold War, it regularly grew bigger but also more unbalanced. Analysts and political leaders were regularly haunted by fears of its "decline." By 1968, the end of the Kennedy–Johnson era, inflation was rising, the trade surplus was vanishing, the dollar was under assault, and the economy was heading into a recession.[5] The continuous economic troubles of the 1970s kept up declinist fears. In 1971, for the first time since the nineteenth century, the U.S. began running trade deficits, widely interpreted as a sign of falling competitiveness and productivity.[6] Currency markets forced Nixon to give up defending the dollar's fixed exchange rate, which depreciated sharply and repeatedly, thereby ending the Bretton Woods monetary system. As the dollar fell, the accompanying inflation – including the remarkable oil shocks of 1973–1974 – provided further grist for declinist mills. Thereafter, the economy combined inflation and stagnation, as the trade balance continued to deteriorate and Japan emerged as an exceptionally formidable competitor for American industry. In 1979, renewed oil and currency shocks sent the dollar into a new tailspin and abruptly constrained the Federal Reserve to embrace a much stricter monetary policy.

The 1980s witnessed the unorthodox economic policies of the Reagan administration. Real defense outlays doubled but were accompanied by major tax cuts. The fiscal deficit shot upward and very big fiscal deficits became the norm. Meanwhile, the Federal Reserve continued its restrictive monetary policy to prevent inflation and support the dollar. The result was a severe credit crunch, with record interest rates attracting foreign capital and generating a spectacularly high exchange rate for the dollar. The high dollar was a great disadvantage for American products and soon the record fiscal deficit had a "twin" – a very big external or "current account" deficit that regularly needed massive financing from the rest of the world. The Federal Reserve was periodically forced to loosen credit to avoid major financial bankruptcies. The result was a febrile alternation of bubbles and crashes – the most severe of which was the stock market crash of October 1987. In this overheated atmosphere, fear that the big twin deficits would "overstretch" the economy and lead to "decline" became a major popular concern. Paul Kennedy's best seller of the late 1980s, *The Rise and Fall of the Great Powers*, threatened Ronald Reagan's profligate United States with the bankrupt fate of Habsburg Spain and Bourbon France.[7]

But although the U.S. was accumulating federal debt at what seemed an alarming rate, partisans of Reaganomics observed that the economy was also growing more rapidly than in most other countries.[8] All along, moreover, the U.S. had little trouble financing its huge debt. True, the formula had changed from one decade to the next. In the 1960s, the Bretton Woods system acted to compel other countries to hold dollars in their reserves. In effect, these holdings were forced loans. But when under Nixon speculation against the dollar exploded and the fixed rate system finally broke down, the U.S. adjusted easily to floating rates. It pumped out a vast supply of dollars that financed not only America's deficits but carried much of the rest of the world through the oil shocks. When rampant inflation finally forced an end to the cheap dollar, and the Fed sharply tightened domestic credit, the U.S. administration found it easy enough to finance its deficits by borrowing abroad. Under Nixon and Carter the U.S. exported dollars. Under Reagan it borrowed them back. In short, classical economists might fret and historians might preach cautionary tales but, one way or another, the American economy regularly found the credit it needed – a critical support for its hegemonic ambitions.[9]

Clinton's Renewal

The end of the Cold War finally brought the U.S. back to more conventional economic principles. Big cuts in defense spending, starting in 1989, significantly relieved the budget. Instead of parallel tax cuts, the administrations of the 1990s used this "peace dividend" to restore federal finances. At one point, the elder Bush actually raised taxes.[10] But given the recessionary conditions early in the decade, his administration nevertheless continued running very large fiscal deficits. He failed to be reelected in 1992, despite his success in managing the end of the Cold War and the limited war in Iraq.[11] In the campaign, Bush faced not only Clinton but the maverick third-party candidate Ross Perot, whose declinist themes about the dangers of deficits and free trade dominated the election debates. Perot took 18.7% of the popular vote and Clinton took the election.[12]

Clinton seemed a good compromise. He was clearly knowledgeable and intelligent about economic issues and his lack of interest in military prowess seemed patent. His enthusiasm for welfare reform, globalization in general and information technology in particular, all helped to burnish his image as a leader with communitarian rhetoric but conservative and internationalist discipline. Once in office, Clinton first tried to reform America's extravagant but inadequate health-care system. Congress would not support him. Clinton became, *faute de mieux*, the champion of fiscal balance. Continuing drops in defense spending made his task much easier.[13]

Clinton's fundamentally conservative economic policies were remarkably successful. Balancing the budget and liberalizing the economy appeared to have the beneficial effects classical economists had always predicted. Unemployment was at near-record lows and inflation scarcely visible. When Clinton left office in 2000, the federal budget was pointed toward a large surplus.[14] For the first time since World War II, American productivity growth began regularly outpacing that of Europe and Japan.[15] Favorable macroeconomic conditions were matched by a major technology boom. The U.S. appeared to be the leader in developing and applying the new technologies that were transforming the globe. Buoyed by this heady economic success, America's political imagination turned from economic declinism to economic triumphalism.

European troubles reinforced America's triumphal mood. As the U.S. began enjoying the prudent use of its peace dividend, both Europe and Japan seemed heavily burdened with old and new problems. The Soviet collapse brought Europe new opportunities and incentives but also urgent and major complications. The European confederacy, advancing toward monetary union, suddenly had also to cope with the immediate consequences of a reunited Germany and a liberated Eastern

Europe. Europe also had serious long-term economic problems, as "globalization" was creating a more competitive international economy. With Europe's populations aging rapidly, supporting generous pensions and health care could be expected to put heavier and heavier burdens on fewer and fewer workers. Even many ardent defenders of Europe's corporatist welfare capitalism began to admit that maintaining its postwar success would require a broad reform of labor laws, pensions, and welfare systems. Managing such reforms politically was difficult, particularly in the big continental states, France, Germany, and Italy. Global trends were thus thought to favor the Americans. Once "declining" America had suddenly become the world's economic model.

American declinism, however, was only slumbering. Even in the otherwise exemplary Clinton years, certain key features of the declinist syndrome lingered, in particular the large and growing external or current account deficit.[16] Having such a deficit meant that America's economy was continuing to absorb – consume and invest – substantially more than it was producing. Strictly speaking, the U.S. was living beyond its means. Its external deficits had to be financed by the savings of other nations. In the 1990s, however, this dependence on foreign capital seemed to reflect America's strength rather than its weakness. The American economy was the envy of the world, a huge magnet for investment. Private foreign investors, attracted above all by the technology boom, regularly flooded the U.S. with more than enough capital to cover the domestic economy's external deficit.[17] The trade deficit could thus be portrayed as a natural consequence of foreign eagerness to invest in America.[18] Rather than worry about their deficit, Americans could congratulate themselves on the attractiveness of their huge and fast-expanding economy. And although the big external and domestic debts kept growing, in the late 1990s the booming economy's GDP grew still faster. In other words, America's debts were actually shrinking in proportion to the size of its economy.

Inflation?

Traditional economists did sometimes warn about the boom's insubstantial foundations. America's GDP growth, for example, depended heavily on continuing high domestic consumption, which depended in turn on an ever-growing consumer debt. In these years, the private savings rate was often close to negative.[19] Moreover, the new wealth that offset the growing debt came mostly from capital gains derived from booming equity and real estate markets. To a classic monetarist, this mushrooming growth had the marks of "asset inflation."[20] Nevertheless, conventional inflation – rising prices and wages – failed to develop. The reasons have been a subject of hot dispute. Alan Greenspan at the Federal Reserve and studies at the World Bank credited record American gains in productivity. Others credited free-trade policies that permitted fierce competition from low-wage countries, especially China.[21]

Both explanations are doubtless partly true. But as the American car and steel industries went into steep decline, trade explanations grew more plausible. It is harsh competition, above all, that seems to have limited the growth of most American incomes and kept down price inflation in general. For the majority of Americans, to earn more income, if possible at all, generally meant working more hours, often at relatively low-paying, part-time, additional jobs. By contrast, those able to profit from booming equity and real estate markets rapidly grew much richer. In short, market competition disciplined the middle class while asset inflation indulged the very rich; hence, the unprecedented income gap that developed between the very rich and the rest.[22]

As might be expected, the issue has grown highly charged politically. On the one hand, crediting (or blaming) productivity for the income gap is a relatively benign explanation that suggests growing wealth for all, even if not ideally distributed. Blaming the Chinese, on the other hand, implies a long deflationary future – favorable to the profits of corporations able to take advantage of Asian inputs but promising no correction of the growing income gap and perhaps pointing to a protectionist future.

Nevertheless, during the Clinton years general optimism was high. The U.S. economy did grow rapidly, and unemployment was dramatically lower than in most of continental Europe. Despite heavy debts, low wages, and stingy welfare – or rather because of them – the American formula of the 1990s seemed dynamic and competitive. By contrast, Japan and most of Europe appeared stagnant. Among the major European states, Britain was the exception; it was also the economy whose market culture seemed closest to that of the United States.[23]

Neodeclinism

Since the turn of the century, however, the American economic model has grown beleaguered. The Clinton boom did not long survive the Clinton administration. In 2001, the vaulting stock market collapsed, and the new Bush administration faced a recession.[24] Bush and the Congress reacted with very substantial tax cuts and, after the atrocities of 9/11, with renewed defense spending on a Cold War scale. Big fiscal deficits returned, while the already big external deficits continued growing. Moreover, even after the recession was over, America's debt grew faster than its GDP.[25] And there was a very important further difference from the Clinton era: foreign private direct investment in America fell sharply.[26]

Given the big trade and current account deficits, which kept growing, the significant drop in direct investment from abroad threatened to put the dollar into a steep decline. In the early years of the new century, other foreign buyers stepped into the breach. Foreign holdings of U.S. long-term securities rose sharply.[27] Central banks, above all Japanese and Chinese, were heavy buyers, presumably to bolster the dollar's exchange rate to preserve the competitiveness of their own export industries.[28] These official purchases, however, were insufficient to keep the dollar from falling substantially. Between 2000 and 2004, it dropped some 25% against the euro. By mid-2005, it had recovered somewhat, but the external deficit remained huge. Between July 2006 and July 2008, the dollar fell an additional 23%.[29] As Bush's second term progressed, fears of inflation began to spook markets and the old declinist questions reappeared: With faith in the dollar eroding, how long could America continue to finance its fast-growing fiscal and external deficits? Would supporting the dollar require tight money and high interest rates? What would be the consequences for the bloated real estate and credit markets, whose explosive growth had been financing America's huge private debt?

Until 2008 Americans could be forgiven a certain complacency about these questions. For decades, successive administrations had periodically faced big deficits and an unstable dollar. Invariably, some solution had emerged. The U.S. had found it easy to finance its global policies throughout the Cold War. It was America's "unsound" finance, after all, that was saving Europe and the world from Soviet domination. Nor, in retrospect, did America's national economy appear to have suffered unduly from its half century of "overstretch." Why should old declinist fears for America be taken seriously?

There are two sorts of answers. One draws on conventional economics. The other relies on international relations theory. The two answers – economic and political – live in separate intellectual universes. In the real world, however, they are closely entwined. By 2008, the real world had intruded into the complacent lucubrations of the economists.

Economics and Power

For conventional economists, America's continued ability to finance growing debts by summoning cheap capital from others has posed a fundamental intellectual challenge. Since the days of Adam Smith, the whole discipline has rested on the assumption that economic success flows from economic virtue. The U.S., however, does not practice economic virtue. It does not save to invest; it consumes more than anyone and saves hardly at all. It nevertheless also invests hugely. To keep up these expensive habits, Americans have either printed money or borrowed the savings of everyone else. How long can this practice continue? There are conventional economic answers. So long as the U.S. is seen as the world's prime generator and producer of new products and new industries, its economy will be a magnet for foreign investment. Whether this magnetism would remain sufficient to finance the ever-growing consumer-driven external deficits was always an issue. But the U.S. has done well for a long time, even if, from a conventional economic perspective, the risks seem high and rising.[30]

Only a very naïve economist, however, would ascribe America's power to attract foreign capital to purely economic factors. International relations theory can easily provide a powerful supplementary explanation: So long as America has its hegemonic position, the money it needs will flow to it. In other words, American hegemony includes the ability to summon cheap and ready credit from the rest of the world. That credit allows the U.S. to pay for the guns and butter that sustain its hegemonic lifestyle.

America's military and financial hegemony have been interdependent since World War II. The various postwar monetary systems – Bretton Woods and the floating rate system that succeeded it – have made it easy for the U.S. to borrow freely from the rest of the world. But this persisting privilege cannot be explained without taking the Cold War itself into account. America's affluent allies – the West Europeans and the Japanese – lived comfortably under an American military protectorate. Americans seemed to be spending more on the defense of their allies than were the allies themselves. For the allies, financing the Americans by accepting their surplus dollars was a sort of imperial tax, easy to justify and awkward to refuse.

Without a threatening Soviet Union, however, Europe no longer depended on the U.S. for its security. America's ability to create or summon the world's money at will seemed more and more an "exorbitant privilege." Before the EU's monetary union, moreover, currency instability, often touched off by the dollar, was, on the whole, much more disruptive among Europe's distinct but closely integrated economies than within the U.S. itself. As the Soviet threat disintegrated, it was not surprising that the heirs of Monnet, Adenauer, and de Gaulle pressed forward to create their own common currency. In doing so, however, they put in place monetary arrangements that implied a more balanced, multilateral, and rules-based global system. Europe's new common currency is a major alternative to the dollar – both as a currency for transactions and as an international store of value. If American policy makes the dollar unstable, actors in the international economy now have alternative money. That money, moreover, serves what is probably the world's biggest collective economy and financial center. The euro's very existence thus challenges the dollar's primacy. Under present conditions the euro has proved a far better store of value. At the very least, its existence points toward a world of multiple reserve currencies, one that seems likely to constrain America's traditional ability to borrow easily and cheaply or otherwise create whatever credit it needs.[31]

In short, two of the traditional reasons for Europe to support the dollar are now much eroded. Europe no longer urgently needs American military protection, nor does it lack an alternative reserve and transactions currency. The dollar's global position seems ripe for a great fall. What, if anything, stands in the way? Inertia is perhaps the most important remaining support.

It will doubtless take time for the new dispensation to reveal itself. Europeans have long wished to rein in American monetary power but not to usurp it. European challenges to the U.S., in the monetary sphere, as in most others, are ambivalent and half concealed. Europeans have too much to lose. Trade with the U.S. is important for most European countries. European firms have colossal direct investments in the American economy.[32] Europeans have giant financial holdings in dollars. Today's Europe is not only too rich and comfortable for revolutionary adventures but also too divided. Its states are still far from united around common monetary ambitions. Its central bank, although powerfully protected, lacks the legitimacy needed to conduct a commanding global policy. Only a massive wave of exported American inflation or real financial panic seem likely to compel the Europeans to abandon the dollar. Unfortunately, by the fall of 2008 the inflation was far from unimaginable and the panic seemed to have arrived. After the Clinton years, moreover, Europeans substantially reduced their private investment flows to the U.S.[33] Increasingly, the dollar's exchange rate came to depend on the support of central banks, in particular the central banks of Japan and China.[34]

China's suddenly critical role indicated that America's unipolar economic pretensions are being challenged by more radical global changes than a fitfully uniting Europe. The most significant such change is the rising power and wealth of the nascent Asian superpowers – China and India. If anything, the rise of these countries seems long overdue. The past gives no reason to assume that China and India must be poor and the West rich. Throughout much of history, things have been otherwise.[35] But keeping the peace while making room for Asia's rising giants presents an immense challenge for the new century. Asia's rise has already altered the global economy's dimensions and seems bound to provoke major changes in the way it is governed.

The challenge is both immediate and long term. In the near term, severe problems appear to lie in wait for the dollar. Since the early 1990s, China's economy has grown at a furious rate. China's growth is linked intimately to America's burgeoning current account deficit. That deficit reflects not only America's increasingly resented role as the world's biggest borrower but also its still welcome role as the global "consumer of last resort." Suppliers around the world, China most of all, have prospered from America's voracious consumption. That consumption explains America's need to borrow the world's savings. Because private foreign investing no longer covers our external deficit, our habitual easy credit now depends, more and more, on the central banks of Japan and China. By holding America's surplus dollars in their reserves, they finance America's consumption of their countries' exports.

Japan, rich and stagnant, has done this for decades and may well continue.[36] But going on with this practice seems particularly problematic for China. The country still has vast areas of domestic poverty and urgently needs massive investments for developing its own national infrastructure. To be sure, juggling the wildly divergent parts of the huge economy creates all sorts of formidable problems for China's policymakers. In the short run, it may seem easier to subsidize exports than to deal with the general dislocation and mass unemployment that would follow in China if the U.S. were forced to cut its imports sharply. Sooner or later, however, China seems likely to find a more satisfactory use of its savings than subsidizing America's consumption, let alone its growing military presence around the world.[37] The financial crisis of 2008 appears to have accelerated this evolution, as China has announced a giant program of $586 billion for domestic infrastructure and welfare.[38]

If, to build up their own domestic investment and consumption, the Chinese seriously reduce their outsized support for the dollar, the dollar's exchange rate will almost certainly fall sharply against most currencies. Indeed, from the turn of the century to July 2008 the dollar had already lost roughly half its value against the euro.[39] Prices of America's exports and imports will change accordingly. America's consumption of foreign goods will almost certainly falter. This may help to revive America's own manufacturing and reverse the declining trade balance. But logically, it will also bring a painful drop in America's living standards, one that will be particularly severe to low-income families who benefit the most from being able to buy cheap imports. It will also be disadvantageous for firms abroad that have become America's habitual suppliers, including the American firms that have outsourced their production to those foreign suppliers.

Attracting the foreign capital to stabilize the falling dollar will logically require higher U.S. interest rates, constraining Americans to pay more for their domestic and foreign borrowing. Major geopolitical consequences would seem to follow, as our familiar global military ascendancy will grow more onerous to finance.[40] The assumption of unlimited resources, implanted in the unipolar vision, will be difficult to sustain. In short, market forces will no longer conspire to finance America's unipolar role. Instead, economics will more and more constrain America's unipolar pretensions.

Quite apart from the immediate difficulties of the dollar, the longer term problems of absorbing rising China into the global system are redoubtable. Foreign-policy analysts focus on the danger that a much wealthier China will turn more aggressive militarily. But China's "threat" may simply be that it grows too fast for the rest of the world to adjust. Respectable projections see the Chinese GDP overtaking that of the United States in a few decades. One OECD study sees this happening by 2015. More startling still, it predicts new Chinese growth between 1995 and 2015 that is equal to the actual size of the U.S. economy in 1995. In other words, China's growth over a twenty-year period is expected to be equivalent to adding another U.S. to the world economy.[41] Insofar as this immense Chinese growth is at the expense of other producers in the global economy, the consequences can be expected to be severe for the losers. Even if China's growth is not at anyone's expense, but is simply an addition to world production, the probable consequences for energy use, raw materials prices, and environmental damage are also highly disturbing.[42] Many of these consequences are already familiar.

Nothing, of course, guarantees that China's rapid growth will continue. Even sophisticated projections can easily mislead. As has happened so often in modern times, war and revolution may rob this gifted people of the fruits of their labor and talent. But if China's rise does collapse, the rest of the world is unlikely to escape unscathed. China should continue to grow rapidly for a long time. There is still a huge reserve of Chinese labor to draw on plus an enormous gap between Chinese and Western wages.[43] Cheap labor, of course, is not in itself a competitive advantage. More expensive work forces may keep their competitive edge because they are better educated and more effectively trained and disciplined. They may have more capital and better technology and therefore be more productive. But against China and India, these normal advantages of more developed economies do not always apply. Although Chinese and Indian populations are, on average, still among the world's poorest, parts of them are also among the world's better educated.[44] China, moreover, has no trouble attracting foreign capital. In any event, its own savings rate is phenomenal by

Western standards.[45] China also has little trouble acquiring Western technology. More importantly, it has the scientific and technological infrastructure to make effective use of that technology. Indeed, it is rapidly becoming a major scientific power in its own right.[46]

China's continuing success will undoubtedly shake things up in the world. Not only will its GDP eventually overtake that of the U.S. and the EU, and perhaps go well beyond either, but its competitive prowess also gravely threatens Western living standards. Why should that be? So long as China is not dedicating itself to the military domination of its neighbors, classical economics would tell us not to fear its phenomenal growth. Old competitive patterns will doubtless be disrupted, Adam Smith might say, but the new patterns should be more efficient and generate greater wealth all around. This view seems to describe well the rapid postwar growth of Japan and of Asia's "Little Tigers" – South Korea, Taiwan, Hong Kong, Thailand, Singapore, and Malaysia. By the 1970s, their competition was severely challenging old industries in the West. In due course, however, markets adjusted. Wages in many Asian countries rose sharply – even to Western levels. New Asian markets appeared for Western industries. At home, Western labor redeployed to industries and services that had grown more competitive; Western production thus grew overall more efficient. Everyone, as Adam Smith and David Ricardo had taught, was eventually better off.

China and India, however, introduce an unprecedented problem of scale. The earlier rising Asian economies had populations of small or middle-sized European states. Even Japan's population is smaller than that of France and Germany combined. As competition drove Japanese and Western wages toward a common average, the pressure on Japanese wages to go up was greater than on Western wages to go down.[47] Bringing the huge populations of China and India into the global workforce will have a different impact. Logically, given the relatively huge size of the new labor potentially available, as respective wage levels adjust toward each other, the new global average will be well below the initial Western wages.[48] Those in the West who compete directly with Chinese labor will do very badly. Others who are in a position to receive the fruits of China's low labor costs will do well. Competition with the big Asian economies is thus already linked to major changes in income distribution within Western societies, changes that have significant implications for class structure and political influence. Naturally, Western workforces will fight to insulate themselves to preserve their living standards and their welfare systems.[49] Under such circumstances, wide-scale protectionism of one sort or another seems a likely political imperative. At the same time the giant Asian states will exert their growing power to demand an increasing share of the world's prosperity.

What do these massive trends imply for global governance in the future? Economically, today's world is not growing more unipolar. Instead of a closely integrated and U.S.–dominated world economy, we should probably expect one that is more segmented and politically regulated. Countries with relatively compatible economies will probably group into large blocs, perhaps built around a dominant or common currency, or a relatively stable monetary union. Ideally, these blocs will remain reasonably open to each other. But the occasions for severe conflict – both within countries and among them – will be very great. In other words, today's unfolding trends do not promise automatic abundance and peace. Instead, they point to a harsh confrontation between Asian growth and Western prosperity. The liberal vision of harmony through competition is not adequate. Neither is the rival American fantasy of order kept through unipolar power. Certainly, the exorbitant privilege of unlimited global credit for America will grow harder and harder to sustain. If there is to be a peace in this century, the great states, including our own, will have to give up ambitions for domination, however well-intentioned, and learn the arts of mutual appeasement. A benign order in this new century will be the product of policies and institutions appropriate to managing a plural system of distinctive and self-determining regions. Arguably, such a model will look more like a pluralist *Pax Europea* than a unipolar *Pax Americana*. Very likely Europe's postwar experience is more relevant to the global political economy of the future than is our own. It remains to be seen if the current economic crisis accelerates or blocks peaceful adaptation to a more plural sharing of global wealth.

Notes

1. See "Rank Order – GDP (Purchasing Power Parity)," in The CIA World Factbook 2008, https://www.cia.gov/library/publications/the-world-factbook/geos/xx.html#Econ; and see *International Trade Statistics 2007: Most Frequently Accessed Tables: Who Are the Leading Traders* (New

York, NY: The World Trade Organization, 2005), p. 12, http://www.wto. org/english/res_e/statis_e/its2007_e/its07_toc_e.htm.

2. As the data below show, in recent years the United States has generally led the world's states in FDI inflows. The aggregate inflow to the states of the European Union, however, is much greater.

Inward FDI Flows by Country (Millions of USD)

Region/Economy	1995	2002	2003	2004	2005	2006
European Union	131,345	307,345	256,707	204,245	486,409	530,976
United States	58,772	74,457	53,146	135,826	101,025	175,394
United Kingdom	19,969	24,029	16,778	55,963	193,693	139,543
China	37,521	52,743	53,505	60,630	72,406	69,468
France	23,673	49,035	42,498	32,560	81,063	81,076
Belgium	–	16,251	33,476	43,558	33,918	71,997
Germany	12,025	53,520	32,369	–9,195	35,867	42,870
Spain	8,070	39,214	25,820	24,761	25,020	20,016
Hong Kong, China	6,213	9,682	13,624	34,032	33,618	42,892
Netherlands	12,304	25,038	21,043	2,123	41,456	4,371

"Inward FDI Flows by Host Region and Economy (1970–2006)," UNCTAD World Investment Database, July 4, 2008, http://www.unctad. org/Templates/Page.asp?intItemID=3277&lang=1.

3. According to "Fortune's Global 500, 2007," 162 of the world's largest corporations by revenue are headquartered in the United States. Japan is second with 67, whereas France has 38, Germany has 37, Britain has 33, and Italy has 10. The European Union, seen as an economic bloc, contains within its borders 161 of the 500 largest corporations. See "Fortune's Global 500, 2007," *Fortune Magazine,* http://money.cnn.com/magazines/ fortune/global500/2007/countries/US.html.

4. In 2007, foreign students accounted for 3.8% of the total U.S. university student population. The U.S. was the top destination in the world, hosting 22% of all international postsecondary students, followed by the United Kingdom (13%), France (10%), and Germany (9%). In the United States, foreign students are disproportionately distributed to the hard sciences and engineering. See *The Atlas of Student Mobility* (New York: Institute of International Education), at http://atlas.iienetwork.org/ for more detail.

5. The recession did not occur although the U.S. economy did slow to a mere 0.2% growth rate by 1970. Low economic growth continued until 1974–1975, following record inflation in 1973 and the first oil shock. For the economic conditions of the late 1960s, see David P. Calleo, *The Imperious Economy* (Cambridge, MA: Harvard University Press, 1982),

Chs. 1–6. For GDP performance, see *The Economic Report of the President* (Washington, DC: U.S. Government Printing Office, 2005), pp. 211.

6. The Petersen Report of March 1970 was commissioned by President Richard Nixon to address the role of the United States in the world economy. Among its conclusions was the fear that the relative decline of the U.S. share of world exports, and the subsequent trade imbalances that resulted, presaged falling U.S. competitiveness. For my discussion of the report in the context of U.S. economic problems in the late 1960s and 1970s, see David P. Calleo, *The Imperious Economy* (Cambridge, MA: Harvard University Press, 1982), Chs. 4–6.

7. Paul Kennedy, *The Rise and Fall of Great Powers: Economic Change and Military Conflict from 1500 to 2000* (New York: Random House, 1987). For my own analysis of American "decline" see David P. Calleo, *Beyond American Hegemony* (New York, NY: Basic Books, 1987), Part II, and *The Bankrupting of America: How the Federal Budget Is Impoverishing the Nation* (New York, NY: William Morrow & Company, 1992).

8. In aggregate terms, the U.S. average annual growth rate for period between 1981 and 1990 was 3.3%, almost a full percentage point higher than the EU-15's average growth rate of 2.4%. Federal debt, meanwhile, increased in real terms from 25.8% of GDP in 1981 to 42.0% in 1989. See *Country Data for EU-15 and the United States* (London, UK: The Economist Intelligence Unit, 2006).

   In constant 2000 dollars, U.S. GDP grew from $1.77 trillion in 1950 to $6.98 in 1989, a gain of 394% in real terms. The debt as a percentage of GDP shrank from 94.1% to 53.1% in the same period. GDP data taken from "Real Gross Domestic Product, Chained Dollars," Bureau of Economic Analysis, January 31, 2007, http://www.bea.gov/bea/dn/nipaweb/SelectTable.asp?Selected=Y#S3. Debt-to-GDP ratios taken from *The Economic Report of the President* (Washington, DC: U.S. Government Printing Office, 2005).

9. See David P. Calleo, *The Bankrupting of America, op. cit.*, Ch. 6. See also W. Carl Biven, *Jimmy Carter's Economy: Policy in an Age of Limits* (Chapel Hill, NC: University of North Carolina Press, 2002), pp. 95–121.

10. In reality, however, over the whole of the George H. W. Bush presidency, effective tax rates changed little. For effective federal tax data, see "Effective Federal Tax Rates, 1979–1997," Congressional Budget Office, 2001, http://www.cbo.gov/showdoc.cfm?index=3089&sequence=0.

11. According to the National Bureau for Economic Research, the recession of the early 1990s began in July 1990 and ended in March 1991. The recovery was quite slow, however, and the recession's effects lingered well into the 1992 presidential campaign. See "NBER Business Cycle Dating Committee Determines That Recession Ended in March 1991,"

22 December 1992 (Cambridge: National Bureau for Economic Research, 1992). The Federal Reserve suggests the recession had three proximate causes: falling consumer and business confidence due to the Iraqi invasion of Kuwait and the subsequent Gulf War, an overly restrictive monetary policy, and falling demand for domestically produced output. See Carl E. Walsh, "What Caused the 1990–1991 Recession?" *Economic Review*, no. 2 (San Francisco: Federal Reserve Bank of San Francisco, 1993). For a review of the recession's probable causes in light of standard macroeconomic theory, see Robert E. Hall, "Macro Theory and the Recession of 1990–1991," *The American Economic Review*, Vol. 83(2), pp. 275–279, available at http://links.jstor.org/sici?sici=0002-8282(199305)83%3A2%3C275%3AMTATRO%3E2.0.CO%3B2-T.

12. Clinton campaigned with the slogan: "It's the economy, stupid!" He proposed tax increases for the wealthy and cuts for the middle class and a new series of investment credits in education, the environment, and job training to alleviate the recession. But whereas Clinton and Bush were aligned on free trade, and in particular the looming North American Free Trade Agreement, Ross Perot ran on populist grounds, opposing free trade and predicting a "great sucking sound" to the south as U.S. businesses fled high labor and regulatory costs for the more business-friendly Mexico.

    Clinton's economic prescriptions helped him carry the election against aggressive Republican campaigning on his supposed character defects. Exit polling and media surveys suggested that voters were largely dissatisfied with Bush's economic performance and saw Perot as too risky an alternative compared to the Arkansas governor. Perot's campaign was manifestly a criticism of Bush. Some studies of electoral returns and exit polling suggest Perot took votes equally from Clinton, but I find this conclusion implausible. Studies of electoral returns and exit polling suggest that Perot, by providing an economic policy alternative to Bush, who lacked the troubling character issues of Clinton, took votes from both candidates equally.

    For a summary of the Bush and Clinton campaigning platforms on the economy, see David E. Rosenblum, "The 1992 Campaign Issues: Economic Philosophy, Candidates Sharply Divided on Prescription for the Economy," *The New York Times*, October 9, 1991: A1. For a characteristically trenchant discussion of the electoral results and their economic basis, see R. W. Apple, Jr., "The 1992 Elections, News Analysis: The Economy's Causality," *The New York Times*, November 4, 1992: A1.

13. For my analysis of the 1996 election and the Clinton administration's foreign and fiscal policy going into its second term, see David P. Calleo, "A New Era of Overstretch?," *World Policy Journal*, 15(1), 1998, pp. 11–25.

In real terms, defense spending fell from $450.7 billion to $370.3 billion in constant 2000 dollars between 1992 and 2000. It was even lower in the mid-1990s. Defense spending as a percentage of GDP fell from 4.8% to 3%, whereas the budget as a percentage of GDP fell even further, from 22.1% to 18.4%. Meanwhile, the economic boom produced an explosion of tax revenues. Between 1992 and 2000, tax revenues increased by 85% while total spending increased only 23%. Of the major budgetary line items, only defense and international affairs spending were flat in nominal terms during this period. All other items increased in nominal terms (and most in real terms, given inflation of 23% total during this period): health (72%); medicare (66%); income security (27%); social security (42%); debt interest (15%); and "other" (39%). See *The Economic Report of the President* (Washington, DC: U.S. Government Printing Office, 2005), pp. 211, 305. The real decline in defense spending cannot, in itself, fully account for the balanced budgets of the late 1990s. A full explanation reasonably requires weighing the favorable effects of a return to fiscal balance on investment and growth. See note 20 below.

14. A budget surplus of $166 billion was predicted for 2000 and $184 billion for 2001. See *The Economic Report of the President* (Washington, DC: U.S. Government Printing Office, 2000), p. 397.

15. The 1990s saw the United States overtake the EU-15 in overall productivity growth. Although the EU-15 did better in the period 1990–1995, averaging 1.9% per annum (U.S. 1.1%), in the latter half of the decade, U.S. productivity grew at 2.5% per annum (EU-15 1.4%).

   This shift appears tied to the use of information and computer technology (ICT). In the United States the productivity of ICT-using industries grew nine times faster than that of other industries. In the EU-15, the ICT multiplier generated only a twofold difference in growth rates. Moreover, a larger proportion of U.S. GDP was composed of ICT-using sectors than in the EU (30.6% vs. 27.0%). Finally, the sectors experiencing the highest productivity growth – i.e., retail and wholesale trade, and financial securities – benefit within the United States from much larger economies of scale than in the E.U.-15, where cross-border consolidation remains a contentious issue. See Bart van Ark, Robert Inkaar, and Robert McGuckin, "Changing Gear: Productivity, ICT, and Services Industries: Europe and the United States" *Research Memorandum GD-60* (Groningen: Groningen Growth and Development Center, 2002), at http://www.ggdc.net/workpap.html. In Japan, lack of growth in ICT assets was also responsible for slower productivity growth. See Tsutomu Miyagawa, Yukiko Ito, and Nobuyuki Harada, "The IT Revolution and Productivity Growth in Japan," *Journal of the Japanese and International Economies*, Vol. 18(3), 2004, pp. 362–389.

16. Between 1992 and 2000, the U.S. current account deficit grew more than tenfold, from $36.9 billion to $396.6 billion. The Congressional Budget Office argues that the rapid expansion of the U.S. economy during this period was a primary driver of the widening deficit between imports and exports, just as it was in the mid-1980s. As in that period, consumption demand outstripped capacity, and U.S. demand growth exceeded that of America's major trading partners. The deficit's decline in the late 1980s is attributed to the slowing U.S. economy amid declining consumer demand. See "Causes and Consequences of the Trade Deficit: An Overview" The Congressional Budget Office, February 1, 2000, http://www.cbo.gov/showdoc.cfm?index=1897&sequence=0.

Another significant factor was the falling value of the dollar after the conclusion of the Plaza Accords. The real trade weighted value of the dollar (as measured by the Federal Reserve's ten-country index) fell 36% between 1985 and 1987; there was a corresponding 40% fall in the trade deficit. For a discussion of the role of the dollar in U.S. trade balances, see Martin Feldstein, "The Dollar and the Trade Deficit in the 1980s: A Personal View," *NBER Working Papers Series*, no. 4325 (Cambridge: National Bureau for Economic Research, 1993).

17. From 1997 to 2000, annual FDI in the U.S. went from $682 billion to $1,257 billion, an increase of $575 billion, and 84% on a historical cost basis. In the same period, the annual current account deficit grew by $275 billion dollars. Capital inflow growth thus exceeded trade deficit deterioration by approximately $300 billion. Of this FDI increase, 40%, or $228 billion, went to four sectors: computers and electronic products, electronic equipment, information, and professional/scientific/technical services. For FDI data, see "Direct Investment: Foreign Direct Investment in the U.S." and for data on the trade balance, see "Balance of Payments (International Transactions)," Bureau of Economic Analysis, http://www.bea.gov/bea/di1.htm.

18. Trade deficits and investment inflows represent two sides of the same macroeconomic identity. Having one requires having the other, but says nothing about which one causes the other. Distinguished economists of both the left and right joined in denigrating the importance of the current-account deficit. Robert Heilbroner, in line with Milton Friedman, argued that the twin deficits, far from being a sign of America's weakness, reflected its strength. Quoting Friedman, Heilbroner saw the willingness of the Japanese to invest in the U.S. economy rather than their own as "a sign of U.S. strength and Japanese weakness." Heilbroner argued that foreigners would be willing to invest in the U.S. and thereby sustain Americans' outsized consumption and investment, so long as the U.S. maintained an internationally competitive economy with high returns to

investment. See Robert Heilbroner and Peter Bernstein, *The Debt and the Deficit: False Alarms and Real Possibilities* (New York, NY: W. W. Norton & Company, 1989).

19. The U.S. entered the 1990s with a household savings rate as a percentage of disposable income of 7%. This steadily declined and the United States entered the new century with a savings rate of 2.3%. On average, Americans in the 1990s saved 5.2% of their disposable income. In comparison, the Japanese saved 13.9% of disposable income in 1990 and 10.7% in 2000 and the Germans 13.9% and 9.5%, respectively. See "Macroeconomic Trends: Economic Growth: Household Saving," in OECD Factbook 2006: Economic, Environmental, and Social Statistics, January 29, 2007, http://lysander.sourceoecd.org/vl=8881248/cl=13/nw=1/rpsv/factbook/.

20. The administration argued that the fall in the federal deficit made possible higher private investment without raising interest rates. Continuing low interest rates also made possible booming real estate and asset prices. For a neoclassical economist like Friedrich Hayek, booming corporate profits with a concomitant rise in stock prices is an early sign of inflation. Rising profits and asset prices become an embedded expectation, which cannot be satisfied except by increasing inflation. See also footnote 13. For Hayek's thoughts on asset inflation, see Friedrich A. Hayek, *The Constitution of Liberty* (Chicago, IL: University of Chicago Press, 1978), pp. 331–332.

21. The low inflation during the 1990s growth cycle was puzzling from the start. Early on, unemployment, fell below the NAIRU (non-accelerating inflation rate of unemployment), but price inflation did not follow. Economists wondered whether structural changes in the economy had pushed the inflation rate lower than in past expansions. The long period of relatively low inflation following the 1970s was thought to have moderated inflationary expectations and therefore wage demands. But by the second half of the 1990s, with wages rising at twice the rate of inflation, inflation still did not accelerate. Federal Reserve Chairman Alan Greenspan argued in the mid-1990s that the rate of technology adoption meant that U.S. productivity growth made real wage increases possible without inflation, and at the same time also led to lower unemployment.

Some analysts blame Greenspan's confidence about productivity gains for his easy monetary policy that, they maintain, allowed an asset and stock market bubble to develop. Greenspan himself seems to have recognized this danger, most famously in his 1996 "Irrational Exuberance" speech. The exuberance came to an end just as Greenspan had feared it might, with the fall of the stock market following the dot-com collapse and a wave of corporate reporting scandals. Meanwhile, the high consumer indebtedness of the 1990s remained. For Greenspan's thinking at the height of the 1990s boom, see "Statement by Alan Greenspan, Chairman, Board of Governors of the Federal Reserve System, before the Joint Economic Committee of the United States Congress," June 17, 1999, at http://www.house.gov/jec/hearings/grnspn4.htm. For critics, see Stephen S. Roach, "Think Again: Alan Greenspan," *Foreign Policy*, Issue 146, January/February 2005, pp. 18–24, and "Original Sin," Morgan Stanley Global Economic Forum, http://www.morganstanley.com/GEFdata/digests/20050425-mon.html.

Later arguments gave more weight to the deflationary effects of cheap imports, Chinese in particular. As the World Bank has argued, excessive rates of private saving in China have resulted in overinvestment and overcapacity in Chinese export industries. Between 1996 and 2002, the pressure on these industries to channel their excess output into global markets lowered Chinese export prices by an average of 15%. The result was falling prices for many consumer goods within the U.S. economy. Hence, as the volume of Chinese exports to the U.S. jumped from $15.2 to $100 billion between 1990 and 2000, the U.S. in effect imported deflation into its economy. See "China Is Becoming the World's Manufacturing Powerhouse," *Beyond Transition, World Bank Transition Newsletter*, Vol. 13(6), 2002. See also Denise Yang, "China: Exporting More Deflation," in *Global Economic Forum* (New York, NY: Morgan Stanley, 2002). The reports of the Council of Economic Advisers argued that falling import prices did lower inflationary expectations but only by 0.3 percentage points. See *The Economic Report of the President* (Washington, DC: United States Government Printing Office, 1997, 1998, 1999).

Critics of this view note that much of the Chinese import growth came at the expense of equally cheap imports from other developing economies. Therefore, given the already-high volume of consumer goods imports from Asia, the deflationary impact of these imports should already have been present in the U.S. economy. For skepticism about China's disinflationary effect, see Steven B. Kamin, Mario Marazzi, and John W. Schindler, "Is China 'Exporting Deflation'?" *International Finance Discussion Paper 791* (Washington, DC: Board of Governors of the Federal Reserve System, 2004) and "Deflation: Determinants, Risks, and Policy Options – Findings of an Interdepartmental Task Force" (Washington, DC: International Monetary Fund, 2003).

Other studies suggest China's deflationary effect may be greater than previously thought thanks to the changing nature of U.S. retailing, in particular the role of giant firms like Wal-Mart that import heavily from China. A recent study from the National Bureau of Economic Research estimates that the effect of Wal-Mart's "everyday low prices" on local grocery markets was underestimated by 14–18.3%. Correcting for this in the Consumer Price Index would have lowered the official estimate of inflation by 15%! For Wal-Mart's operations and their effects on inflation, see Anthony Bianco and Wendy Zellner, "Is Wal-Mart too Powerful?" *Business Week*, October 6, 2003, p. 100, and Gene Koretz, "Wal-Mart versus Inflation," *Business Week*, May 13, 2002, p. 32. For evidence of methodological bias in CPI calculations stemming from undercounting the effect of big-box stores, see Jerry Hausman and Ephraim Leibtag, "CPI Bias from Supercenters: Does the BLS Know That Wal-Mart Exists?," *NBER Working Papers*, no. 10712 (Cambridge, MA: National Bureau for Economic Research, 2004).

22. America's income gap varies with the statistical model and population groupings used. Nevertheless, all signs point to increased income inequality. The United States Census Bureau, for example, reports a broad growth in income inequality in the period 1995–2005.

% of Total Income Owned by

Quintile	2005	1994
Top	50.4	49.1
Middle 3	46.2	47.3
Bottom	3.4	3.6

See *Income, Poverty, and Health Insurance Coverage in the United States: 2005* (Washington, DC: United States Census Bureau, 2006); and *Income, Poverty, and Valuation of Noncash Benefits: 1994* (Washington, DC: United States Census Bureau, 1995).

A closer breakdown reveals growing inequality within the top quintile itself. In 1997, the pretax income threshold for the top quintile was $167,500. But the top 1% of earners made at minimum six times more or $1.02 million. Moreover, between 1979 and 1997, the share of national pretax income going to this top 1% increased from 9% to 16%, a 78% increase, even as the income going to the top quintile as a whole increased by 50%. Meanwhile, the bottom quintile's share of national pretax income declined from 5% to 4%. *Historical Effective Tax Rates, 1979–1997: Preliminary Edition* (Washington, DC: Congressional Budget Office, 2001), pp. 74–75. See also "The Rich, the Poor, and the Growing Gap between Them," *The Economist*, June 15, 2006. For a more critical analysis of this trend and its potential costs to the United States, see Paul Krugman, "For Richer," *The New York Times*, October 20, 2002: F62.

The same trends do not yet appear to apply to the stock of wealth. Estate tax returns for the 1916–2000 period suggest that wealth in the top 2% of wealth holders has declined since its postwar high of 32.5% in 1960 and since 1976 has fluctuated within a band of 25–28%. See Wojiech Kopczuk and Emmanuel Saez, "Top Wealth Shares in the United States, 1916–2000: Evidence from Estate Tax Returns" *NBER Working Papers Series*, no. 10399 (Cambridge, MA: National Bureau of Economic Research, 2004).

23. From 1990 to 2000, the U.S. compound annual growth rate of GDP was 3.0% compared to the EU-15's 2.2% and Japan's 1.1%. Unemployment in the United States averaged 5.6% compared to 10.0% in the EU-15 and 3.2% in Japan. Among the major states, Germany, struggling under the fiscal and economic burdens of unification, sustained a compound annual growth rate of GDP for the period 1991–2000 of only 1.6%. France was only slightly better at 1.8%. Japan, still reeling from the banking collapse of the late 1980s, grew at a mere 0.9% annually. But the UK's rate was 2.6%, second only to the United States within the G7. Thatcher's deregulatory efforts of the previous decade are often given credit, but Britain's exit from the European Monetary System after the 1992 sterling crisis was also important. It isolated Britain from the follow-on effects of German reunification, transmitted to the rest of the Eurozone via the exchange rate requirements of EMS membership. For the benefits of Britain's exit from the EMS, see David P. Calleo, *Rethinking Europe's Future* (Princeton, NJ: Princeton University Press, 2001), pp. 190–191. For unemployment and GDP growth data, see "The Economist Intelligence Unit (EIU), Japan, the United States, and Europe, Country Data 1980–Present," EIU Limited, September 21, 2006, www.eiu.com.

24. As the Council of Economic Advisers notes, the economy as of 2001 was still recovering from the dot-com collapse and the subsequent revelations of corporate malfeasance. The surge in private-sector investment characteristic of the 1990s ended with double-digit declines as its principal investment target, computer infrastructure, reached saturation. Coupled with the fall in consumer spending, the collapse of overall demand pushed the economy into recession by late 2000. An emerging recovery was postponed by the economic shock of the September 11, 2001 terrorist attacks on the heart of the financial system. See *The Economic Report of the President* (Washington, DC: United States Government Printing Office, 2001), pp. 23–30.

25. For the duration of the recession, see Nell Henderson, "Economists Say Recession Started in 2000," *The Washington Post*, January 22, 2004, available at http://www.washingtonpost.com/ac2/wp-dyn/A38826–2004 Jan22?language=printer. During this period, the debt continued to rise. From 2000 to 2004, gross federal debt grew by 31%, whereas U.S. GDP

in that same period grew by 19%. Data derived from *The Economic Report of the President* (Washington, DC: U.S. Government Printing Office, 2005), p. 303.

26. The Economist Intelligence Unit reports that foreign direct investment in the United States, having risen from 0.83% of GDP in 1990 to 3.199% in 2000, fell to a nadir of 0.485% in 2003 before recovering slightly to 0.812% by 2005. The estimate for 2007 indicated FDI flows into the U.S. were 1.3% of GDP. "The Economist Intelligence Unit (EIU), Japan, the United States, and Europe, Country Data 1980–Present," EIU Limited, July 4, 2008, www.eiu.com.

27. Foreign ownership of U.S. government and private securities and assets has increased greatly after the mid-1990s. From 1994 to 2004, the percentage of United States government debt owned by foreign entities increased from 19.1% to 43.9%. Geographical distribution of the ownership also changed, Europe remained the largest holder, but Asia was rising somewhat more rapidly. From June 2002 to June 2005, foreign holdings of U.S. long-term securities increased by $2.336 trillion. Of this, the Asian nations accounted for nearly half or $1.037 trillion. Europe accounted for only slightly less, adding $1.033 trillion to its stock of dollar-denominated assets. Europeans were more inclined to buy equities and the Asians long-term debt securities. See *Report on Foreign Holdings of US Securities as of June 30, 2005* (Washington, DC: Department of the Treasury, 2005). It is worth noting that the main foreign holders were foreign central banks and government investment funds. See Kenneth Rogoff, "Foreign Holdings of U.S. Debt: Is Our Economy Vulnerable?" Brookings, June 26, 2007, http://www.brookings.edu/testimony/2007/0626budgetdeficit_rogoff.aspx.

28. Official U.S. data show Japan and China as the major holders, as the table below indicates:

Major Foreign Holders of Treasury Securities (Billions of USD)

Country	Jun-02	Jun-03	Jun-04	Jun-05	Jun-06	Jun-07	Dec-07	Apr-08
Japan	349.4	460.5	667.6	666.4	613.9	622.3	581.2	592.2
China	96.5	147.1	194.2	297.8	372.2	477.2	477.6	502.0
United Kingdom	50.1	52.1	46.1	50.4	51.8	47.9	156.7	251.4
Oil Exporters	n.a.	n.a.	n.a.	n.a.	n.a.	133.0	137.9	153.9
Brazil	11.2	12.0	13.8	22.4	33.3	94.8	129.9	149.5
Hong Kong	43.1	43.0	45.6	44.3	48.6	56.9	51.0	63.1
Russia	3.7	3.8	3.0	1.3	4.5	3.4	32.7	60.2
Germany	39.3	41.5	47.1	46.1	41.8	45.9	41.7	44.0
Taiwan	36.8	43.0	67.0	67.8	63.4	44.7	38.2	42.6
Korea	32.6	60.2	44.5	62.9	65.6	43.6	39.2	40.5
Mexico	30.0	28.1	38.4	29.2	46.1	34.1	34.4	38.0

For more data, see "Major Foreign Holders of Treasury Securities," United States Department of the Treasury, July 7, 2008, http://www. ustreas.gov/tic/mfh.txt.

For China's motives, as seen from the U.S. Treasury, see "China's Exchange Rate Regime and its Effects on the U.S. Economy," John B. Taylor, Under Secretary of Treasury for International Affairs, Testimony before the Subcommittee on Domestic and International Monetary Policy, Trade, and Technology House Committee on Financial Services October 1, 2003," United States Department of the Treasury, October 2003, http://www.treas.gov/press/releases/js774.htm. For a broader perspective, see Martin Wolf, "America's Deficits Are More Than Just China's Problem," *The Financial Times*, April 20, 2005, p. 17. For growing U.S. dependence on foreign central banks rather than private investors to finance the external deficits, see Brad Setser's article "Taking Stock of the Dollar's Global Role," *RGE Monitor*, May 11, 2008, available at http://www.rgemonitor.com/blog/setser/252597/.

29. The dollar/euro interbank rate stood at 1.0155 on January 3, 2000, fell to 1.2592 on January 2, 2004, recovered slightly to 1.2232 on June 1, 2005, and was 1.2808 by November 15, 2006, By July 3, 2008, it had dropped precipitously to 1.5708. See "Foreign Exchange Rates, 2000-Present," Federal Reserve, http://www.federalreserve.gov/releases/H10/hist/.

30. Martin Wolf argued that the U.S. deficit situation was unsustainable from any perspective. The U.S. fiscal situation left the stability of the dollar a function mostly of intervention by foreign governments for their own economic reasons. See Martin Wolf, "The World Must Adjust to the Dollar's Inevitable Fall," *The Financial Times*, November 24, 2004, p. 21.

31. For my own analysis at various stages, see David P. Calleo, *Beyond American Hegemony, a Twentieth Century Fund Book* (New York, NY: Basic Books, 1987), Chs. 6–7; *The Bankrupting of America* (New York, NY: William Morrow & Co., 1992), Ch. 6; "The Strategic Implications of the Euro," *Survival*, 41(1), 1999, pp. 5–19, and *Rethinking Europe's Future*, *op. cit.*, pp. 200–205.

32. See Daniel S. Hamilton and Joseph P. Quinlan, *Transatlantic Economy 2006 Annual Survey of Jobs, Trade, and Investment between the United States and Europe* (Washington, DC: Center for Transatlantic Relations, 2006).

33. See CRS Report For Congress. European Union-US Trade and Investment Relations: Key Issues. February 14, 2008, p. 23.

34. See Table 4.

35. In 1750, China and India/Pakistan together are thought to have accounted for 57.3% of world manufacturing output with Europe at only 23.2%.

Over the next 150 years, the positions reversed. By 1900, Europe accounted for 62% of global output, with China and India/Pakistan combined a mere 7.9%. See Paul Kennedy, *The Rise and Fall of Great Powers*, pp. 1–98, 190. For the decline of the Muslim Middle East following the Middle Ages, see Bernard Lewis, *What Went Wrong?: Western Impact and Middle Eastern Response* (New York, NY: Oxford University Press, 2001).

36. Susan Strange once described Japan as a "black hole" for dollar deficits. See pp. 275–278 of "International Monetary Relations" in Andrew Shonfield (ed.), *International Economic Relations of the Western World, 1959–1971* (London, UK: Oxford University Press, 1976).

37. Shifting China's massive private savings into internal consumption and investment probably requires a strong appreciation of the currency; the Chinese government allowed a 2% rise of the yuan in July 2005 when the People's Bank of China stopped pegging to the dollar. As of January 2008, the yuan had appreciated by 14% more. The yuan rose 3.3% against the dollar in 2006 and by a full 0.9% in the last week of 2007 alone. See "Revaluation by Stealth," *Economist*, January 10, 2008; and Keith Bradsher, "China Lets Currency Appreciate a Bit Faster," *The New York Times*, December 29, 2007. Section B, p. 1.

Skeptics note that the regime, having legitimated itself with economic growth, fears any threat to the powerful export sector and the economic prosperity it brings. Floating has its dangers, as China's Asian neighbors have demonstrated in repeated currency crises. Steven Hanke of *Forbes* magazine cites Robert Mundell, the Nobel laureate, as telling some guests at a party in 2005 that a revaluation would "cut foreign direct investment, cut China's growth rate, delay convertibility, increase bad loans, increase unemployment, cause deflation distress in rural areas, destabilize Southeast Asia, reward speculators, set in motion more revaluation pressures, weaken the external role of the renminbi and undermine China's compliance with World Trade Organization rules," Steven H. Hanke, "Why China Won't Revalue," February 28, 2005, http://www.forbes.com/columnists/business/global/2005/0228/048.html.

Rising internal discontent very likely does increase pressure to preserve economic stability. Rapid development has generated rising income inequality, substantial environmental damage, and tension between the wealthy coast and much poorer interior. On the rise of political discontent, see Murray Scot Tanner, "Testimony Before the US-China Economic and Security Review Commission" (Santa Monica: The RAND Corporation, 2005), at http://www.rand.org/pubs/testimonies/2005/RAND_CT240.pdf, and Albert Keidel, *Policy Brief 48: China's Social Unrest: The Story Behind the Stories* (Washington, DC: The Carnegie Endowment for

International Peace, 2006), and Edward Cody, "In Face of Rural Unrest, China Rolls Out Reforms," *The Washington Post*, January 28, 2006: A01, available at http://www.washingtonpost.com/wp-dyn/content/article/ 2006/01/27/AR2006012701588.html. Meanwhile, Chinese goods are meeting new export barriers. The EU in 2006 imposed a two-year 16.5% tariff on Chinese imports of shoewear. See Theo Leggett, "Brussels Extends Asia Shoe Tariff," *BBC News*, October 4, 2006, http://news.bbc.co.uk/2/hi/business/5405898.stm.

For environmental problems, see "100 Tonnes of Pollutants Spilling into Chinese River," *The Guardian*, November 25, 2005, http:// www.guardian.co.uk/china/story/0,7369,1650786,00.html; and Andreas Lorenz, "Choking on Chemicals in China," *Der Spiegel*, November 28, 2005, http://www.spiegel.de/international/spiegel/0,1518,387392,00 .html. See also *The New York Times* ten-part series called "Choking on Growth," published in 2007, which can be found at http://www.nytimes. com/interactive/2007/08/26/world/asia/choking_on_growth.html.

38. See announcement from Bloomberg news http://www.bloomberg.com/ apps/news?pid=20601068&sid=aIpq7IF4BM9Q&refer=home.

For the official announcement in Mandarin, see the State Council http://www.gov.cn/ldhd/2008-11/09/content_1143689.htm.

39. See footnote 29.

40. Joseph Stiglitz and Linda Blimes state in *The Three Trillion War* (New York, NY: W. W. Norton & Company, 2008) that the Bush administration drastically underestimated the cost of the Iraq war. The original government estimates of $50–$60 billion were quickly surpassed. The cost, counting only money officially appropriated, reached $600 billion sometime around when the book was published in 2008. Deficit spending has given the illusion of a cheap war, but someday the full financial costs, including equipment replacement, long-term health care for servicepeople, and the economic effects due to higher deficits, will be spectacularly higher than officially anticipated. For an excerpt of the book, see http://www.vanityfair.com/politics/features/2008/04/stiglitz200804. For an earlier estimate, see Chapter 4, footnote 28.

41. In 1998, Angus Maddison estimated that China's GDP (measured in 1995 dollars) would match that of the United States in 2015 and comprise 17% of the global economy – slightly more than the United States. This was based on a conservative average annual GDP growth rate for China of 5.5% and per capita growth rates of 4.5%. Angus Maddison, "General Economics & Future Studies: Development Centre Studies: Chinese Economic Performance in the Long Run," *OECD*, Vol. 1998(7), pp. 1–196. In 2003, a Goldman Sachs team considered the global effects if the BRICs (Brazil, Russia, India, and China) continued to grow at their

current potential until 2050. In 2003, these countries accounted for 20% of world growth and slightly less than 10% of the global economy. By 2025, they could well account for 40% of world growth and constitute close to 30% of the global economy, with enormous implications for global energy demand, income distribution, capital markets, and the environment. The team estimated that the BRICs' share of global GDP will have easily overtaken that of the G6 by 2050, with China the world's largest economy and India and the United States vying for second place. See "Dreaming with BRICs: The Path to 2050," *Goldman Sachs Global Economic Paper No. 99*, October 1, 2003, http://www2. goldmansachs.com/ideas/brics/book/99-dreaming.pdf; and "The BRICs and Global Markets: Crude, Cars and Capital," *Goldman Sachs Global Economics Paper No. 118*, October 2004, http://www2.goldmansachs. com/ceoconfidential/CEO-2004-09.pdf.

According to the Goldman Sachs research team, by 2050, China will have added another four 2003 U.S. economies to the global economy and India another three, whereas the U.S. itself would have added another two and a half ("Dreaming with BRICs: The Path to 2050," *op. cit.*).

Critics of the Goldman Sachs report find several of their baseline assumptions incorrect. China will face significant problems extending the growth along the prosperous eastern coastline to the interior, where social and political unrest is rising. India, although democratic, faces entrenched poverty supported by a caste system, and a poorly developed educational system. Russia depends heavily on oil development, historically a hindrance to overall economic development, resulting in the so-called Dutch disease.

Finally, although the Goldman Sachs report assumes relatively pacific international economic and strategic conditions, new economic powers rarely arise without international discord, as the nineteenth and early twentieth century's experience with Germany, the United States, and Japan might suggest. For critiques of the Goldman Sachs report, see "BRIC – The Major Issues" (Danske Bank, 2006) at http://danskeresearch. danskebank.com/link/PresentationAndreMarkeder27062006/$file/ BRIC27062006.pdf.

42. IMF studies attribute to China a large percentage of the notably increased demand for a wide range of commodities, including foodstuffs, metals, chemicals, and oil products. Reportedly, China will also overtake the United States in 2009 as the world's leading emitter of carbon dioxide – thought to be the principal source of global warming. For China and world commodity demand, see *World Economic Outlook: Housing and Business Cycles* (Washington, DC: The International Monetary Fund, 2008), pp. 46–62. For China's growing emissions,

see the Netherlands Environmental Asessment Agency report, "China Contributing Two Thirds to Increase in CO2 Emissions," which can be found at http://www.mnp.nl/en/service/pressreleases/2008/20080613 ChinacontributingtwothirdstoincreaseinCO2emissions.html and David Adams, "China Carbon Emissions Soaring Past the US," *The Guardian*, June 13, 2008.

43. The labor force in the United States was estimated to be 149.3 million in 2005, whereas it was 231.9 million in the EU, 790.1 million in China, and 497.0 million in India. By 2007, the U.S. labor market comprised 153.1 million workers, and the E.U.-15 comprised 188.6 million workers, whereas all of Europe, excluding Turkey, had 228.7 million workers. Meanwhile, by 2007 the Chinese labor market had grown to 803.3 million and India's had grown to 516.4 million. Labor costs in 2004 (measured in 1996 dollar terms) were $21.40/hour in the EU and $23.60/hour in the United States, compared to $1.20/hour in China and $1.10/hour in India. By 2007, U.S. labor costs were $25.60/hour and still only $1.63/hour in China. "The Economist Intelligence Unit (EIU), China, India, the United States, and Europe, Country Data 1980–Present," EIU Limited, 2007, www.eiu.com. Retrieved February 1, 2007, and July 8, 2008.

44. In 2000 approximately 100 million students were enrolled in universities worldwide: 38% in Asia, excluding Japan, and only 15% in the United States. Of the 38% in Asia, the majority were studying science and engineering (S&E). In 2003, for example, China graduated 700,000 S&E students and the United States only 60,000. In 1975, the United States accounted for 50% of the world's PhDs; by the early years of the new century, that figure dropped to only 22%. If current trends persist, this figure will have dropped to approximately 15% by 2010. Richard B. Freeman, "Doubling the Global Work Force: The Challenge of Integrating China, India, and the Former Soviet Bloc into the World Economy," presentation given at the Institute for International Economics, Washington DC, November 8, 2004, available at http://www.iie.com/ publications/papers/freeman1104.pdf. According to the Institute of International Education, in the 2003–2004 school year, Indian students made up 13.9% of all foreign students in the United States, the majority of whom came to study at the graduate level. Furthermore, India is the leading place of origin for international students (79,736 abroad in 2004), http://opendoors.iienetwork.org/?p=50137. "International Student Enrollments Declined by 2.4% in 2003/04 Graduate Enrollments Increased Slightly While Undergraduate Numbers Dropped." Institute for Internation Education, November 10, 2004.

45. In 2004, China's gross national savings rate was 48.5% of GDP ($3.66 trillion), India's 22.7% ($0.78 trillion), the EU's 19.8% ($2.48 trillion), and the United States's 10.8% ($1.29 trillion). See "Economist

Intelligence Unit (EIU), China, India, the United States, and Europe, Country Data 1980-Present," EIU Limited, London, 2007, www.eiu. com. Retrieved February 1, 2007.

46. In October 2003, China became the third country in history to send a human being into space. The mission was relatively modest by U.S. or Russian standards – the rocket orbited the globe 14 times in 22 hours. By October 12, 2005, China launched its second manned space mission – sending two astronauts into orbit for a five-day trip with experiments conducted. The National Science Foundation estimates that in 2000 only the U.S., South Korea, and Japan outspent China's $50.3 billion on general R&D. "National Patterns of Research Development Resources," National Science Foundation, 2003, http://www.nsf.gov/statistics/nsf05308/sectd.htm#note29.

47. Nominal hourly compensation for Japanese labor increased sharply through the late 1980s, overtaking American compensation rates in 1992. See "Economist Intelligence Unit (EIU), Japan, the United States, and Europe, Country Data 1980–Present," EIU Limited, London, 2007, www.eiu.com. Retrieved February 1, 2007.

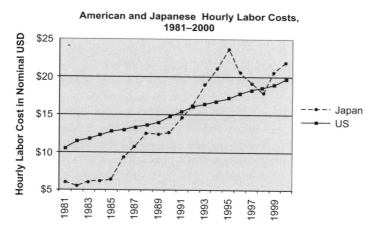

American and Japanese Hourly Labor Costs, 1981–2000

For the effects of Japanese competition, see Robert Z. Lawrence et al., Vol. 1993, no. 2 "International Trade and American Wages in the 1980s: Giant Sucking Sound or Small Hiccup," *Brookings Papers on Economic Activity: Microeconomics*, 1993(2), pp. 161–226; and Lawrence Katz and Ana L. Revenga, "Changes in the Structure of Wages: The U.S. vs. Japan," *NBER Working Papers Series*, no. 3021 (Washington, DC: National Bureau for Economic Research, 1989).

48. In 2004, U.S. per-capita income was $39,876. Chinese per-capita income was $1,490. In a "perfect" global labor market, the incomes would equalize. Given such a market in 2004, with 2004 populations in both

countries, the equalized 2004 per-capita wealth figure for China and the United States would stand at $8,581. This would be 575% of the initial Chinese income and 21.5% of the initial U.S. income. Although obviously a crude approximation of real conditions, the calculation strongly suggests that integrating the Chinese economy into the world economy will result in rigorous international labor competition; depressed real wages in today's high-income countries seem likely.

Current data appear to reinforce this expectation. In 2004, average real wages increased 9.9% in China and 54.7% in India, part of a violent adjustment that then moderated to an average of 2.6% per annum growth for 2005–2009, including forecasts. Wages in the EU-15 increased by 0.5% in 2004 and declined 0.5% in the United States. Predictions to 2008 show these relative growth figures remaining almost constant. "The Economist Intelligence Unit (EIU), China, India, Japan, the United States, and Europe, Country Data 1980–Present," EIU Limited, London, 2007, www.eiu.com. Retrieved July 4, 2008.

Of course, wage dynamics are also affected by job loss and displacement from competition. Studies of data spanning 1979–1999 show American manufacturing workers displaced from import-competing sectors suffering short-term weekly earnings losses of 13% on finding a new job, with estimates of long-term losses still greater. Only 63% managed to find reemployment, and only 35% of these were getting at least the same salary, whereas 25% reported a wage cut of 30% or more. Although the U.S. Congress made provision for these displaced workers in the 1993 North America Free Trade Agreement Implementation Act, by 1999, only 36,910 of the 295,000 eligible for readjustment allowances were receiving them. See Lori G. Kletzer, *Job Loss from Imports: Measuring the Costs* (Washington DC, Institute for International Economics, 2001), available at http://bookstore.petersoninstitute.org/book-store/110.html.

In recent years, white-collar jobs have also begun to be lost to lower-wage Chinese workers. Estimates from the Cambridge-based research group Forrester Inc. show 850,000 American white-collar jobs lost to outsourcing to India and China in 2005. By 2015, 3.3 million middle-class job positions may be lost, along with real wage losses of 13% for displaced manufacturing jobs. Hence, the increasing bifurcation of America's labor market, where high- and low-income jobs within the service sector have been growing at the expense of middle-income jobs, within both manufacturing and service sectors. See Robert D. Atkinson, "Understanding the Offshoring Challenge," Progressive Policy Institute, May 2004, http://www.ppionline.org/documents/Offshoring_0504.pdf.

For a positive assessment of the long-term effects of outsourcing, see Hans Fehr, Sabine Jokisch, and Laurence J. Kotlikoff, "Will China Eat

Our Lunch or Take Us out to Dinner? Simulating the Transition Pathway of the U.S., E.U., Japan, and China," *NBER Working Papers Series*, no. 12038 (Cambridge, MA: National Bureau for Economic Research, 2005). Their model is consistent with observed effects of outsourcing – namely the divergence of skilled and unskilled wages resulting in higher average incomes but not higher median incomes. For a quantitative discussion of this effect, see James J. Heckman and Lance Lochner, "Explaining Rising Wage Inequality: Explorations with a Dynamic General Equilibrium Model of Labor Earnings with Heterogeneous Agents," *Review of Economic Dynamics*, 1, 1998, pp. 1–58. The authors, in their zeal for economic efficiency, yearn for a perfect market in populations that would permit massive and rapid transfers of population and capital – a dubious expectation. For per-capita income data and populations in China and the United States, see "Key Development Data and Statistics," The World Bank, 2005, http://web.worldbank.org/WBSITE/EXTERNAL/DATASTATISTICS/0,,contentMDK:20535285~menuPK:1192694~pagePK:64133150~piPK:64133175~theSitePK:239419,00.html.

49. For example, reactions to the 1998 Asian and Russian economic crises spawned major criticisms of globalization, as in Serge Halimi, "From Market Madness to Recession: Liberal Dogma Shipwrecked," *Le Monde Diplomatique*, October 1998, pp. 1, 10–11. For an analysis of French responses, see Jonah Levy, "Economic Policy and Policy-Making," in Alistair Cole, Patrick Le Galès, and Jonah Levy (eds.), *Developments in French Politics 3* (New York, NY: Palgrave Macmillan, 2005).

6

Power and Legitimacy among Western States

Sovereignty and Consent

America's unipolar vision derives from consciousness of its own match-less power. It also reflects a view about that power's unique legitimacy and benevolence. Fewer and fewer people in the rest of the world appear to share this view, even among our traditional allies. Particularly in Europe, ideas about international order and legitimacy have evolved in a direction that does not favor American pretensions to unipolar status. Because America's global positions depend heavily on European support – economic, diplomatic, and even military – it pays to consider where Europe's different ideas about the legitimacy of power have come from and where they appear to lead.

Philosophers have been speculating about the nature of political power for millennia. Nevertheless, it remains an elusive concept, coming in many forms and flowing from myriad sources.[1] To help sort out a definition, a distinction is often drawn between power and influence. Power may be seen as the capacity to compel by physical coercion, whereas influence is the capacity to persuade without force. In recent years, analysts also speak of "soft" and "hard" power, a distinction that parallels that of influence and coercion, but perhaps better implies their close linkage.[2] In practice, the arts of persuasion and coercion are not easy to separate, nor is soft from hard power. Power is seldom merely physical. Its efficacy often depends heavily on the consent of those over whom it is exercised. In Rousseau's classic formulation: "The strongest is never strong enough to always be the master, unless he transforms his might into right, and obedience into duty."[3] In other words, to endure, power must be considered *legitimate* by those over whom it is exercised. Over the centuries, the study of political power and legitimacy has encompassed two distinct dimensions: power within a single state or political community and power among such states – in other words, within some system of interacting states.

In the Western world, early modern philosophers of the state were preoccupied with the concept of domestic *sovereignty*. A well-ordered state was deemed to require a supreme or sovereign authority able to compel obedience in its own territory and from its own population. According to the great English theorist of the early seventeenth century, Thomas Hobbes (1588–1679), the justification for this supreme power was rooted in human nature itself.[4] In Hobbes's "realist" view, humans are selfish and aggressive. If not restrained by official power, human society is "a mere war of all against all" and human lives are "solitary and poor, nasty, brutish, and short."[5] Thus, for Hobbes, even an oppressive sovereign is better than no sovereign at all. Self-interest, Hobbes taught, should prompt citizens to enter a social contract to create a commonwealth dominated by a sovereign government.[6] In effect, Hobbes's teachings were a secular and philosophical defense of absolutism.

In Hobbes's lifetime, with England wracked by pitiless civil and religious war, his analysis had great force. Even today, it remains a powerful rationale for governmental authority. In the end, however, his appeal is to the citizen's self-interest, a way of reasoning implying that the civil power, which he taught should be absolute, is nevertheless actually contractual. It depends on the consent, or at least the acquiescence, of the governed.[7] What Hobbes hinted timidly, numerous later Western political philosophers trumpeted boldly: Government within a state cannot for long be based on force alone. As England's poet-philosopher Samuel Taylor Coleridge (1772–1834) wrote in the early nineteenth century, "... without the Laws the sword is but a piece of iron."[8] To be effective, a government's power requires legitimacy. To be legitimate, subjects must consider their government to be rightful. They must feel obliged to obey it – not merely from fear but from duty. To earn legitimacy, the government of a state must rule by law and its laws must be rational. Above all, the laws and the government must enjoy the consent of the governed.

The basic idea that power, to be legitimate, requires the consent of the governed has, by and large, triumphed in the West. Much of modern political philosophy is a search for the conditions that make a government based on consent possible. Most agree that governments must rule by laws that are rational and consistent. Beyond are several distinct theories about sustaining consensus.

The Liberal State

Hobbes's own century saw the birth of English *liberal* theory, closely associated with Hobbes's rival, John Locke (1632–1704). Written a few decades after Hobbes', Locke's theory of the state distinguished sharply between the commonwealth, a contract among citizens where the majority was sovereign (supreme in the Hobbesian sense), and its government, which could be rightfully overthrown when the sovereign people withdrew their support. Among the people forming the commonwealth, Locke saw a majority arising naturally from the common interest in preserving property, including personal rights and liberties.[9] A century later, at the time of the American and French revolutions, liberals like Thomas Paine (1737–1809) added an expanded portfolio of citizens' rights, reflecting self-evident natural law.[10] In 1776, Thomas Jefferson's Declaration of Independence summed up the portfolio as "life, liberty and the pursuit of happiness." In that same year Adam Smith's (1723–1790) *Wealth of Nations* added the pursuit of wealth through free markets. In the minds of these Enlightenment liberals, a state with a consensus formed around natural rights brought itself into harmony with a benevolent natural order – one where citizens, free to pursue their own self-interest under law, would naturally give rise to a harmonious society free from tyrants, monopolists, and empires. By installing and defending liberal rights, governments earned their domestic legitimacy. Liberal economists threw in a bonus: peace among nations practicing free trade. Kant added perpetual peace among liberal republics.[11]

Many of the classical liberal political philosophers of the eighteenth century began life as British subjects. Despite its relatively advanced parliamentary system, the government in London was often a major obstacle to liberal principles. Eighteenth-century Britain, intent on pursuing a global empire, was perpetually at war. The mercantilist economics that Adam Smith sought to overthrow was the practical system with which Britain was financing its imperial wars. The Navigation Acts, which eventually drove the American colonies to revolt, were a key part of imperial policy. British liberal teachings were thus implicitly revolutionary. Clearing away obstructions to the liberal's natural order meant eliminating the imperial regime, a project that could easily take a violent turn. This is what happened in the American Revolution. Many British liberals found it easy to sympathize with the rebels and some, like Paine, actually joined them. A few years later liberal ideas fired up the still more violent French Revolution and its Napoleonic aftermath. A revolution that began by trying to empower bourgeois liberals ended by rejuvenating both autocracy and imperialism. Liberal and Hobbesian perspectives, in practice, reached common ground.

A quarter century before the French Revolution, this darker side to liberal expectations had been anticipated by the brilliantly iconoclastic French-Swiss philosopher Jean-Jacques Rousseau (1712–1778) in his *Social Contract* (1762). Rousseau was far more pessimistic than liberals about the durability of any political consensus based on private interests alone.[12] But unlike Hobbes, Rousseau rejected an authoritarian solution. Instead, his version of the social contract stressed how a state, to sustain its legitimacy, must be a psychological community, one whose interests are broader and more comprehensive than those of the individual citizen, but with which his private self identifies closely. Without such a broad collective identity to result in a public "general will," Rousseau did not believe a consensual community could be expected to last. On occasion, Rousseau also saw the consensual community requiring an ethical foundation. A state was legitimate because it provides a framework that brings out the best from its citizens. Here Rousseau returned to the teachings of Plato and Aristotle, for whom the state was meant to provide the collective moral framework necessary for citizens to pursue virtuous lives. Rousseau brought that Idealist past into the modern world. For some analysts, of course, Rousseau also offers more than a glimpse of a totalitarian future.[13]

For those who lived through the French Revolution and Napoleonic Empire, the tyrannical potential of liberal revolutions was hard to ignore. Although few liberals mourned the fall of the Bourbon monarchy, many soon came to fear the Revolution itself. On the whole, bourgeois liberals wanted a state that protected their private liberty and property, not one that imposed mob rule, dictatorship, demonic military adventures, or socialism. First-hand experience with social and political upheaval encouraged a more sober view of human nature in politics, one less sanguine about an easy compatibility between freedom and order. Hardier liberals were nevertheless unwilling to abandon their aspirations and embrace the Hobbesian absolutism of the *ancien régime*. They searched for a broader political doctrine better able to reconcile liberal freedom with continuity and order. At the same time, many conservatives searched for broader formulae able to appease liberal aspirations without opening the way either to revolutionary chaos or to counterrevolutionary tyranny.[14]

The Constitutional State

This mutual quest of liberal and conservative moderates encouraged interest in a third stream of Western ideas about power – one that was neither entirely absolutist nor entirely liberal. This was the *constitutionalist* view of the state, stretching back to the Middle Ages and mediated into the modern world by writers like the Englishman Richard Hooker (1554–1600) or the French writer the Baron de Montesquieu (1689–1755).[15] According to this tradition, if a diverse society is to hold together while liberties are preserved, official power must be limited and balanced. This was the guiding principle for America's founding fathers, writing their remarkable Constitution of 1789.[16] Constitutionalism also informed the thinking of European "conservatives," like Burke, Coleridge, or Talleyrand, reacting against the tyrannical excesses both of revolutionary France and of the reactionary continental regimes that fought it. Sustaining a state's consensus around legitimate power and rights depends, they argued, not on the abstract perfection of institutions or the absolute virtue of rulers but on a practical balance of power among a state's constituent elements. Controlling the conflicts endemic to human society is best accomplished, they thought, through balanced and long-standing institutions, with which a nation's people identify and are accustomed to obey. Such institutions not only can confirm governments in their legitimate sphere of action but also protect liberties, encourage official competence and responsiveness, and discourage imperial adventures. As many constitutionalists noted, however, these habits of balance and self-restraint or civic loyalties deeply shared among the population cannot be induced rapidly or quickly tailored to measure.[17] They are most reliably rooted in a community with a shared "national culture," reflecting a continuous development of ideas and institutions over a long period.

The Nation-State

Linking legitimate power to cultural consensus and continuity fitted well with the new forces of nationalism that sprang up around the French Revolution. Already in the late eighteenth century, the "father" of German nationalism, Johann Gottfried Herder, was spreading the idea that a culture could protect itself only if it possessed an independent state of its own.[18] That idea served not only conservatives, using home-grown nationalism to oppose Revolutionary and Napoleonic France, but also liberals proposing to replace autocratic empires with democratic nation-states. It pointed toward the creation of modern Italy and Germany, together with the breakup of the Ottoman, Habsburg, and Russian empires.

Liberalism and nationalism thus continued to have strong symbiotic affinities throughout the nineteenth century. In an era of rapid economic and social change, with violent revolution in the air, moderate liberals and conservatives alike increasingly realized that containing social conflicts without heavy coercion required a strong underlying sense of community and shared identity. A nation-state's inherent cultural and social consensus seemed the natural and generally indispensable requisite for sustaining a liberal society. Liberalism and the doctrine of national self-determination seemed natural partners.[19]

Romantic Idealism and the Nation-State

As the nineteenth century progressed, moderates of various schools (liberal, constitutionalist, conservative, and nationalist) blended together to seed a modern "Idealist" school. Writers like Burke, Hegel, Coleridge, John Stewart Mill, Mazzini, Greene, Bradley, and Bosanquet linked a state's legitimacy to its capacity to support a national "Good

Society" – one that limited official power and left citizens with a wide range of liberty but also encouraged them to honor and serve the community as a whole.[20]

These Idealist, nationalist, and constitutionalist traditions were generally informed and enriched by the broad Romantic world view of the time. Whereas earlier varieties of liberalism, constitutionalism, and Idealism reflected the rather mechanical and perfectionist worldview of the Enlightenment, later Romantic versions of these traditions had a more dynamic, organic, and vitalist view of history, one that expected change, even when it was regretted. As this Romantic spirit flowed through liberal, conservative, and constitutionalist traditions, it helped to rescue them from their own too static and mechanistic tendencies. Romanticism made it seem only natural that, in a world of revolutionary change, sustaining national consensus requires a government that is a "living legitimacy" – a constitutional system that restrains and refines power but also constantly enables government to serve the common good proactively. Romanticism encouraged a communitarian, neomedieval view of economic relations – one where the strong felt obliged to help the weak. Romanticism also encouraged a different view of political leaders – heroes who intuitively grasp the forces of history and who can guide their society through its inevitable storms toward the better prospects inherent in its historical situation. Since World War II, we have tended to focus on the dangers in the Romantic view of politics, but its contribution to our modern ideas about the state was critical.

In the years before World War I, several of the great Western political schools – Hobbesian, liberal, constitutionalist, nationalist, Idealist – seemed to be reaching broad if uneasy agreement about what legitimized and controlled power within a modern state. Although Europe's nation-states remained highly individual, most were socially conservative but constitutionalist. Capitalism and nationalism blended together with a growing communitarianism that pointed toward the modern welfare state. All featured some form of balanced representative government and a widening popular franchise. Given the economic, social, and political progress of the nineteenth century, optimism about the future of the West's constitutional nation-states seemed not unreasonable.

Optimism Deceived

There were, of course, disturbing portents, not least in the world of political philosophy. Even in Western Europe and America, where liberal and constitutionalist traditions were most fully developed, alternative ideas about power and legitimacy had grown deeply rooted. Among these alternative doctrines were anarchism, social Darwinism, imperialism, racism, revolutionary Marxist socialism, along with what might be called "aesthetic" realism – the essentially artistic legitimation of power preached by Nietzsche and Wagner. For them, power was the oxygen permitting the "superman" to elaborate his excellence.[21] In the comfortable European world of the late nineteenth century, these alternative ideals, although promoting violence in theory, seemed only marginal in practice.

A more urgent threat to the peace of bourgeois Europe was emerging from capitalism itself. Although rapid growth brought great prosperity to the increasingly dominant bourgeois class, and, in due course, radical improvement in general living standards, the instability that often accompanied capitalist growth was proving more and more disturbing to peace at home and abroad. After the great boom of the 1860s and early 1870s came the crash of 1873, followed by the Great Depression that lasted until 1896.[22] Very rapid growth had inspired overinvestment leading to industrial overproduction and a collapse of profits. Meanwhile, dramatic improvements in global transport led to glutted markets for agricultural products. The consequent depression in both industry and agriculture meant periodic high unemployment, with severe consequences for ordinary living standards.

As economic competition grew more brutal, economics itself grew less liberal – less expecting harmony – and more Darwinian. Political life inevitably reacted. Labor movements and socialist parties rose rapidly and hoped to appropriate state power to improve working class incomes, employment, and security. New coalitions formed to press for tariffs and subsidies as agrarian and industrial interests also turned to the state for relief. Parties inspired by Marxism arose to challenge the bourgeois social order itself. In due course, all the great powers except Britain turned to protectionism. State interference with trade fed fear of being kept from selling to lucrative markets controlled by a rival or of being denied access to vital raw materials. Such fears encouraged a "new imperialism," with the great powers, led by Britain, scrambling to annex territory, above all in Africa. In effect, mercantilist imperialism, driven by overproduction, increasingly linked economic competition with state power. Successful trade, needed to sustain domestic employment and growth, required military control of overseas territory. With capitalism ailing, trade became another form of conflict.

Once formed, the neomercantilist pattern provided its own momentum. Even when the depression ended in the 1890s, the new fusion of state power with economic competition persisted. By the nineteenth century's end, Britain's rapid economic rise earlier in the century was being repeated in most of the other traditional great powers. The world began to seem too small for the relentless growth and burgeoning territorial ambitions of old and new capitalist powers. This uneven and laggard development threatened stability in both the European and global state systems.[23]

The twentieth century thus opened with two conflicting patterns: In domestic politics, advanced states were progressing toward a consensual constitutionalist model, limiting class conflict and reconciling liberty and change with reasonable security and order. Capitalism was providing the wealth and opportunity needed to power this social and political progress. To limit the disruptions that accompanied capitalist development, states turned to subsidies, welfare, protectionism, and imperialism. This gave rise to a second pattern, where states, driven by fear of economic disruption and social conflict, set out on a mercantilist and imperialist course that soothed domestic problems but risked economic and military collisions with other states. As it happened, these conflicts could not be reconciled within the state system of the day.[24] The ideas and institutions that favored social and political consensus within states found no complementary ideas and institutions to sustain a peaceful consensus among states. The means used to keep peace at home proved incompatible with keeping peace in the world. It was this failure of the interstate system to develop in parallel with the nation-states composing it that made possible the two world wars and the Cold War of the last century. The early twentieth century rediscovered brutally what European history has revealed again and again: A good nation-state is never a purely domestic accomplishment. A good national order cannot long endure undisturbed unless reinforced by a state system favorable to the stability and prosperity of the continent as a whole. In Europe, "living legitimacy" can never be a purely national affair. The fate of nations depends on the state system that is their intimate and inescapable environment.

Legitimacy in the State System

Western political thought has long featured a caesura between principles that should govern the state internally and those that should govern a "system" of states. This discontinuity has mainly worked to favor Hobbesian views of international relations. Thus, although the influence of Hobbes faded in the evolving constitutionalist and communitarian vision of the domestic national state, it remained vigorous in theories of the international state system. Hobbesians could convincingly argue that the state system is most emphatically not a community with a legitimating consensus. Rather, it is a close approximation to Hobbes's vision. Seeing the international system as Hobbes's anarchical state of nature implies a Hobbesian solution – a dominant hegemonic power, able to keep order among otherwise quarrelling states. Failing a hegemon, states are condemned to rely on their own coercive power over their neighbors.[25]

The Hobbesian view of hegemony, of course, encompasses soft as well as hard power. Ideological prestige and cultural attractiveness can augment a hegemon's authority and coercive prowess. Above all, Hobbesians are inclined to be "mercantilists." For them, economic power is hard power, vital for sustaining military force. Economic sanctions, moreover, may be used to coerce other states. Hobbesians tend to see the global economy as itself relentlessly competitive – often a zero-sum game among states. Trade is war by other means. It is this view of the world economy that distinguishes Hobbesian hegemonists most clearly from classical internationalist liberals.

Today's descendants of classical liberals reject the Hobbesian view of a relentlessly conflictual state system, just as they reject the mercantilist view of zero-sum market competition. Instead, they stress the growing prosperity of an integrating global economy. Like domestic liberals, they see harmonious progress as the natural outcome of free competition, once economic and political monopolists are removed from the system. It is now common to present these old liberal arguments as "peace theory," wrapped in fashionable globalist rhetoric. In today's version economic development is supposed to bring about a progressive erosion of state sovereignty. The global economy offers more and more scope for private international organizations. As they intensify their commercial and political activities, they progressively open up national societies and economies to outside forces. Governments find themselves marginalized as international actors. As their ability to interfere with the market is progressively curtailed, the old mercantilist states grow unable to pursue their traditional preoccupation with power. Privatized competition and the activism of nongovernmental organizations leads to a benign "interdependence" – an environment that makes warfare difficult and unprofitable.[26]

Constitutionalism and the State System

In some sense, these old Hobbesian and liberal arguments about the state system seem not to have advanced much since the eighteenth century. Left in their pure forms, the rival models risk seeming irrelevant – the Hobbesians perversely pessimistic and the liberals artlessly naïve.[27] But just as constitutionalist ideas have rejuvenated theories of the nation-state, so constitutionalists have sought to rebuild the state system. The most ambitious efforts have called for a sort of global government – the League of Nations and the United Nations. But the most successful interstate structure has been regional – the European Union. The EU springs from Europe's history. It embodies the vital idea that Europe is now a community of nations deciding to travel together through history. Like a nation-state, the EU has been customized to fit its participating societies, histories, cultures, geographies, and economic and social situations. In some senses, today's idea of European Union is the interstate equivalent of the old Idealist model of the national state. It embodies and consolidates the liberal, constitutional, and communitarian cultures of Europe's nation-states. It is the highly creative reaction of those nation-states to their reduced status in the world. Above all, it is their reaction to the destructive traumas that Europeans inflicted on themselves in the last century.

In some respects, European states have yet to recover from World War I. Its hideous destruction and abandoned brutality, brought on by an explosion of unmeasured ambitions, was a terrible defeat for the rational and principled conduct of human affairs. In several major countries – Russia, Italy, Germany, Spain, and even France – the breakdown of the state system reverberated to destroy the constitutionalist states themselves, thus opening the way to lunatic alternatives. Thereafter, and for most of the twentieth century, the Western constitutional state found itself severely challenged by a variety of "totalitarian" models. In the end, however, the constitutionalist model did survive its Fascist, Nazi, and Soviet rivals. Arguably, that was the real significance of the Soviet disintegration. It marked not merely the defeat of the totalitarian model but the triumph of the Western nation-state. But as painful experience had made clear, Europe could not preserve its system of nation-states without building a regional superstructure to confine their conflicts.

This is what Europe's states have been attempting with the European Union. If we try to infer a theory for the constitution of today's EU, we emerge with a complex hybrid. European constitutionalists, like Hobbesians, can claim to have a realist view.[28] Unlike the old-fashioned liberals, they do not anticipate an automatic and perpetual peace among nations. But like liberals, they believe the EU's function is to defend human rights. And unlike Hobbesians, the states that have built the EU have not been looking for a benevolent hegemon. But neither are they seeking to dissolve themselves in a federation. Instead, they maintain a *collaborative balance of power* – where no single state or combination of states can easily dominate the others. The result is a confederal interstate system with institutions that encourage mutual appeasement.

Pax Europea and Pax Americana

The European approach to interstate relations is strikingly different from the approach of many American liberals who, although constitutionalists at home, tend to be Hobbesians abroad. Inside the U.S. they prefer, in principle at least, power to be dispersed and contained within a liberal and constitutional framework. Outside the U.S., however, they want American power focused to dominate. These are America's hybrid liberals. They may retain their faith in the virtues of global free markets and popular democracies but believe that such a global system can work only with a benevolent and omnipotent hegemon. Only the U.S., they believe, can play this vital role.[29] When they search for historical validation they find inspiration not from the Concert of Europe – an arrangement suited to a plural system – but from the mid-nineteenth-century *Pax Britannica*, a global system thought to have been both hegemonic and liberal, a model, they believe, for world order today.[30]

In today's Europe, such a compartmentalization of ideas has grown increasingly difficult to sustain. Centuries of Western speculation have reached certain broad philosophical conclusions about the nature of legitimate civil authority within a single state. These conclusions have grown hard to banish from analyses of states considered in relation to each other. National and international theories of legitimacy have had a tendency to coalesce. Individual states have evolved from absolutism to democratic communitarianism. Why should the interstate system not also evolve away from Hobbesian power politics toward constitutionalist rules and communitarian relationships? The question is particularly insistent in Western Europe, where individual national sovereignties and the regional state system as a whole are less distinct than elsewhere.

The more an international system begins to be considered a community, rather than a Hobbesian cockpit of warring states, the greater the tendency to consider the whole body of Western thought about legitimizing power within the nation-state as relevant to legitimizing power among states. If Hobbesian hegemony is not sustainable within each state individually, why should it be expected to endure among closely related states? Since World War II, a large part of interstate diplomacy within the West has been conducted on the assumption that at least a contingent liberal harmony of interests can exist among nation-states. By now, European experience suggests that, given the proper worldview and multilateral machinery, a group of states can, over time, be fashioned into a community. A concert or even a union of states can replace Hobbesian anarchy. Such a community of states cannot expect to abolish conflict among themselves but can hope to overcome it.[31] In effect, constitutionalism in Europe has jumped from advanced nation-states to an advanced state system. Interstate conflict does not disappear but, with effort and luck, balanced and cooperative institutions can manage that conflict. Moreover, these institutions appear to gain in strength as success in one sphere tends to "spill over" into others.[32]

Until the end of the Cold War, at least, this constitutionalist way of looking at things also prevailed in postwar Western Europe's relations with the United States, relations that were generally conducted in multilateral frameworks – military, political, and economic – where American leadership was seldom absolute or unchallenged. By and large, Atlantic institutions have since failed to adapt to the end of the Cold War or to today's more unified Europe. Such failure is one of the costs of America's post-Soviet infatuation with the unipolar world view.[33] But although transatlantic constitutionalism has been stalled, the post-Soviet era has seen a great flourishing of cooperative interstate communities elsewhere, not only in Europe but also in Asia.[34]

Postwar experience with interstate institutions has, by now, profoundly shaped the worldview of many states and their publics about what legitimizes international power. The result has been a mushrooming multilateral culture. It is within this culture that America's vigorous pretensions to unipolar power have come as such a rude shock. The United States of the Bush administration appeared a startling reincarnation from Hobbes's dread seventeenth century – a rogue Leviathan on the loose. Thus, according to the multilateral ethic that many states have come to value highly, America's power, exercised unilaterally, has rapidly been losing legitimacy.[35] Lacking legitimacy, it has been greatly devalued.

Many American analysts argue, of course, that Europeans are wrong to deny legitimacy to American power. In doing so, the argument runs, they are undermining the international order that protects them. Thanks to American power, Europeans can live in a civilized but decadent dream world of their own imagining. Beyond the protected West, however, the real world is a Hobbesian jungle.[36] In some respects, American critics of Europe are probably right. Surely the future does have great potential for conflict. But for all the reasons previous chapters have tried to spell out, unipolar American hegemony cannot manage that conflict. If a successful and legitimate international order is unlikely to be inspired by unipolar America, does Europe's model offer a plausible alternative?

Notes

1. From the vast bibliography on power, let me cite three of my old teachers from Yale. Robert A. Dahl, *Modern Political Analysis* (Englewood Cliffs, NJ: Prentice Hall, 1963); Harold D. Lasswell and Abraham Kaplan, *Power and Society: A Framework for Political Inquiry* (New Haven, CT: Yale University Press, 1965); and Arnold Wolfers, *Discord and Collaboration: Essays on International Politics* (Baltimore: Johns Hopkins Press, 1962); also an old friend, Susan Strange, *The Retreat of the State: The Diffusion of Power in the World Economy* (New York, NY: Cambridge University Press, 1996). Like most people in our discipline, I have learned a great deal from Max Weber, *Wirtschaft und Gesellschaft* (Berlin: Paul Siebeck, 1922). In my own case I should add Bertrand de Jouvenel, *Du pouvoir: Histoire naturelle de sa croissance* (Paris: Hachette, 1972).

2. Robert Keohane and Joseph Nye distinguish between "behavioral power" ("the ability to obtain outcomes you want") and "resource power" ("the possession of the resources that are usually associated with the ability to get the outcomes you want"), Keohane and Nye further divide "behavioral power" into "hard" and "soft" power. Hard power, they contend, is "the ability to get others to do what they otherwise would not do through threat of punishment or promise of reward," and soft power is "the ability to get desired outcomes through attraction rather than coercion. If a state can make its power legitimate in the eyes of others and establish international institutions that encourage others to define their interests in compatible ways, it may not need to expend as many costly traditional economic or military resources. Hard and soft power are related, but they are not the same" (p. 86). Robert O. Keohane and Joseph S. Nye, Jr., "Power and Interdependence in the Information Age," *Foreign Affairs*, 77(5), 1998, pp. 80–94.

3. Frederick Watkins (ed. and trans.). *Jean-Jacques Rousseau: Political Writings* (New York, NY: Thomas Nelson and Sons, 1953), pp. 6–7.

4. The classic theorists of sovereignty, Jean Bodin (1530–1596) and Thomas Hobbes (1588–1679), both concerned primarily with domestic sovereignty, wrote in the context of religious wars destroying the stability of France and England. Both sought a durable system of authority that would be acknowledged as legitimate, regardless of religious affiliation. Both endorsed a highly centralized authority structure and rejected any right of revolt. See Jean Bodin, *Les Six Livres de la république* (1576), translated by Julian Franklin as *On Sovereignty* (Cambridge, UK: Cambridge University Press, 1992). Thomas Hobbes, *Leviathan* (1651) (Cambridge, UK: Cambridge University Press, 1996), and *De Cive* (1642) (Oxford, UK: Clarendon Press, 1983). Also, Preston King, *The Ideology*

of Order: A Comparative Analysis of Jean Bodin & Thomas Hobbes (London, UK: Allen & Unwin, 1974), Stephen D. Krasner, "Rethinking the Sovereign State Model," *Review of International Studies* (2001), 27, 17–42 (p. 20) and "Sovereignty," *Foreign Policy*, January/February 2001, pp. 20–27.

5. Thomas Hobbes, *De Cive* (Oxford, UK: Clarendon Press, 1983), p 34.

6. Thomas Hobbes, *Leviathan* (Cambridge, UK: University Press, 1996), p. 89.

7. Hobbes' concept of sovereignty reflects an Enlightenment worldview and is very different in its philosophical foundations from the "divine right of Kings" preached by Jacques-Bénigne Bossuet (1627–1704) in his *Politics Derived from Holy Writ* (1709), Translated & reprinted as: *Politics Derived from the Words of Holy Scripture* edited by Keith Michael Beker (Chicago: The University of Chicago Press, 1987). Which tied royal authority to divine bestowal. For absolutism based on a patriarchal theory of government, see Sir Robert Filmer (d. 1653), *Patriarcha, or The Natural Power of Kings* (London: Walter Davis, 1680). For further analysis see J. N. Figgis, *The Theory of the Divine Right of Kings* (Cambridge, UK: Cambridge University Press, 1896, reprinted 1965), and *The Divine Right of Kings* (Cambridge, UK: Cambridge University Press, 1914); also F. Kern, *Kingship and Law in the Middle Ages* (New York, NY: Harper & Row, 1956).

8. Samuel Taylor Coleridge, *Collected Works*; Barbara E. Hooke (ed.), *The Friend* (1809–1810) (Princeton, NJ: Princeton University Press, 1969), p. 173.

9. John Locke (1632–1704), *Two Treatises of Government (1690)* (Cambridge, UK: Cambridge University Press, 1988). The first treatise is a refutation of Filmer (see footnote 7). The second is the most relevant to our argument here.

10. Thomas Paine (1757–1809), after defending the American Revolution (*Common Sense.* London: J. Almon, 1776), returned to England and wrote *The Rights of Man* (London: J. S. Jordan, 1791, 1792), a vigorous defense of the French Revolution on the grounds that only democratic governments could guarantee man's natural rights. He was prosecuted for treason and fled to Paris, where he took a prominent role in the Revolution and was soon imprisoned by the Jacobins. He eventually returned to the U.S. where his attacks on Christianity (*The Age of Reason.* London: Barrois, 1794, 1795) and George Washington (*Letter to Washington*, Philadelphia: Benjamin Franklin, 1796) made him unpopular. He died in poverty.

11. Thomas Jefferson, *The Declaration of Independence* (1776); Adam Smith, *An Inquiry into the Nature and Causes of the Wealth of Nations* (1776), Alan Krueger (ed.) (New York, NY: Bantam Classics, 2003);

and Immanuel Kant, *Perpetual Peace* (New York, NY: Cosimo, 2005).
For a discussion of peace theory, see my *Rethinking Europe's Future*
(Princeton, NJ: Princeton University Press, 2003), pp. 357ff.

12. Jean-Jacques Rousseau, *The Social Contract* (1762), *op. cit.* My understanding of Rousseau owes a good deal to my old Yale mentor, Frederick Watkins. See his *The Philosophical Tradition of the West: A Study
in the Development of Modern Liberalism* (Cambridge, MA: Harvard
University Press, 1948). Another old teacher and colleague is Karl
Deutsch, *Political Community at the International Level: Problems of
Definition and Measurement* (Princeton, NJ: Princeton University Press,
1957) and *Nationalism and Social Communication: An Inquiry into the
Foundations of Nationality* (Cambridge, UK: Cambridge University Press,
1953). My views of the state also owe much to my earlier study of the
political thought of Samuel Taylor Coleridge; David P. Calleo, *Coleridge
and the Idea of the Modern State* (New Haven, CT: Yale University
Press, 1966) and also to my studies of the British Idealist writer Bernard
Bosanquet. See his *The Philosophical Theory of the State* (London, UK:
Macmillan, 1923). I was put on to both these seminal thinkers by another
old Yale teacher and friend, Lewis Perry Curtis.

13. See, for example, John W. Chapman, *Rousseau – Totalitarian or Liberal?*
(New York, NY: Oxford University Press, 1956); Alfred Cobban,
Rousseau and the Modern State (London, UK: Allen & Unwin, 1934). For
a broad study of the links among liberalism, nationalism, and imperial-
ism, see Hannah Arendt, *The Origins of Totalitarianism* (Cleveland, OH:
World Publishing Company, 1958), especially Part 2, "Imperialism."

14. For a particularly poignant example of this quest, see Samuel Taylor
Coleridge, *The Friend* (1809–1810) (Princeton, NJ: Princeton University
Press, 1969). For my early effort to link Coleridge's Romantic philoso-
phy to the development of English constitutionalism, see David P. Calleo,
Coleridge and the Idea of the Modern State (New Haven, CT: Yale Uni-
versity Press, 1966).

15. Richard Hooker: *The Laws of Ecclesiastical Polity*. A complete edition
appeared in 1666, including a celebrated biography by Izaak Walton
(1665). The standard complete edition is John Keble (ed.), 1836. A newer
edition is available from Cambridge University Press (Cambridge, UK:
Cambridge University Press, 1989). Hooker deeply influenced Locke.
Charles Louis de Secondat, Baron de la Brède et de Montesquieu, was
a French jurist from Bordeaux. His major work is *Spirit of the Laws*
(1748) (Cambridge, UK: Cambridge University Press, 1989), and it shows
a strong influence from Locke. See also his *Persian Letters* (1721) (Indi-
anapolis, IN: Bobbs-Merrill, 1999) and his *Considérations sur les causes
de la grandeur des Romaines et de leur décadence* (1734).

16. Alexander Hamilton, James Madison, and John Jay, *The Federalist Papers*
(1787–1788), Clinton Rossiter (ed) (New York, NY: Signet, 1961). For

a survey and analysis of competing ideas at the American Constitutional Convention, see Charles A. Beard, *An Economic Interpretation of the Constitution* (1913) (New York, NY: The Macmillan Company, 1935; reprint, Union, NJ: Lawbook Exchange, 2001); Max Farrand, *Fathers of the Constitution* (1921) (New Haven, Connecticut: Yale University Press, 1921); Carl van Doren, *The Great Rehearsal* (1948) (Westport, CT: Greenwood Press, 1982); and Forest McDonald, *We the People: The Economic Origins of the Constitution* (1958) (Edison, NJ: Transaction, 1991).

17. Edmund Burke, *Reflections on the Revolution in France* (Oxford, UK: New York, NY: Oxford University Press, 1999); Samuel Taylor Coleridge, *On the Constitution of Church and State according to the Idea of Each*, John Barrell (ed.) (London: Deut, 1972). For my own analysis of Coleridge, see note 14. For Talleyrand, see *The Correspondence of Prince Talleyrand and King Louis XVIII during the Congress of Vienna* (New York, NY: Da Capo Press, 1973). See also Guglielmo Ferrero and Theodore R. Jaeckel (trans.), *The Reconstruction of Europe: Talleyrand and the Congress of Vienna, 1814–1815.* (New York, NY: Norton 1963); and Samuel J. Hurwitz, *The Two French Revolutions, 1789–1796*, Guglielmo Ferrero (trans.) (New York, NY: Basic Books, 1968).

18. Robert Reinhold Ergang, *Herder and the Foundations of German Nationalism* (New York, NY: Columbia University Press, 1931).

19. Alfred Cobban, *National Self-Determination* (New York, NY: Oxford University Press, 1970).

20. Giuseppe Mazzini, *The Duties of Man*, E. A. Venturi (trans.) (London, UK: Chapman & Hall, 1862); John Stuart Mill, *The Basic Writings of John Stuart Mill: On Liberty* (1859), *The Subjection of Women* (1869), and *Utilitarianism* (1863) (New York, NY: Modern Library, 2002); also *The Principles of Political Economy* (1848) William J. Ashley (ed.) (London, UK: Longmans, Green and Co., 1909). Edmund Burke, *Reflections on the Revolution in France* (1790) (Oxford, UK: New York, NY: Oxford University Press, 1999); Charles Taylor, *Hegel* (Cambridge, UK: Cambridge University Press, 2006); Francis H. Bradley, *Collected Essays* (New York, NY: Oxford University Press, 1970); Thomas H. Green, *Lectures on the Principles of Political Obligation* (Ann Arbor, MI: Michigan University Press, 1967); Bernard Bosanquet, *The Philosophical Theory of the State* (London, UK: Macmillan, 1910).

21. Friedrich Nietzsche (1844–1900), *Thus Spoke Zarathustra: A Book for Everyone and No One* (1883–1885), Walter Kaufmann (ed. and trans.) (New York, NY: Penguin, 1966). *Beyond Good and Evil: Prelude to a Philosophy of the Future* (1886), R. J. Hollingdale (trans.) (New York, NY: Penguin, 1973).

22. For a masterful discussion of the whole period see Eric Hobsbawn, *The Age of Empire: 1875–1914* (New York, NY: Vintage Books, 1989). For

my own analysis of how the late nineteenth Century's Great Depression affected German foreign policy with a further bibliography, see my *The German Problem Reconsidered: Germany and the World Order, 1870 to the Present* (Cambridge, UK: Cambridge University Press, 1978).

23. For the classic exposition of imperialist capitalism as the underlying cause of World War I, see V. I. Lenin, *Imperialism, the Highest Stage of Capitalism* (London, UK: Lawrence and Wishart, 1948).

24. For my own attempt to sort out the causes of World War I see my *The German Problem Reconsidered: Germany and the World Order, 1870 to the Present* (Cambridge, UK: Cambridge University Press, 1978), Chs. 3 and 4.

25. For more on Hobbes's anarchic state of nature as it applies to international relations, see Kenneth Waltz, *Theory of International Politics* (New York, NY: Random House, 1979). For more information on the role of a hegemon in such a system, see Robert Gilpin, *War and Change in World Politics* (Cambridge, UK: Cambridge University Press, 1981). The theoretical need for a hegemon in the economic sphere is presented in Charles Kindleberger, *The World in Depression: 1929–1939* (Berkeley, CA: University of California Press, 1973).

26. See, for example, Kenichi Ohmae, *The Borderless World: Power and Strategy in the Interlinked Economy* (rev. ed., New York, NY: Collins, 1999). For an example of a liberal institutionalist persective see Robert Keohane, *Power and Governance in a Partially Globalized World* (New York, NY: Routledge, 2002). For my further analysis, see David P. Calleo, *Rethinking Europe's Future* (Princeton, NJ: Princeton University Press, 2001), especially Ch. 3.

27. For a discussion of the intellectual confusion of the "Realism" vs. "Idealism" debate, see Barry J. Balleck, "Psychometry and Semantics," *Peace Psychology Review*, Vol. 1(1), 1994, pp. 38–44.

28. For a cogent discussion of the distinctions, see Robert Jervis, "Realism, Neoliberalism and Cooperation – Understanding the Debate," *International Security*, Vol. 24(1), 1999, pp. 42–63.

29. For discussions of these views and their ascendancy in the Bush administration, see James Mann, *Rise of the Vulcans: The History of Bush's War Cabinet* (New York, NY: Viking Penguin, 2004); and Peter J. Boyer, "The Believer: Paul Wolfowitz Defends His War," *The New Yorker*, November 1, 2004, available at http://www.newyorker.com/archive/2004/11/01/041101fa_fact [accessed 11/11/2008].

30. See Niall Ferguson, *Empire: The Rise and Demise of the British World Order and the Lessons for Global Power* (London, UK: Allan Lane, 2000); Niall Ferguson, *Colossus: The Rise and Fall of the American Empire* (London, UK: Penguin Books, 2004); Charles Kindleberger, "Dominance and Leadership in International Economy: Exploitation, Public Goods, and Free Rides," *International Studies Quarterly*, No. 25, 1981,

pp. 242–254; and Robert W. Tucker, *Nation or Empire? The Debate over American Foreign Policy* (Baltimore, MD: Johns Hopkins University Press, 1968).

31. See Amitai Etzioni, *From Empire to Community: A New Approach to International Relations* (New York, NY: Palgrave Macmillan, 2004), pp. 195–198.

32. For my own extended analysis of the theory implicit in the EU's historical development, see *Rethinking Europe's Future* (Princeton, NJ: Princeton University Press, 2001), especially Chapter 8.

33. NATO is sometimes seen as the Atlanticist rival to the EU. Its focus is relatively narrow but critically important. Since the Soviet demise, finding a common interest sufficient to weld NATO's member states closely together has grown more difficult. NATO's membership is more diverse than the EU's. Having an American as its Supreme Commander and the U.S. as its principal contributor of military resources lends a hegemonic bias to the whole institution. It is sometimes described as a "toolbox" of European resources available for American-led projects beyond Europe. U.S. policy has worked to block institutional changes that would favor some sort of European "pillar" and thus result in a more balanced alliance. This was broadly acceptable during the Cold War but seems less so now. U.S. initiatives like the Iraq War or quarrels with Russia and Iran arguably add to Europe's insecurity and preempt more productive efforts at cooperation. The reaction of Europe's major powers – Germany and France in particular – has been to withdraw from a very active role. NATO thus seems unlikely to progress toward a more intimate union. However, it seems unlikely to disappear. It remains the chief institutional tie between the U.S. and Europe. It is useful in coordinating counterterrorism measures and perhaps other interventions, as today in Afghanistan. European states probably still value the American security guarantee highly, but especially new or aspiring NATO and EU members from Eastern Europe and Central Asia, countries still preoccupied with Russian dominance. The major West European states still hope membership gives them a certain handle on American military policy. In short, everyone benefits marginally, a situation likely to persist unless the U.S. insists on NATO projects clearly not in the interest of the major European powers. For further discussion, see Ch. 3.

34. See Ch. 7 and, in particular, footnotes 27 and 28.

35. See Robert Cooper, *The Breaking of Nations: Order and Chaos in the Twenty-First Century* (New York, NY: Grove/Atlantic, 2003), p. 167.

36. See Robert Kagan, *Of Paradise and Power: America and Europe in the New World Order* (New York, NY: Random House, 2003) and my critique "Power, Wealth and Wisdom," *National Interest*, 72, 2003, pp. 5–16.

PART III

WORLD ORDER IN THE NEW CENTURY

7

American and European Models

Hobbes without a Hegemon

Deflating America's hegemonic pretensions does not, in itself, produce a convincing rival. If the United States cannot be the world's unipolar hegemon, surely no one else can either. Any other nation would have even more limited prospects. Eventually, several great powers may be able to challenge anyone else's global dominance. China, for example, might grow strong enough, even by itself, to prevent American hegemony in Asia. Nevertheless, China would still be very far – culturally, diplomatically, militarily, or economically – from being able to impose its own global or perhaps even regional supremacy. Nor is anyone else likely to possess the universal appeal, or the intellectual, military, diplomatic, or economic means to play a global hegemonic role. Arguably, the most plausible alternative to America would be Europe, which has a still living history of global domination and now has potential resources that, in theory, rival those of the United States. But to bid for global hegemony, Europe would have to focus its power and centralize its own governance – in other words, transform itself into a centralized federation like the United States. Europe probably will move in this direction but nevertheless stop far short of where the U.S. is today.

Today's trends belie not only realist expectations of Hobbesian hegemony but also liberal expectations of Kantian perpetual peace. An increasingly plural world system presents abundant prospects for

conflict. The rise of China, for example, points toward violent confrontations among Asian growth, Western prosperity, and the world's
physical environment.[1] Present trends also suggest a continuing sur-
feit and proliferation of nuclear weapons.[2] In effect, an unsentimental
vision of the future supports a Hobbesian diagnosis, even if it denies
a Hobbesian prescription. There will be conflict but no hegemon to
suppress it.

Under such circumstances some form of multilateral governance
seems the only practical approach. The world's great powers, rising
and otherwise, will have to learn to conciliate each other's reasonable dreams and develop machinery to anticipate and resolve problems before they grow unmanageable. Although Hobbesians say this
is impossible without a hegemon, Hobbes does not have the last word
on the topic.

Recent historical trends, even if they discourage facile liberal hopes,
do offer some encouragement. In recent decades, parts of the West
have seen a remarkable transformation of thinking about international order. Chapter 6 spells out an increasing tendency, especially
in Europe, to approach the problem of freedom and order among
states in the same constitutionalist fashion as those problems have traditionally been approached within states. The result is Europe's hybrid
interstate system – resolutely confederal but with critical federal elements. A constitutional balance of international power that blocks
hegemony among states makes possible a system of rules, rights, and
institutions that gives states the courage and means to cooperate. As
such it is a major advance for the nation-state formula. As Western
Europe has developed this formula, the caesura between domestic state
theory and international relations theory has been closing. The United
States, possessed by its unipolar fantasy, has been inclined to evolve
differently.

Old America

For more than two centuries, America has been home to the modern
world's most successful experiment in continental union. That union
encompasses a huge continental space, with diverse populations and
cultures, within a constitutional framework that guards liberal rights
and preserves democratic forms. America's model is not one, moreover,

where unity has been bought at the expense of power. On the contrary, the federal center has by now accumulated colossal military and economic power, unmatched by any other government. Indeed, since the Civil War, the American experiment has internally grown more and more Hobbesian. Federal authority has increasingly subordinated the states. Compared to the member states of the European Union, America's states are much restricted in their powers and budgets. The federal budget dwarfs them all and reflects where real power lies.[3] Within the American federal center, moreover, presidential power has been greatly augmented, even under administrations that have ostensibly opposed it.[4] The result is a huge and somewhat conflicted system. America's scale and diversity help to safeguard its liberty, as Madison predicted, but also exact their cost in efficiency, as Hamilton feared.[5]

Coherent federal policies and budgets to match are difficult to generate in America's giant system. An increasingly centralized federation is not always an efficient or otherwise desirable way to govern an entire continental system. The administration of government programs in America is frequently well below the standards of advanced European states. Our arrangements for health care provide a notorious contemporary illustration: the most expensive in the world but far from the most successful. The American defense budget is itself a stunning illustration of competing bureaucracies and private interests run amuck, with a government too divided and distracted to bring things under control. America's weak governing structure goes hand in hand with its abandoned fiscal habits and erratic monetary policies. Macroeconomic indiscipline helps to explain America's perpetual need for subsidy from the rest of the world – a need that, as Chapter 5 explains, makes the U.S. increasingly dependent on the monetary perquisites of its international position.[6] By now the accumulated economic imbalances are such that if the U.S. loses its dominant position in the world, it risks a severe downgrading of its domestic standard of living. Continuing to sustain the power of our government abroad now seems essential for meeting the insistent demands of our overstretched economy.

Building and exerting American global power adds extra strains on the federal system. Almost inevitably it means enhancing presidential power at home. By the same reasoning, sustaining outsized presidential power relies on maintaining an overbearing prominence for security and foreign policy issues in American politics. In other words, there exists for America a symbiosis between world hegemony and presidential primacy. Conversely, too little conflict in the world seems to threaten presidential power at home. In the last decades of the twentieth century, for example, détente and ending the Cold War, both which reduced America's overseas preoccupations, also seriously undermined the presidency and, with it, the stability of the federal system. All three presidencies caught in this process – those of Reagan, the first Bush, and Clinton – found themselves seriously challenged by Congress and the courts. After several presidencies adrift in détente, the "War on Terror" allowed the second Bush administration to reassert the old bipolar global model with unprecedented extensions of presidential power – the "unitary executive," the right to arrest arbitrarily and imprison indefinitely without trial, the official use and defense of torture – ideas and practices that draw their inspiration from another age.

The constitutionalist tradition, however, remains deeply planted in American political culture. States still find imaginative ways to resist or bypass federal encroachment and there are recurring campaigns to cut the presidency down to size. Nevertheless America's huge global military establishment weighs ever more heavily on its constitution. It remains to be seen what new balance will be struck after the elections of 2008. The Congressional elections of 2006 suggested that a countervailing reaction was building against presidential power. But the election of 2008 may well mean a rehabilitation of that power. In any event, without a determined effort to contain the country's external role, little change can probably be expected in the long-standing drift toward presidential federalism.

A domestic political culture traditionally inclined to vaunt the federal executive as the national guardian and engine of progress helps to explain why the American political imagination, confronted with the problem of order in a plural world, turns instinctively to global hegemony as the solution. Having successfully produced a federal government to rule America, why not extend its rule over the rest of the world? But because the rest of the world has different ideas, and we lack the legitimacy and power to impose ourselves, our federalized political imagination has grown dangerously anachronistic. Pursuing unipolar hegemony is not only a dead end for America's foreign policy, it unbalances our own domestic constitution. This is not a problem, moreover, that the United States can resolve by itself. We will almost certainly require help from our European friends.

New Europe

Developments in the West's other great federal experiment have been proceeding along a different path. Starting in the mid-twentieth century, Europe's states began creating a new political formula among themselves. By now Europe's Union, like America's, is a great advance over traditional state systems. So far, at least, the European Union is not a federation in the American sense, nor even such a federation in the making. Rather, it is an association of free and distinctive nation-states, linked by a long history of living together in a crowded continent and sharing a common desire to increase their real sovereign power by cooperating closely. Acting together in their Union, member states believe they can achieve national aims that they could never hope to achieve alone. Such a Union aims not so much to reduce or suppress its member states as to incorporate itself as a vital element within the constitutional structure of each separate member. The Union and its values are internalized; they become a vital part of the sovereignty of the member states themselves. Just as in the writings of Jean-Jacques Rousseau the idea of a "general will" is meant to embody reasonableness in the community, so in today's Europe the idea of Union is meant to embody reasonableness in the continent's interstate system.[7] In effect, the EU provides the national constitution of each member state with an institutionalized superego to discipline national power, thereby making it possible to transform interstate relations from a zero-sum game to one of mutual gain.

Unlike in Adam Smith's vision of the liberal market, however, finding the right policies and outcomes for this Europe of nation-states is not expected to be an automatic process, where each member pursues its own interests and nature somehow provides for the whole. Instead, success requires perpetual study and negotiation to identify and achieve a viable balance between national and common interests and values. The Union provides the machinery for that negotiation. Above all the Union encourages the mindset that favors compromise and mutual appeasement.[8]

As Europe's experience demonstrates, success requires a variety of benign preconditions, together with continuing wise and skillful leadership. A rapidly changing world challenges member states to continue identifying and focusing on their common interests. It helps if an underlying balance of power blocks any one group of states or elite transnational actors from systematically exploiting the others. But it also helps if some states are dedicated to leading the ensemble – states endowed with the resources to pay sometimes more than their share for the common good and with the wisdom to refrain from trying to turn leadership into domination and exploitation. And certainly no reasonable analyst can deny the critical role of the European Commission. It provides the Union with an institutionalized technocracy of high professional quality, one that belongs to no one and to everyone. Its task is to anticipate problems and seek solutions before they are foreclosed by events. It is a major political invention; Europe's experience with it could be of great importance for interstate governance in the future.

Europe's Union, like America's, is not merely the product of clever institutional engineering. Today's EU is the organic outgrowth of postwar Europe's own remarkable moral redemption – the unexpected good that followed the deep plunge into evil and suffering that began with Europe's Great War of 1914. The sense of community that grew up among Europe's ravaged states after World War II was the regional embodiment of what had been developing within the states themselves. The welfare state was a domestic product of Europe's renewal. It reflected what Europeans had learned from the horrors of their own recent history. It drew deeply from many traditions, not least from the premodern principles of Europe's medieval past – compassion and responsibility for the vulnerable, respect for the dignity of the human soul, as well as a sense of a community of souls stretching across political boundaries. This spiritual renewal was the real postwar European miracle. Thus, Europe's welfare states and Europe's Union were conjoined from the start. The welfare state was not merely an accessory to Europe's postwar prosperity. It reflected the moral transformation that enabled postwar Europe to form a community of states.[9]

To what extent should the practical wisdom embodied in the European Union's great experiment with cooperative conciliation be regarded as a public good for the world? In a system of diverse great powers, where hegemony is bound to be strongly resisted, the European constitutionalist model seems more promising for managing global affairs than the American Hobbesian model. Perhaps Europe, which invented the nation-state, has incubated the formula to complete it. The idea is intriguing but not altogether convincing. At the moment, Europe itself has severe problems.

Europe's Challenges

Nothing in human history lasts forever. Europe's great experiment of the last century may not achieve the longevity of America's Union. It may well fail before our new century is over. Europe's postwar generation is nearly gone and has taken its moral grandeur with it. Quite apart from sporadic hostility from the United States, the EU faces dangerous challenges within Europe itself. On the one hand, the challenges are organizational: how to embrace so many diverse new member states without losing coherence and direction. On the other hand, Europe's challenges are social and economic: how to preserve the now overburdened welfare state in a global economy where European labor increasingly has to compete with the labor forces of China and India.

Each challenge is also a dilemma. The EU needs a stable periphery and cannot remain true to itself if it ignores the claims of those European states who were trapped in the Soviet empire. The promise of enlargement has seemed the most effective way to induce those countries to affirm their European character – to undertake constitutional governments and market economies. But although enlarging the EU's membership may stabilize Europe as a whole, and bring great benefits to Central and Eastern Europe in particular, some compensatory centralizing formula is needed to offset the additional diversity. A major attempt to advance the Union's cohesion and strengthen its direction was made in the proposed constitutional treaty in 2004. It required unanimous agreement among the member states. It failed, as voters in two of the European Community's core member states – France and the Netherlands – rejected it outright. Re-presented in 2008, it was voted down in an Irish referendum. Squaring the constitutional circle will not, it seems, be easy.[10]

Along with an institutional overhaul that permits more expeditious and coherent decision-making, the Union also requires the military capacity to support order in its own surroundings. These now stretch into Eurasia, as well as to Africa and the Middle East. Although Europe needs to hang on to its American alliance, it can, less than ever, simply follow America's lead. Europe, for example, urgently needs to recast its own relations with Russia and the Arab world. Its interests in both places are ultimately much greater than America's and, with the best will in the world, are not necessarily identical. Nor do the EU's global interests allow it to be a negligible force in Africa, Asia, or Latin America.

Trying to generate a more forceful and independent diplomacy puts great strains on Europe's own inner cohesion. Old differences among British, French, and Germans recur as the new fault lines of European unity. New member states from the old Communist bloc often have dissonant perspectives on the nature and future of the European Union. So long as the Union remains faithful to its confederal and communitarian character, these states cannot simply be coerced into line. Achieving the necessary consensus promises, at best, to take time. In these circumstances, America's recurring jealous antagonism toward the Union is particularly damaging.

Continental Europe's economic models face a parallel dilemma. Although "communitarian" formulas may be morally superior to the more primitive capitalism vaunted in Bush's America, they generate abuses that can easily lead to a corrupt domestic culture of dependency. Above all, trying to preserve Europe's humane if tainted social values in today's radically more competitive global markets is an increasing challenge. Europe's ageing population already promises severe fiscal strains in the not so distant future. A declining native population exacerbates social and political tension over the substantial and growing immigrant population, particularly given Europe's stubbornly high levels of unemployment.[11] With neighboring Africa's terrible poverty and burgeoning populations, the pressure for large migrations northward may well grow more and more violent. Europe, moreover, is challenged not only to share its prosperity with its own neighbors but also to reconcile that prosperity with the ambitions of a rapidly rising Asia. China, too, claims a right to grow and flourish and will certainly assert that right energetically. It forms a vast and rapidly expanding market, with particular opportunities for Western industries. Europe cannot afford to cut itself off from these most dynamic parts of the new world economy and thereby lose their opportunities.[12]

But how do the rich countries of Europe stay rich when competing with formidable low-wage rivals like China? Upgrading Europe's technology and labor to keep it competitive, despite high labor costs, is the conventional and logical solution. And indeed that is the thrust of the EU's so-called Lisbon Goals.[13] Education and investment are to give Europe a commanding position in the high end of global industry and services. The goals, of course, are admirable and necessary but also insufficient. Given the huge size and potential quality of the Chinese and Indian labor forces, and their extremely low wages, any successful European adaptation to globalism will necessarily involve some political regulation of trade. Moreover, because Europe's strategy – capturing the high end of innovation in goods and services – is also being followed by the U.S., and with very large if inefficient government support, Europe's strategy is unlikely to succeed without heavy subsidies and political backing.

Can Europe enjoy the benefits of protectionism without succumbing to its vices? There are some reasons for optimism. Having a continent-sized common market ought to be a major advantage. Protection within an already large and diverse bloc that is liberal internally should risk far less collateral damage to competitiveness than protection on a merely national scale. In Europe's already large and open market, it should be much harder for special interests to turn protection into a racket. Nevertheless, coming to terms with Asia and America is a severe challenge to Europe's comfortable place in the world.[14]

China's explosive rise today has disturbing similarities to the rapid growth of Germany, Japan, and the United States in the years leading to World War I.[15] Everyone then paid a terrible price because the global system failed to reconcile its old and new powers. Today, China's huge scale – not to mention India's – make those historic problems of the twentieth century seem comparatively trivial. Moreover, the old problem of making room for rising powers is nowadays hugely complicated by an impending ecological crisis. We are unlikely simply to "grow" out of our economic conflicts.[16]

The need to avoid repeating the disastrous failures of the twentieth century is what makes Europe's own postwar accomplishments so important for the world. Europe, although perhaps even more threatened than America, has generated a more hopeful formula for responding. What the new century urgently needs is the EU's gift for appeasing rival interests – for building institutions that can transform conflict into cooperation. It helps that the EU has never been a liberal paradise, where the common interest has always been easy to find or achieve. Europe's model offers no magic liberal formula for prosperous harmony. Instead, it promises nothing better than perpetual negotiation and compromise. In this, the model reflects the intrinsic realism of the constitutionalist worldview, backed up with Europe's rich postwar experience. For all its problems, the EU is the most promising political achievement of our time.

Europe for Export?

To what extent can Europe's postwar experience contribute to world order in the twenty-first century? The question can be broken into three parts: Can Europe be a model for other regional systems? Can Europe be a model for the global system as a whole? And what role is a successful European Union likely to play in the global system? Inseparable from this last question is the issue of Europe's future relations with America.

The EU's present difficulties should make clear that its model cannot be transplanted easily, particularly to regions without comparable historical experiences and cultural ties or with radically different political and economic infrastructures. Nevertheless, in regions not predisposed to accept the hegemony of a big neighbor, Europe is perhaps a model with something to offer. And even in a neighborhood with a dominant country, the European model suggests a multilateral constitutional and regulatory framework that may trammel raw hegemonic power and be more likely to produce regional governance in the general interest.

The EU does already have significant regional imitators, in particular ASEAN and ASEAN+3 in Asia and Mercosur in Latin America.[17] Probably the most significant geopolitical use of the European model lies in recent Chinese attempts to create a geostrategic concert in Eurasia, a "Shanghai Cooperation Organization" that includes Russia, Kazakhstan, Kyrgyzstan, Tajikistan, and Uzbekistan. China has also been trying to bring India and Iran into this nexus.[18] China's aim presumably is to preempt the U.S. from building an implicit anti-Chinese alliance within China's own neighborhood. The most exalted hope is that forming an indigenous concert might foster in Asia the cooperative regional attitudes, habits, and structures typical of post-war Western Europe. Rather than a bipolar Asia divided between the U.S. and China, there might grow up a cooperative Union of Asian States. The critical test is probably whether China and Japan can reach a genuine reconciliation and partnership.[19] If so, this might have the same catalyzing effect for an Asian Community as the Franco-German entente has had for the EU.

Would a balanced Asian Union of this sort serve America's strategic interest or China's? It would not if either was aiming to dominate the region. But it would be ideal if both China and America were primarily interested in finding a way to stabilize the region without a perpetual arms race and with a low risk of war. Any economic integration that emerged as a by-product might well be a bonus for the whole region. As things stand, however, the implicit anti-American bias is the Shanghai project's greatest weakness. Without the U.S. as a balancing force, fear of China seems likely to stand in the way of intimate regional collaboration. But a bigger, more open Asian Union, with room not only for Japan, India, and Russia but also Europe and, in some fashion, the U.S. itself, might help to keep China's too-powerful embrace from threatening to suffocate its neighbors.

This hope of blending global elements in a regional system moves us on to our second question: Could Europe's system be a model for the global system itself? Surely, no one should expect a global-scale EU. But conceivably the experience of the EU does have something to offer the United Nations. Politically, the two organizations are very different. In the EU, all twenty-seven of its member states are formally equal. All sit in the European Council. Although various schemes for weighted voting have been introduced, in theory each state has a veto.[20] The UN, by contrast, has over 190 member states. All sit in the General Assembly, but real authority normally rests with the Security Council, and more particularly with its five permanent members, each with a right of veto – Britain, China, France, Russia, and the U.S. – historic great powers with serious nuclear deterrents.[21] Until now, permanent membership on the Security Council has remained frozen. None of the defeated Axis great powers of World War II – Germany, Italy, and Japan – has yet been admitted to permanent membership. Neither have the nascent great powers likely to emerge in our new century – giant states like Brazil or India. In effect, the UN, with its present configuration, has little chance of evolving into the global concert of great powers that the plural world of our new century calls for. This points to what is an old issue.

At the very beginning of the UN, Roosevelt and Churchill disputed the character and function of the Security Council. Roosevelt saw the UN as instrumental – multilateral machinery needed for global governance based on liberal principles and American power. Its purpose was to legitimate America's leadership and provide allies to defeat "aggression." Together with the International Monetary Fund and World Bank, it would defend a liberal and integrated global order installed by the U.S. Churchill, by contrast, saw the Security Council as a political concert, with a variety of independent great powers, each with particular regional responsibilities. Churchill insisted, for example, that France be made a permanent member, with a veto, a move Roosevelt resisted. As Churchill saw the Council's function, it should promote peaceful adjustments among the different political and economic blocs built around the great regional powers. At heart, the issue was whether the UN's machinery would imply and reinforce a hegemonic or a plural world system.[22] Within a few years, the Cold War suppressed this earlier Western argument. Stalin forced the West into a single bloc and transformed the UN into much more of a bipolar arena.[23] Now, with the Cold War over, the old Western argument is ready to resume. The Iraq war may well prove the catalyst.

Recent history gives hints as to how the UN might function as a concert in a plural world system. In particular, it suggests answers to our third question: How would having a stronger Europe affect a plural world system? Chapter 3 spells out how continental Europe's two leading powers (France and Germany) challenged the U.S. over Iraq and were supported by two other Eurasian great powers (China and Russia). The confrontation suggested a new era of geopolitical flux and allowed the glimpse of a new configuration of global power. Momentarily, at least, the UN Security Council was proclaiming its plural nature. Public opinion around the world seemed strongly supportive.[24] Nevertheless, the U.S., joined by Britain, went ahead with its military invasion and was able to "punish" France and Germany by exposing the EU's own disunity.

Subsequent events have worked toward healing the transatlantic breach. Limiting the damage from America's disastrous military and diplomatic defeat provided the U.S. and "Old Europe" with an immediate common interest. At the same time, European states, including the increasingly disillusioned British, have found further incentive to mend their own unity. As American and Israeli policy toward Iran seemed to point to a general regional conflagration, European diplomacy, drawing support from Russia and China, began to assert itself with unaccustomed force. The U.S. gradually found itself maneuvered into new positions toward Iran, Lebanon, and Palestine. By late 2006, it was possible at least to imagine the world being run by a concert.[25] Brave hopes revive sporadically that Europe may finally be generating a more effective military power of its own. Britain and France have been refashioning their militaries since the 1990s; Germany, reluctantly, sometimes appears to be joining them.[26] By 2007, new leaders were installed in Germany, France, and Britain. New faces brought fresh hope.

Meanwhile, America's unipolar world view fell at least temporarily into eclipse. The Congressional elections of November 2006 suggested that Americans themselves were growing wary of their country's outsized pretensions. By 2007 the Bush administration seemed to realize the need for allies and adopted, at least superficially, a more multilateral and conciliatory style in dealing with its European partners. European governments, themselves, grew more wary of the dangers of open transatlantic disunity. The unfolding economic disasters demonstrated how much each side depended on the other. The urgent need for a pooling of resources and coordination of policies was obvious to all. The European Union provided unexpectedly timely and skillful reactions to the financial crisis, as well as to the Russian incursion into Georgia. The French Presidency of the European Council gave a hint that Europe might be growing stronger and what might be the result.

The Future of the West

The election of Barack Obama in November 2008 brought a spectacular rejuvenation of American prestige among publics in Europe and most of the rest of the world. The atmosphere seemed right for a more balanced and harmonious transatlantic relationship. Whether such a relationship will actually evolve depends less on general goodwill than on the particular policies that emerge.

Obama's election could mean a more restrained, conciliatory, and collaborative American foreign policy, but it could also provide a new lease on life for America's hegemonic ambitions. Above all, the transatlantic relationship depends on whether Europe and the United States can come to a satisfactory understanding on certain fundamental geopolitical interests.

The collapse of the Soviet Union, the explosion of Muslim discontent, and the rise of the Asian superpowers all call on the West for major adjustments. For Europe, finding stable and productive relationships with the Muslim world and Russia are particularly critical challenges. In both cases, geography and demography weigh quite differently on Europe and the United States. Europe abuts the Muslim world of North Africa and the Middle East, which has one of the world's highest birth rates, while Europe's is among the lowest. Immigrants from the Muslim world already form a significant element in West European populations. Although speaking of a war of civilizations with the Muslim world is merely a rhetorical exaggeration in the U.S., in Europe the very idea signals catastrophe. Whereas American support for Israel sometimes seems unconditional, Europe's vital interest demands an equitable and durable settlement between Israelis and Palestinians.

Similarly, making a success of relations with Russia is far less urgent for the U.S. than for Russia's European neighbors. For the latter, Russia is a troubling but not-too-distant cousin, intimately juxtaposed in a common "near abroad." Russia's vast resources complement Europe's needs and offer big opportunities for Western capital. Whereas the U.S. is still inclined to see Russia through the lens of military competition, Europeans downplay that perspective. They hope to avoid the heavy fiscal burdens of a renewed Cold War, not to mention the disadvantages of once more being highly dependent on an American military alliance. Just as postwar West European states learned to live together in cooperative prosperity, the states of today's EU need institutions that will allow them to cohabit amicably with their giant Eastern relation. Otherwise there seems scant hope for a happy European future. Something of the same distinction exists between

American and European approaches to China. The U.S. sees China as a rival for regional military and naval hegemony. European states have no interest in entering such a competition. Instead they prefer to emphasize, perhaps unwisely, the advantages of peaceful economic collaboration.

In summary, European states tend to have a fundamentally different approach from the United States. The European approach is mutual appeasement organized through multilateral constitutionalist structures. The strategy is to catch up neighbors in an expanding network of mutually beneficial rules and bargains. American critics fault this European approach for basing security on the wiles of Venus rather than the strength of Mars. Europeans take this approach, it is said, because they lack the strength or determination to do otherwise.[27] Of course, the difference of approach also mirrors the fundamental distinction between America's unipolar view – preoccupied with hegemonic military and economic power – and the constitutionalist perspective embodied in the European Union. Europe is disposed to come to terms with a plural world; the United States is not.

As noted earlier, these contrasting American and European approaches tend to be mutually self-defeating. Europeans deny legitimacy to American strength, and therefore devalue it. Americans, throwing their weight around the world, create an embittered atmosphere that not only discourages European efforts at organized conciliation but also divides Europeans from one another.

Both Americans and Europeans require a fresh retuning of their political imaginations. Both need to expand their visions beyond the confines of their postwar experiences and roles. Unfortunately, both show a strong tendency to remain frozen in admiration of their past accomplishments. Both Europe and the U.S. see their postwar era as an unprecedented success, albeit in opposite ways. Europe built its Union. Its states turned inward – away from their near-suicidal competition for global power. Together they tamed their inner devils and constructed a cooperative regional system permitting unprecedented domestic development and social peace. Postwar America's accomplishments lay in the opposite direction. The U.S. turned outward – to build a global economy and to protect Europe and Japan from the great external evils that threatened them. Neither the U.S. nor Europe could have succeeded without the assistance of the other. Europe's great experiment with internal healing was unlikely to have worked without America's protecting presence, which gave the wounded West European states the security to cooperate. At the same time, Europe's internal peace and prosperity made a relatively open global economy possible, while the Atlantic Alliance reinforced and legitimized America's world leadership. With Europe's collaboration and assistance, the U.S. could finally fulfill its Wilsonian dream of leading the world by invitation. NATO provided a multilateral structure that helped the U.S. use its new power well.[28]

For both America and Europe, however, too much success in the twentieth century has become a danger for the twenty-first. Both are trapped in unproductive nostalgia. In this book my focus has been on the United States. Convinced that "victory" in the Cold War confirms its hegemony, an America dangerously enamored of global power clings stubbornly to its protector's role and privileges. That the U.S. will go on playing a leading role in any future world system goes without saying. But an American imagination that remains obstinately fixated on overblown Roman dreams creates enemies rather than friends. It blights prospects for a concert of cooperative powers. Instead, it arouses and confirms those ancient patterns of frightened and uncompromising national egoism that substantiate the Hobbesian view of international relations. By now, we should know how much America's continuing anxious pursuit of hegemony threatens our prosperity and crowds our liberty. We should recognize unipolar views for what they are: facile doctrines that mask a too-ardent taste for domination. To be worthy and successful at leadership in a plural world, the United States must exorcise the demon of unipolarity.

Purging America's political imagination of its unipolar bias is a task for liberals and conservatives alike. Liberals will have to overcome their traditional vice – enthusiasm for arrogant abstractions rolled forward, heedless of what is trampled in the process. Conservatives will need to rediscover their own traditional virtues: a constitutional respect for institutions and balance – for good manners within and among nations, together with a healthy reserve toward overheated and self-serving idealism. With luck, liberals and conservatives together can give us an America that is better adapted to our new century – less assertive and more self-confident.

At the same time, Europe has its own transformation to make: to consolidate its own unity and accept the responsibilities of its own great resources. If America is too strong for its own good, it is not least because Europe remains too weak. Nothing condemns the U.S. and Europe to be antagonists – quite the contrary. But to save their friendship requires a better balance between them. At present, each often caters to the worst features of the other. Imperious America, bemused with its unipolar fantasy, encourages European passivity and free-riding. Rich Europe – weak and divided – is a standing invitation to American overextension. A strong Europe is thus essential not only for protecting Europe's interests in a challenging world but also for America to recover its own inner equilibrium.

Like all great powers, the U.S. needs to be checked and balanced. With so much power concentrated in Washington, to preserve America's own domestic balance, something beyond a purely national constitutional framework is required. Keeping power in check at home requires balancing it abroad. Balance among states requires balance within them. Two world wars exacted a terrible price before Europe's states learned this lesson. Their expensive education led to the EU. Their subsequent progress suggests a more general historical lesson: Among states, as among individuals, balancing is often better done among friends than between enemies; in other words, in a cooperative rather than a zero-sum relationship. To be Europe's stabilizing friend was America's vital postwar role. Europe must now assume that role for the overstretched and disoriented constitution of post-Soviet America. The Iraq misadventure has shown how urgently America needs to be contained by its friends – by those who share the values of liberty at home and respect for the rights of other peoples. Restoring balance to America requires more political and military weight for Europe. To succeed, each will need the other. When America and Europe are genuinely together, the experience of each side can hugely enrich the other. When they are apart, each repairs to a dangerously provincial worldview, inadequate for the challenges that lie ahead.

If the West is unable to build and sustain a collaborative equilibrium within itself, the prospects for concord in the rest of the world are grim. But if America's political imagination regains its balance, and Europe rises to the occasion, there may be hope that the West can accommodate the new Asia and perhaps even avoid a dismal degradation of the Earth's environment. The twenty-first century may then come to reflect Europe's new model for peace rather than its old model for war.

Notes

1. For a similar view, see John Gray, "Global Delusions," *New York Review of Books*, April 27, 2006, pp. 20–23.

2. Chaim Kaufmann, "Why Nuclear Proliferation Is Getting Easier," *Peace Review*, Vol. 18(3), 2006, pp. 315–324; for the possibility of nuclear terrorism, see Charles D. Ferguson, William C. Potter, et al., *The Four Faces of Nuclear Terrorism* (Monterey, CA: Center for Nonproliferation Studies, 2004). For a more optimistic view about prevention, see Graham Allison, *Nuclear Terrorism: The Ultimate Preventable Catastrophe* (New York, NY: Times Books, 2004).

3. Aggregate U.S. state budgets were $57.8 billion in fiscal year 2006, according to the National Conference of State Legislatures; federal spending was $2.472 trillion, according to the Congressional Budget Office. For information on the state budgets, see the National Conference of State Legislatures' publication titled, "State Budget Actions: FY 2006 and FY 2007" February 2008, http://www.ncsl.org/programs/fiscal/sba06sum.htm#execsum. For information on the U.S. federal budget, see http://www.cbo.gov/budget/data/historical.shtml.

4. See Andrew Rudalevige, "The Contemporary Presidency: The Decline and Resurgence and Decline (and Resurgence?) of Congress: Charting a New Imperial Presidency," *Presidential Studies Quarterly*, 36(3), 2006, pp. 506–524, and also John Owens, "Presidential Power and Congressional Acquiescence in the 'War' on Terrorism: A New Constitutional Equilibrium?," *Politics & Policy*, 34(2), 2006, pp. 258–303.

5. For how "enlarging the orbit" protects liberty, see "Federalist #10." For Hamilton's fears, see "Federalist #9," in Alexander Hamilton, James Madison, John Jay, Clinton Rossiter (eds.), *The Federalist Papers* (New York, NY: Signet, 1961).

6. For my own study of the inefficiencies of the American federal model and how they are compensated for internationally, see David P. Calleo, *The Bankrupting of America* (New York, NY: Morrow, 1992), Chs. 4 and 6.

7. For this view of Rousseau's general will as idealized rational common interest, see Bernard Bosanquet, *The Philosophical Theory of the State*, ed. 2 (London, UK: Macmillan, 1920), Ch. 3. However, Bosanquet, unlike Rousseau, believes the general is more likely to be expressed through the state's constitutional institutions than through spontaneous expressions of popular will. The great eighteenth-century English jurist,

Sir William Blackstone, offers a similarly conditional view of the crown as idealized reason. When acting in a fashion "prejudicial to the commonwealth," royal authority, he thought, was no longer valid. William Blackstone, *Commentaries on the Laws of England, Vol. 1: A Facsimile of the First Edition of 1765–1769* (Chicago, IL: University of Chicago Press, 1979), p. 239 [facsimile of first edition, 1765–1769].

8. See my *Rethinking Europe's Future* (Princeton, NJ: Princeton University Press, 2003), especially Ch. 13. Also, for a view emphasizing how EU states seek their own national advantage and economic interest, see Andrew Moravcsik, *The Choice for Europe: Social Purpose and State Power from Messina to Maastricht* (Ithaca, NY: Cornell University Press, 1998).

9. Tony Judt, *Postwar: A History of Europe since 1945* (New York, NY: The Penguin Press, 2005), p. 77, celebrates eloquently the centrality of the welfare state but does not, as far as I can tell, perceive the domestic welfare state and Europe's Union as two sides of the same coin.

10. For more information on the French and Dutch rejections of the EU constitution in 2005, see Simon Jeffery, "Q&A: The European Constitution," *The Guardian*, June 2, 2005, available at http://www.guardian. co.uk/world/2005/jun/02/eu.france2. See also footnote 12 in Ch. 3. For additional information on the recent Irish rejection of the Lisbon treaty, see "Ireland's Voters Speak," *The Economist*, June 21, 2008, p. 57; John Thornhill, "Irish 'No' Leads to Yet Another European Psychodrama," *Financial Times*, June 14, 2008, p. 7. For French President Sarkozy's early plans to relaunch the EU's constitutional reform, and also for a hint of more extreme remedies, see Tony Barber, "Sarkozy Warns of Need for Multi-Tier Europe," *Financial Times*, July 11, 2008, p. 4.

11. In the European area as a whole the unemployment percentage (standardized unemployment rate) remained around 10% for most of the 1990s, dropping to 7.1 by April 2008. German and French levels in April 2008 were 7.4% and 7.8%, respectively. Source: OECD, www.stats.oecd.org. An OECD study shows a general increase in the trend of legal immigration into Europe. In 2000 about 2.2 million legal immigrants were reported as having permanently moved to the EU-25 nations that reported statistics to the OECD. In 2005 that number was 2.5 million. Estimating the flow of illegal immigrants is much more difficult, but judging from the rise in legal immigration, especially into southern European states, the flow of illegal immigrants likely has also increased. *International Migration Outlook 2007.* (Paris: OECD Publications, 2007).

12. For European and Chinese trade and investment figures, see Chapter 5, footnotes 2 and 35.

13. Proclaimed by European Union leaders in 2000, the Lisbon Goals aimed at increasing R&D to 3% of GDP, reducing red tape to promote

entrepreneurship, and achieving an employment rate of 70% (60% for women). In 2004, the Commission urged fresh impetus with three priority areas:

- "Investment in networks and knowledge: starting the priority projects approved in the 'European Growth Initiative';
- Strengthening competitiveness in industry and services: stepping up efforts in the areas of industrial policy, the services market and environmental technologies;
- Increasing labour market participation of older people: promoting active ageing by encouraging older workers to work for longer." See http://www.euractiv.com/en/agenda2004/lisbon-agenda/ article-117510.

14. For a discussion of the limits to European protectionism, see "European Comment: The Right Kind of Champion," *The Financial Times,* June 8, 2004. For examples of the rising competition between the EU and America (such as the Boeing-Airbus dispute), see http://trade.ec.europa.eu/ doclib/docs/2007/february/tradoc_133279.pdf. For more recent information on the dispute, see Mark Landler, "Ruling near on Boeing Airbus Dispute," *The New York Times,* May 29, 2008, http://www.nytimes.com/ 2008/05/29/business/worldbusiness/29trade.html. After having won the contract in early 2008, Airbus's parent company, EADS, now faces an overturned decision and may have to compete against Boeing again for the Air Force contract; Caroline Brothers and Micheline Maynard, "Air Tanker Contract Pits Airbus against Boeing on Global Stage," *New York Times,* July 15, 2008, http://www.nytimes.com/2008/07/ 15/business/worldbusiness/15tanker.html?scp=3&sq=boeing&st=cse. See also my *Rethinking Europe's Future, op. cit.,* Ch. 12.

15. For the rapid growth of Germany, Japan, and the United States before World War I, see Paul Kennedy, *The Rise and Fall of Great Powers: Economic Change and Military Conflict from 1500 to 2000* (New York, NY: Random House, 1987), especially Ch. 5. For current Chinese growth rates going back to 1980, see World Economic Outlook Database, www.imf.org.

16. For this argument richly developed, see John Gray, "Global Delusions," *op. cit.* For the costs associated with climate change, see Sir Nicolas Stern's report to the British Prime Minister, "The Economics of Climate Change," October 30, 2006, http://www.hm-treasury.gov.uk/Independent_ Reviews/stern_review_economics_climate_change/sternreview_index.cfm. For China's environmental challenges see Elizabeth C. Economy, *The River Runs Black: The Environmental Challenge to China's Future* (Ithaca, NY: Cornell University Press, 2004).

17. For similarities and differences between the EU and its imitators, see Richard Kirkham and Paul James Cardwell, "The European Union: A Role Model for Regional Governance?" *European Public Law*, Vol. 12(3), 2006, pp. 403–431. For an analysis of the lessons that ASEAN and the AEC might derive from the European Union's experience with economic integration see Michael G. Plummer, "The ASEAN Economic Community and the European Experience." Hamburg Institute of International Economics, http://www.hwwi.org/4_The_ASEAN_Economi.751.0.html. For recent deepening trade ties in the energy and services sectors, as well as discussions of ASEAN's role in Asia, see Carlos H. Conde, "China and Asean in Services Pact," *The New York Times*, January 15, 2007: C2; Goh Sui Noi, "Question Mark over Future Shape of East Asia Summit: Some Countries Want It to Be Developed into a Community, While Others See It in a Peripheral Role," *The Straits Times* (Singapore), January 16, 2007; and Roel Landinginand and John Burton, "China and Asean Sign Key Trade Deal," *Financial Times*, January 15, 2007, p. 8.

18. Iran, Pakistan, and India became observers in 2005. For a short history of the Shanghai Cooperation Organization and Iran's possible entry, see Lionel Beehner, *The Shanghai Cooperation Organization*, Council of Foreign Relations backgrounder, April 8, 2008, at http://www.cfr.org/publication/10883/#2. For a discussion of Chinese participation in multilateral institutions, see Evan S. Medeiros and M. Taylor Fravel, "China's New Diplomacy," *Foreign Affairs*, Vol. 82(6), November/December, 2003, pp. 22–35.

19. Lanxin Xiang, "China's Eurasian Experiment," *Survival*, Vol. 46(2), 2004, pp. 109–122. See also David P. Calleo, "The Atlantic Alliance in a Global System," *Asia-Pacific Review*, Vol. 14(1), 2007, pp. 72–89.

20. For a discussion of how the EU's Nice treaty has altered its voting procedure, see my *Rethinking Europe's Future*, op. cit., Ch. 13. For how the proposed new constitutional treaty would change voting procedure, see "Treaty of Lisbon – The Treaty at a Glance," Europa, http://europa.eu/lisbon_treaty/glance/index_en.htm. See also "What the Lisbon Treaty Will Do," Foreign and Commonwealth Office, http://www.fco.gov.uk/en/fco-in-action/institutions/britain-in-the-european-union/global-europe/eu-lisbon-treaty/what-the-lisbon-treaty-will-do.

21. The General Assembly elects ten rotating members of the Security Council. Changes in the UN Security Council's membership and procedures require the approval of both the General Assembly and the Security Council itself. On three occasions, the "Uniting for Peace" procedure has been used, whereby a two-thirds vote of the General Assembly can recommend a use of force. When a vetoing power is in a clear minority, such a vote might lend *de facto* legitimacy to an intervention. See Thomas G.

Weiss, "The Illusion of UN Security Council Reform," *The Washington Quarterly*, Vol. 26, Autumn, 2003, pp. 147–161.

22. For Roosevelt and Churchill's conflicting views, see Francis L. Loewenheim et al., *Roosevelt and Churchill: Their Secret Wartime Correspondence* (Cambridge, MA: Da Capo Press, 1990). For Roosevelt's shifting views in the 1930s, including interest in a global order of regional blocs, see Benjamin M. Rowland, editor, *Balance of Power or Hegemony* (New York, NY: NYU Press, 1976), in particular Rowland's own Ch. 5, "Preparing the American Ascendancy: The Transfer of Economic Power from Britain to the United States, 1933–1944," and Robert J. A. Skidelsky's Ch. 4, "Retreat from Leadership: The Evolution of British Economic Foreign Policy, 1870–1939." For an account of the United Nations' beginnings, see Stephen C. Schlesinger, *Act of Creation: The Founding of the United Nations* (Boulder, CO: Westview Press, 2003).

23. For the persisting Third World and the Non-Aligned Movements during the bipolar era see Peter Willetts, *The Non-Aligned Movement: The Origins of a Third World Alliance* (London, UK: Frances Pinter, 1979).

24. See Ch. 3, footnote 10. See also poll conducted by GlobeScan/Program on International Policy Attitudes (PIPA), March 2005, available http://65.109.167.118/pipa/pdf/apr05/LeadWorld_Apr05_rpt.pdf. The summary reads as follows: "In 20 of 23 Countries Polled Citizens Want Europe to Be More Influential Than US; France Most Widely Seen as Having a Positive Influence in World; US and Russia Mostly Seen as Negative Influences; Britain and China Mostly Viewed Positively."

25. On European diplomacy with Iran, see Ian Traynor, "US Joins Europe in Dispute over Iran," *The Guardian,* March 12, 2005, p. 15; and Daniel Dombey and Gareth Smyth, "E.U. to Continue Talks with Tehran Despite Passing of UN Deadline," *Financial Times*, August 31, 2006; p. 7. On the European role in Lebanon, see "Abroad Be Dangers: The European Union in the world," *The Economist,* August 26, 2006; Ewen MacAskill and David Gow, "Middle East Crisis: E.U. to Commit Biggest Force in Its History to Keep the Peace," *The Guardian,* August 26, 2006; p. 14; and "Charlemagne: Just a Moment, or Possibly More," *The Economist,* September 2, 2006. See also Nicola Casarini and Costanza Musu (eds.), *European Foreign Policy in an Evolving International System* (Basingstoke, UK: Palgrave Macmillan, 2007); Charles A. Kupchan, "Europe and America in the Middle East," Council of Foreign Relations, March 2007, http://www.cfr.org/publication/12761/europe_and_america_in_the_middle_east.html.

26. For recent changes in French military doctrine, see *Défense et Sécurité Nationale, Le Livre Blanc* (Paris: Odile Jacob, La Documentation Française, June 2006).

27.　See Robert Kagan, *Of Paradise and Power: America and Europe in the New World Order* (New York, NY: Random House, 2003).

28.　See Geir Lundestad, "Empire by Invitation? The United States and Western Europe, 1945–1952," *Journal of Peace Research*, Vol. 23(3), 1986, pp. 263–277.

Index

DATE DUE